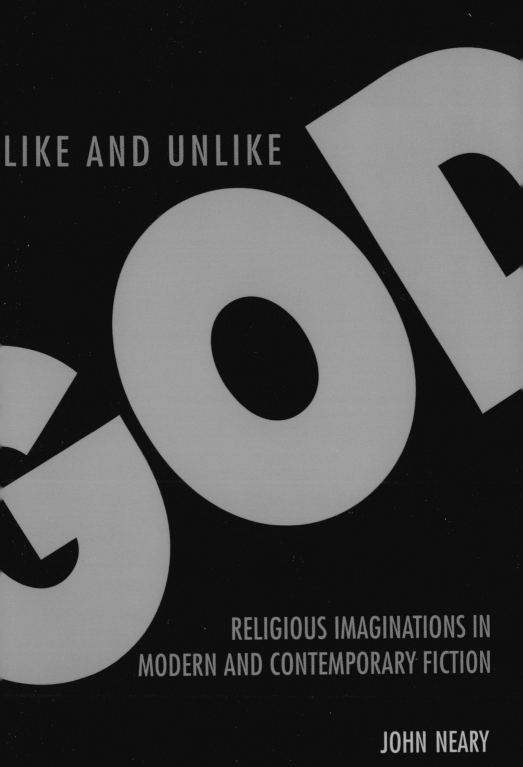

LIKE AND UNLIKE GOD

RELIGIOUS IMAGINATIONS IN MODERN AND CONTEMPORARY FICTION

JOHN NEARY

LIKE AND UNLIKE GOD

AAR

American Academy of Religion
Reflection and Theory in the Study of Religion

Editor
Mary McClintock Fulkerson

Number 13
LIKE AND UNLIKE GOD
Religious Imaginations in Modern
and Contemporary Fiction

by
John Neary

LIKE AND UNLIKE GOD

Religious Imaginations in Modern and Contemporary Fiction

by
John Neary

Scholars Press
Atlanta, Georgia

LIKE AND UNLIKE GOD
Religious Imaginations in Modern and Contemporary Fiction

by
John Neary

Library of Congress Cataloging in Publication Data

Neary, John, 1952–
    Like and unlike God : religious imaginations in modern and
contemporary fiction / by John Neary.
       p.   cm. — (Reflection and theory in the study of religion ;
no. 13)
    Includes bibliographical references.
    ISBN 0-7885-0573-4 (pbk. : alk. paper)
    1. Religious fiction, American—History and criticism.
2. Christianity and literature—United States—History—20th
century. 3. Christianity and literature—Great Britain—
History—20th century. 4. American fiction—20th century—History
and criticism. 5. English fiction—20th century—History and criticism.
6. Religious fiction—History and criticism—Theory, etc.
7. Christian fiction—History and criticism—Theory, etc.
8. Religious fiction, English—History and criticism. 9. Religion
and literature—History—20th century. 10. Christian fiction—
History and criticism. 11. God in literature.   I. Title.
II. Series.
PS374.R47N43 1999
813'.509382—dc21
                            99-16272
                            CIP

08 07 06 05 04 03 02 01 00 99   5 4 3 2 1

Printed in the United States of America
on acid-free paper

To Laura, Kevin, and Kyle

and to Howard, who gave me the idea

Contents

Acknowledgments   ix

Preface:
Twin Peaks and *Columbo*   xi

1

Introduction:
Dialectical and Analogical Imaginations   1

2

Conrad and Joyce:
Modernist Imaginations   47

3

Three Christian Critics:
Nathan Scott, William Lynch, and Cesáreo Bandera   107

4

Realism/Postmodernism:
Contemporary Religious Imaginations   147

Works Cited   197

Acknowledgments

I wish to thank the following publishers, who have given me permission to use extended quotations from copyrighted works. Excerpts from David Tracy's *The Analogical Imagination: Christian Theology and the Culture of Pluralism* (New York: Crossroad, 1981) are reproduced with the permission of the publisher. Excerpts from Nathan Scott's *The Wild Prayer of Longing* (New Haven: Yale University Press, 1971) appear with the permission of the publisher. Excerpts from Cesáreo Bandera's *The Sacred Game: The Role of the Sacred in the Genesis of Modern Literary Fiction* (University Park: Pennsylvania State University Press, 1994; copyright 1994 by the Pennsylvania State University) are reproduced by the permission of the publisher.

The excerpts from John Updike's *Roger's Version,* copyright © 1986 by John Updike, and from Anne Tyler's *Saint Maybe,* copyright © 1991 by Anne Tyler Modarressi, are reprinted by permission of Alfred A. Knopf, Inc. Excerpts from *Voices from the Moon* (1984), by Andre Dubus, are reprinted by permission of David R. Godine Publishers. Excerpts from *The Crying of Lot 49*—copyright © 1965, 1966, and copyright © renewed 1993, 1994 by Thomas Pynchon—are reprinted by permission of HarperCollins Publishers, Inc. And excerpts from James Joyce's *Ulysses* are reprinted with the kind permission of the Estate of James Joyce.

Portions of the preface and of chapter 1 appeared in *The Way,* Heythrop College, Kensington Square, London, England. Portions of chapter 3 appeared in *Christian Spirituality Bulletin: Journal of the Society for the Study of Christian Spirituality* 3, no. 2 (Fall 1995): 31–32. Reprint permission has been granted by *Christian Spirituality Bulletin,* Loyola Marymount University, Los Angeles, California.

I wish to thank the St. Norbert College Faculty Personnel Committee for graciously granting me a sabbatical leave to begin work on this book. I also thank Dr. Ken Zahorski, director of Faculty Development, St. Norbert College, and the St. Norbert Faculty Development Committee for a generous summer grant that further helped me with my work. And I am especially grateful to Dr. Bradford Hinze, associate professor of Theology at Marquette University, for painstakingly leading me through the Christian theological tradition and for working closely with me on my first two chapters, and to Dr. Howard Ebert, assistant professor of Religious Studies at St. Norbert College, for many hours of conversation about this project.

Preface:
Twin Peaks and *Columbo*

Some years ago I was hooked on film director David Lynch's television series *Twin Peaks*. I was fascinated by the show's twisting, twisted story, eccentric characters, and overall weirdness. But when I mentioned *Twin Peaks* to a good friend who is a Catholic theologian, he told me with some embarrassment that he found the show off-putting; it was "too Protestant," he said.

When I asked my friend what he meant, he handed me an article by Fr. Andrew Greeley from a 1991 issue of *America*. In this article Greeley, invoking theologian David Tracy's "magisterial *The Analogical Imagination*" (285), describes two religious imaginations, two ways of using images to suggest a transcendent reality: the "dialectical" and the "analogical." Borrowing from David Tracy's ideas, Greeley claims that, within modern Christianity, Protestantism tends to nurture a dialectical imagination and Catholicism an analogical or sacramental imagination:

> The analogical or Catholic imagination, to summarize and simplify David Tracy, emphasizes the presence of God in the world. It perceives the world and its creatures and relationships and social structures as metaphors, sacraments of God, hints of what God is like. I often illustrate the theory by noting that Catholics have angels and saints and souls in purgatory and statues and stained glass windows and holy water, and an institutional church that itself is thought to be a sacrament. Protestant denominations, on the other hand, either do not have this imagery or do not put so much emphasis on it. . . .
>
> One side, the Catholic analogical imagination, leans in the direction of immanence; the other, the Protestant dialectical imagination, leans in the direction of transcendence. Which is better? Neither. Which is necessary? Both. ("Catholic Imagination" 286)

My Catholic theologian friend noted that David Lynch's dark, depraved town of Twin Peaks is a place that is dialectically divorced from the good. The hero, FBI agent Dale Cooper, comes from somewhere else, and until late in the series he stays pure, untouched by the depravity around him; he is impeccably well groomed and wholesome, and his worst vice is a passion for coffee and cherry pie. Cooper's access to truth is less through his interaction with the people of Twin Peaks than through insights and visions that transcend the mundane mess around him. My friend said that he preferred *Columbo*, a detective show in which everybody is partly good and partly bad. This show's grumpy, rumpled hero bumbles his way to the truth because the truth is there, available within the imperfect but not hopelessly depraved world around him.

It occurred to me that these two imaginative relationships with ultimate reality have shaped much modern fiction. I decided that an examination of the two imaginations could be a valuable way to reflect on the different views of the Ultimate that inhere in various modern fictional works. That examination gave rise to this book, which in a sense is a long meditation on the difference between *Twin Peaks* and *Columbo*. I quickly discovered that Greeley's assertion that the dialectical imagination is "Protestant" and the analogical is "Catholic" is too facile; Greeley himself acknowledges that "the analogical and the dialectical imaginations are not mutually exclusive. No individual is completely possessed by one or the other, nor does any denomination or group have a monopoly on one or the other" ("Catholic Imagination" 286). But after reading much theology and literary criticism and reflecting on some of the most compelling English-language fiction of the last one hundred years, I am convinced that the overall insight is very fruitful. So in this study I propose that David Tracy's description of two kinds of religious imagination, the "dialectical" and the "analogical," provides a good model for talking about modern fiction and its vision of what Tracy calls the "whole" of reality. For the dialectical imagination, ultimate reality is radically other, unlike earthly reality, while the analogical, sacramental imagination finds metaphors and images that suggest similarities between human reality and the Ultimate.

My first chapter, after placing this study in the context of current examinations of religion and literature and establishing my methodology of close reading, is an introductory exposition of the two religious imaginations. My main sources for exploring these imaginations are texts by such theological writers as Paul, Aquinas, Luther, Barth, Tillich, Lonergan, Rahner, Altizer, McFague, and Tracy, but I have also made use of current literary theory—as does Tracy himself. The chapter ends with illustrations of the two imaginations within contemporary literary texts: John Updike's *Roger's Version* and Andre Dubus's *Voices from the Moon*.

The second chapter discusses the way these two religious imaginations distinguish two seminal modernist fiction writers: Joseph Conrad and James Joyce. The chapter is a close reading of most of Conrad's "Marlow" works and of Joyce's *A Portrait of the Artist as a Young Man* and *Ulysses* in light of my thesis about the two religious imaginations. The third chapter discusses three Christian critics of modern and contemporary prose fiction—Nathan Scott, William Lynch, and Cesáreo Bandera—whose visions of fiction and its purposes illustrate aspects of the analogical and dialectical religious imaginations. The final chapter extends the study to four contemporary writers who integrate the two religious imaginations into differing fictional forms. Two of the writers I discuss—Anne Tyler and Muriel Spark—are, roughly speaking, "traditional" writers, producers of something like "realistic" fiction; I examine the way Tyler uses traditional techniques (in *Saint Maybe*) to embody an analogical imagination, while Spark's vision (in *Symposium*) is primarily dialectical. And the other two writers—Thomas Pynchon and D. M. Thomas—are nonrealistic, postmodernist writers; Pynchon, I argue (using *The Crying of Lot 49*), has a generally dialectical imagination, while Thomas's (in *The White Hotel*) is generally analogical.

I hope I do not side too heavy-handedly with the analogical imagination and against the dialectical. The fact is that although I see great value in the analogical imagination's vision of immanent graciousness (and I love Joyce's profoundly analogical *Ulysses* above all other books), I find *Twin Peaks* more stimulating than *Columbo*; the dialectical imagination has a bracingly astringent edge that the analogical imagination sometimes lacks. To use postmodernist language, each imagination is the other's *supplément*. They need each other to create a vision that is sharp, rich, and whole.

1

Introduction:
Dialectical and Analogical Imaginations

Literature and the Religious in a Postmodern Context

In *Breaking the Fall*, a recent religious analysis of contemporary fiction, Robert Detweiler expresses some surprise at the dearth of recent religious interpretations of literature. Detweiler asserts that various "prominent theorists" (he lists Jacques Derrida, Geoffrey Hartman, and Frank Kermode) "have suggested the value of recent theory for religious interpretation of literary texts" (xi). Detweiler could also mention the fact that the tools of literary theory—theories of narrative and genre, for example—have been assimilated by many current theologians. I agree with Detweiler that it is time for a reintegration of literary analysis with religious issues. The New Critics' distaste for analyses that suggested that literature is connected to the world outside the text, the world of people and nature (and God), has been replaced by an interest in finding connections between literature and other human phenomena. Without falling into earlier, naive notions of one-to-one correspondences between texts and the world, Marxist, feminist, and New Historicist theories are carefully tracing the connections between literature and culture. Similar alliances between theologians and literary theorists seem to me altogether timely and appropriate.

I think, though, that Detweiler does not take seriously enough the extent to which the postmodern suspicion of truth claims has undermined religious viewpoints; this is why, I think, much of the self-consciously postmodern literary academy views religious interests as passé. Those who wish to explore religious issues in literature are likely to believe that such issues have a human, or even transcendent, validity—that they are not just culturally limited, linguistic constructs but that they are in some way deeply real. Much of postmodernism, however, appears to challenge this belief. In *Postmodernity*, a book-length anatomy of postmodernism, Paul Lakeland describes the "linguistic turn"[1] that virtually all contemporary thinkers have taken: "It is not Being or God or *nous* or reason that is the

---

1 See Richard Rorty, ed., *The Linguistic Turn: Recent Essays in Philosophical Method* (Chicago: University of Chicago Press, 1967).

foundation of thinking, and hence of the subject, but language. What can be said lays down the boundaries of what can be thought, and this insight has profound historicizing and contextualizing implications" (19). After the postmodern linguistic turn, Lakeland says, "knowledge cannot be pure, may not even aspire to the condition of purity. Language is not, as Heidegger would have it, the 'house of Being,' but simultaneously its creator and destroyer" (19). The deconstructionist theologian Carl A. Raschke embraces such postmodern suspicion enthusiastically, stating that postmodern thought is no less than "the revelation of the inner vacuity of the much touted 'modern' outlook" (2–3) and that it "shows that the logos of all our latter-day '——ologies,' including theology, has become nought but a ritualistic and compulsive defense against *to kenon* ('the void')" (3). Raschke asserts that postmodern deconstruction, which he calls "the interior drive of twentieth-century theology rather than an alien agenda," is *"the death of God put into writing"* (3).

But such a radical annihilation of religious reality is not the only viable activity for contemporary thinkers. Paul Lakeland argues that postmodernity does contain a "radical historicist perspective" (16), which he considers quite antithetical to a religious viewpoint,[2] but also a conservative "postmodernism of nostalgia" (17) and a moderate "late modernism" (17), both of which are open to religious perspectives. And in *The Trespass of the Sign*, Kevin Hart asserts that even the radical postmodern suspicion of truth claims is not intrinsically atheistic. What is at issue in postmodern skepticism, Hart says, is not the reality of God but only the limitations of human knowledge and the radical incompleteness of all human systems (including Raschke's). Hart argues that postmodern deconstruction, far from being *"the death of God put into writing,"* is "not a collection of first-order propositions about knowledge or being but a second-order discourse on epistemology and ontology, one that traces the effects of their will to totalise" (173). Postmodernism's claim that experience is mediated through representation or sign, that humans experience a deferred or contextualized rather than absolute presence, is similar, Hart suggests, to traditional "negative theology," which emphasizes the fact that any God concept is always already a representation, a sign, not a presence (186). For negative theology, says Hart, "one gains 'knowledge' of God by successively abstracting God from images of Him" (190), hence guaranteeing "that human speech about God is in fact about *God* and not a *concept* of God" (192). Such

---

2 Lakeland claims that this radical perspective is "most frequently associated with the work of Michel Foucault and poststructuralism in general . . . , but also possessing influential variations in the writings of Jacques Derrida, Richard Rorty and the neopragmatist camp, and the whole of French feminist writing represented by Julia Kristeva and Luce Irigaray" (16). For Lakeland, these radical postmodernists do have the fully atheistic agenda that Raschke represents. But Kevin Hart, David Tracy, and others suggest that even a fairly radical reading of Derridean deconstruction leaves room for a religious perspective.

a mystical form of theism, however "negative," is hardly a proclamation of the "death of God."

So I suggest that the current awareness of the thickly particularized contexts within which humans experience reality (contexts governed by historical placement, social position, gender, etc.), and of the fact that these experiences are always linguistically mediated, does not render religious approaches to literature obsolete. Rather, it justifies a close examination of the various ways people have imagined the holy, the specific textures of human representations and signs of God. Robert Detweiler is right: far from rendering religious approaches to literature preciously anachronistic, our contemporary, postmodern situation has the potential to reinvigorate the dialogue between religion and literature. Literature is drenched in religious concerns—modern and contemporary literature at least as much as any other.

Paul Tillich defines religious concerns as those that are "ultimate":

> The ultimate concern is unconditional, independent of all conditions of character, desire, or circumstance. The unconditional concern is total: no part of ourselves or of our world is excluded from it; there is no "place" to flee from it. The total concern is infinite: no moment of relaxation and rest is possible in the face of a religious concern which is ultimate, unconditional, total, and infinite. (*Systematic Theology*, vol. 1, 12)

In theologian Bernard Lonergan's terms, it might be said that humans are driven to Tillich's realm of ultimate concern by the "transcendental exigence"—the inherent, dynamic drive of conscious intentionality for what is beyond itself and beyond what it already possesses (Lonergan considers this dynamic realm of meaning to be where God, the absolutely unconditioned, is discovered). Lonergan states that "human inquiry" possesses an "unrestricted demand for intelligibility," "human judgment" demands "the unconditioned," and "human deliberation" demands "a criterion that criticizes every finite good." Hence, he asserts, humans "can reach basic fulfilment, peace, joy, only by moving beyond the realms of common sense, theory, and interiority and into the realm in which God is known and loved" (83–84).

The theologian whose work inspired this study is David Tracy, and in his 1975 book *Blessed Rage for Order* Tracy uses somewhat different language to express a concept of the "religious" similar to Tillich's and Lonergan's; for Tracy, the religious dimension is marked by its proximity to "limit":

> My contention will be that all significant explicitly religious language and experience (the "religions") and all significant implicitly religious characteristics of our common experience (the "religious dimension") will bear at least the "family resemblance" of articulating or implying a limit-experience, a limit-language, or a limit-dimension. (*Blessed Rage for Order* 93)

But in *Plurality and Ambiguity*, published in 1987, Tracy qualifies both Lonergan's and his own descriptions of the religious; more explicitly than his earlier works, this book takes seriously the "linguistic turn," the postmodern awareness that concepts are never pure but are always deferred, entangled in socially and historically contextualized language. Tracy acknowledges the extent to which postmodernism has disrupted the pure, certain status of phenomenology's conscious intentionality, a factor in both his and Lonergan's descriptions. It is now clear, Tracy says, that consciousness itself is not autonomous but is enmeshed in language and history: "The Enlightenment belief in a purely autonomous consciousness has been as torn apart as Pentheus in the *Bacchae*" (*Plurality and Ambiguity* 16). This destabilizing of the concept of consciousness is, he says, "the major problem for myself in some of my own earlier formulations of the achievements of a phenomenological-transcendental analysis in *Blessed Rage for Order*" (*Plurality and Ambiguity* 134).

But as I have already suggested, this problematizing of human access to the religious need not radically dismantle the concept of the religious altogether. In his 1989 book *Real Presences*, for example, George Steiner argues that something like Lonergan's transcendental exigence is inherent in language itself; Steiner asserts "that any serious consideration of this licentious genius in language, that any serious grammatology and semantic mapping will conduct inquiry towards a valuation, positive or negative, of the theological," and that all discourse is "inextricably enmeshed in the metaphysical and theological or anti-theological question of unbounded saying" (59). Tracy, similarly, is able in *Plurality and Ambiguity* to retrieve the concept of "limit" as a description of the religious. Even if challenges to the autonomy of human consciousness and to the universal meaningfulness of linguistic statements do introduce a new ambiguity and relativity into descriptions of "the religious," they may actually enhance Tracy's claim—and my own throughout these pages—that the religious dimension tends to be related to "limit-experience." Tracy continues to talk, in *Plurality and Ambiguity*, about "religious or limit questions"; indeed, one set of such questions is precisely those provoked by postmodern "resistance" to naive models of certain meaning and autonomous consciousness—"the questions provoked by the sense that in every act of resistance some strange and unnameable hope, however inchoate, betrays itself" (*Plurality and Ambiguity* 87). The religions, Tracy maintains, "join secular postmodernity in resisting all earlier modern, liberal, or neoconservative contentment with the ordinary discourse on rationality and the self" (*Plurality and Ambiguity* 84).

So perhaps even Paul Lakeland's radical postmodernists may be religious after all. In the very act of pushing away categorical concepts that pretend to be absolute but are only relative, postmodernity is settling for nothing less than Tillich's *ultimate concern*; Lonergan's *transcendental exigence* (or language's own implicit *unbounded saying*) drives postmodernism to Tracy's *limit-dimension*. And one great "limit" that thinkers slam against is language. Even Thomas Aquinas, that most orthodox theologian, says that language about God needs to be self-negating in order to indicate that the true being of that which we call "God" can never be made linguistically or conceptually present.[3] Similarly, the deconstructionist literary theorist J. Hillis Miller suggests that linguistic negations may be a way of cracking open the conventional not to engage in utter, scornful skepticism but rather to invoke the never-reached ultimate concern/limit, a ground-that-is-not-a-ground, a "material base" that cannot be reduced to some Marxist physical absolute.[4] The disclosed "base" is an ultimately unfathomable depth that Miller, quoting William Carlos Williams, calls a "radiant gist": "Good reading is . . . productive, performative. Naming the text rightly, it brings the strange phosphorus of the life, what Williams elsewhere calls 'the radiant gist,' back once more above ground" ("Presidential Address" 282). And feminist theologian Sallie McFague argues that the claim that all language is metaphor and that we cannot make present some pure Being or center is valid, but that this need not lead to the conclusion that there is nothing outside language at all: "To claim that all constructions are metaphorical is to insist that one never experiences reality 'raw'; it does not follow from this, however, that there is nothing outside language. All that follows is that our access to reality is in every case mediated and hence partial and relative" (*Models of God* 26).

If answers seem more than ever to be beyond definitive reach, the big questions, the "limit" questions, remain as real and pressing as ever. In the face of postmodern skepticism about the possibility of approaching truth, Tracy, McFague, and other contemporary theologians make it clear that the question of how and to what extent, if at all, metaphor can mediate some deeper reality (divine, transcendent, ultimate concern, radiant gist) is a key modern-day religious question—and one that ought to bring theologians together with literary critics, who study texts explicitly founded on metaphors and fictions. This is a question about religious *imaginations*, about the ways people (theologians, literary artists, ordinary humans) have imagined an ultimate reality—an essentially unnameable reality that is of ultimate concern, that is intended by the transcendental exigence, that is at the limit, that seems to reveal itself even through the web of intertextuality in which postmodern theory has shown the imagining human self to be enmeshed. And I wish to propose that in Christian theological history, two religious imaginations have dominated; borrowing David Tracy's terminology and conceptual framework, I will call them the "dialectical" and the "analogical" imaginations.

---

3 See, for example, *Summa Theologiæ*, Question 13.

4 "The word *materiality*," Miller says, "gives us possession of what it names but only by erasing the named object. What *materiality* names can never be encountered as such because it is always mediated by language or other signs" ("Presidential Address" 289).

Classics and Close Readings

David Tracy's 1981 book, *The Analogical Imagination,* is a careful, detailed presentation of the dialectical and analogical forms of imagination as they are exemplified in the "classics" of the Christian tradition. Tracy, in other words, bases his theology on a literary concept—the "classic"—which many in the world of literary theory have rejected, and I must quickly explain (if not defend) his use of this much-maligned word.

Tracy's definition of "classics"—"those texts, events, images, persons, rituals and symbols which are assumed to disclose permanent possibilities of meaning and truth" (*Analogical Imagination* 68)—might be brushed aside by a postmodernist theorist such as Jane Tompkins, who unites reader-response theory with feminism and cultural criticism, as a remnant of an outmoded and even oppressive foundationalism. Tompkins speaks for many postmodernists when she asserts that "works that have attained the status of classic, and are therefore believed to embody universal values, are in fact embodying only the interests of whatever parties or factions are responsible for maintaining them in their preeminent position" (120). Tompkins, however, does go on to say that she is not claiming that a classic "is simply an 'empty space' or that there is 'nothing there'" (126); she proceeds to formulate a qualified, socially and historically contextualized definition of *classic* that nonetheless does grant the word some status: "[T]he hallmark of the classic work is precisely that it rewards the scrutiny of successive generations of readers, speaking with equal power to people of various persuasions" (126). Tompkins, in other words, sees a classic as a process, not a product.

But Tracy, not a conservative worshiper of the white-male West but a self-described "pluralist," whose image of a "dipolar" God is indebted to process theology, is not as far from Tompkins and her theoretical position as it might appear. Tracy's pluralism guarantees that he will not rigidly fix the meaning of a classic or use it to mandate one cultural norm; he rejects what Lonergan calls "classicism"—"the mistaken view of conceiving culture normatively and of concluding that there is just one human culture" (Lonergan 124). Meaning for Tracy, much as for McFague, is mediated by supple, humanly contextualized metaphors rather than by universal absolutes. Tracy warns, however, that a true pluralism must be suspicious about absolutizing pluralism itself. A retreat into "genial confusion," he says, can be irresponsible—"as Simone de Beauvoir insisted, the perfect ideology for the modern bourgeois mind" (*Plurality and Ambiguity* 90). A true pluralism, it seems, should be open to George Steiner's argument, in *Real Presences*, that an endless play of decentered conversation (the extreme result of the linguistic relativism that Tracy partially endorses in *Plurality and Ambiguity*) is a symptom of the way numbing, commercialized media and careerist academic "research" have blanketed our culture with commentaries on commentaries on commentaries,[5] blocking us from a direct encounter with the challenging, creative "'real presence' or the 'real absence of that presence'" that a genuine experience of music, art, literature, and other classic forms of discourse "must enforce upon us" (*Real Presences* 39). In this spirit of pluralistic wariness of utterly decentered pluralism itself, Tracy calls for a willingness to listen to the classics, including "those other less obvious, only because less intense, classics—the ordinary practices, beliefs, and everyday rituals of all religious persons" (*Plurality and Ambiguity* 97).

In *The Analogical Imagination* Tracy argues, following Hans-Georg Gadamer (245–74), that the very historicity of human culture is a reason for revering, not rejecting, a tradition's "classics." Gadamer, Tracy says, asserts "on strictly philosophical grounds" that "'belonging to' a tradition (presuming it is a major tradition which has produced classics) is unavoidable when one considers the intrinsic, even ontic and ontological historicity of our constitution as human selves. Moreover, tradition is an ambiguous but still enriching, not impoverishing reality" (*Analogical Imagination* 66). Tracy considers a tradition and its classics to be an enriching compensation for "the radical finitude of any single thinker's reflection" (*Analogical Imagination* 66). And he points out that, like it or not, all human selves exist within traditions and it is delusional to suppose otherwise: "There is no more possibility of escape from tradition than there is the possibility of an escape from history or language. No individual reader is any more autonomous than the classic text is" (*Plurality and Ambiguity* 16). He does acknowledge the validity of "the praxis orientation of Jürgen Habermas" (*Analogical Imagination* 73), which assumes a societal situation of "systematically distorted communication" and hence a need for "ideology-critique" (*Analogical Imagination* 75); indeed, in *Plurality and Ambiguity* Tracy says that theologians "should be open to any form of critical theory that helps spot the distortions suspected in the religious classics themselves" (98). But he does not consider such critiques to undermine all interpretations of classics whatsoever, even though "all we can hope for is some relatively adequate interpretations of these disturbing texts" (*Plurality and Ambiguity* 99).

For Jane Tompkins, though, society's systematic distortion of meaning renders traditional classics too radically mutable to provide the enrichment Tracy ascribes to them. With her political emphasis on power and socioeconomic oppression,

---

5 These are expressions of what Paul Lakeland calls the "*obvious*" type of "postmodern humanity," the most truly nihilistic type: "They do not ask the bigger questions of life, they simply do not need to. The twentieth century has washed away the solid cultural ground beneath their feet, and they have learned to survive with no foundations. They are not desperate or morally remiss. On the contrary, they are the public, and the more successful of them are greatly admired, the stuff of TV talk shows, gossip columns, and chic magazines" (9–10).

Tompkins asserts that the thoroughly fluid meaning of a classic is in each historical context created by "quite specific, documentable circumstances having to do
with publishing practices, pedagogical and critical traditions, economic structures,
social networks, and national needs which constitute the text within the framework
of a particular disciplinary hermeneutic" (127). Thus, for theorists like Tompkins
there is no fundamental reality—no human nature, no inherent structure, no "transcendental exigence" or "limit-dimension"—that can mediate even hypothetically
and analogically among various, fluctuating meanings imposed on classics (or
on any other discourse). It is, I think, his emphasis on a "limit-dimension"[6] that
allows Tracy to establish real truth claims without falling into cultural chauvinism.
The affirmation of a limit-dimension, however varied its historical and cultural
shapes, leads Tracy to claim that classics *are* "assumed to disclose permanent possibilities of meaning and truth" (*Analogical Imagination* 68). Acknowledging the
incompleteness and contextuality of the concept of a "religious classic," he does
nonetheless assert the essential reality of its power, its challenging call to conversation: "All interpreters of religion, whether believers or nonbelievers, can employ
something like the theologian's sixth sense that to interpret religion at all demands
being willing to put at risk one's present self-understanding in order to converse
with the claim to attention of the religious classic" (*Plurality and Ambiguity* 98).

As Tracy's analogical and dialectical imaginations have given me the substantive basis of this study, so his concept of a classic supports my methodology. I will
examine the analogical and dialectical imaginations in modern and contemporary
fiction primarily by doing close readings of selected texts, and it is a concept of
the "classic" freed from naive, univocal "classicism" that gives this method credi-
bility in a post–New Critical context.

Postmodernism, as we have seen, warns that classics are not autonomous objects, as New Criticism often assumed. They are compromised: they are always
embedded in a social, political, historical context, and they are fabricated in
language, which defers meaning even as it expresses meaning. But the human encounter with limit and ultimacy—though always local and contextualized—is
nonetheless, even after all the deconstructing and historicizing that postmodernism
can do, a classic experience. My method, then, is to explore religious imaginations
by assuming the reality of classics and hence by doing close readings—aware of
the qualified nature of a close reading, and especially aware that I am engaging not
just in an internal analysis of autonomous works but rather in an exploration of the
classic ways of imaging the religious that infuse these works. Hence, Tracy's
retrieval of the concept of a classic qualifies New Criticism's method of close read-

---

6 As we have seen, Tracy's "limit-dimension" survives the qualifications of the linguistic turn and
even retrieves the notion of a "transcendental exigence," if in a more contextualized, historicized form
than Lonergan envisioned.

ing by acknowledging a something *beyond the text* that the text points toward, and it also qualifies postmodern skepticism by affirming that there is *something* that the text has to express. Close reading of a classic enters into a text and transcends it at the same time; Tracy's definition of classics as "texts" but also "events, images, persons, rituals and symbols which are assumed to disclose permanent possibilities of meaning and truth" (*Analogical Imagination* 68) respects but does not idolize a written text, and I hope it is this moderate and unidolatrous approach to close textual reading that I have adopted in this pages.

Analogical and Dialectical Religious Imaginations

Tracy pulls from the religious "classics" imaginative strands that exemplify his two forms of religious imagination, the dialectical and the analogical. Andrew Greeley, one of the great contemporary popularizers, has very succinctly sketched out a description of these two imaginations; although Greeley's definitions are lacking in nuance, I begin with them:

> The central symbol is God. One's "picture" of God is in fact a metaphorical narrative of God's relationship with the world and the self as part of the world. It was precisely at this point that Tracy's work made its major contribution to my own thinking. His goal in *The Analogical Imagination* was to study the "classics" of the two traditions (the works of men like Luther, Aquinas, and Calvin) to discover the underlying imagery that shapes these crucial works. On the basis of his study, he suggested that the Catholic imagination is "analogical" and the Protestant imagination is "dialectical." The Catholic "classics" assume a God who is present in the world, disclosing Himself in and through creation. The world and all its events, objects, and people tend to be somewhat like God. The Protestant classics, on the other hand, assume a God who is radically absent from the world and who discloses Herself only on rare occasions (especially in Jesus Christ and Him crucified). The world and all its events, objects, and people tend to be radically different from God.
>
> . . . Tracy argues that the two approaches to human society of the respective traditions are shaped by these imaginative pictures. The Catholic tends to see society as a "sacrament" of God, a set of ordered relationships, governed by both justice and love, that reveal, however imperfectly, the presence of God. Society is "natural" and "good," therefore, for humans, and their "natural" response to God is social. The Protestant, on the other hand, tends to see human society as "God-forsaken" and therefore unnatural and oppressive. The individual stands over against society and is not integrated into it. The human becomes fully human only when he is able to break away from social oppression and relate to the absent God as a completely free individual. (*Catholic Myth* 45)

In these definitions, Greeley effectively captures the essential characteristics of each of the two religious imaginations: the dialectical emphasizes the gaps and dissimilarities between things (sacred and secular, human and world, human and transcendence) while the analogical emphasizes the connections, the similarities. Greeley oversimplifies, however, in equating the analogical imagination with Catholicism and the dialectical with Protestantism. Although this equation is handy and often accurate, it needs qualification. When, for instance, Tracy differentiates between Catholic and Protestant religious expressions (*Analogical Imagination* 202–18), he calls Catholic sacramentalism "manifestation" (the disclosure of the sacred within the human world) and Protestant biblicism "proclamation" (the eruption of the Word of the wholly other God, which is radically at odds with the human world). But he describes the theology of Mircea Eliade as a quintessential "manifestation" expression—and Eliade, as we will see, is a deeply dialectical theologian. The categories are somewhat blurred, and they cannot be simply divided along denominational lines.

Certainly there are other frameworks for discussing the religious dimensions of literature. But the concept of the analogical and the dialectical imaginations strikes me as particularly useful in the current literary-theoretical climate because both imaginations are able to take seriously the linguistic turn, which is, after all, a turn away from propositional absolutism[7] and toward metaphor and narrative. Both kinds of imagination are grounded in the insight that the transcendent "limit-dimension" is an absent presence that can be mediated only metaphorically. Where these imaginative visions differ is in their attitudes toward this insight—their willingness or unwillingness to go ahead and use positive metaphors to suggest that which is beyond literal naming. The dialectical imagination, hyper-aware of the metaphoricity of religious language and image, constantly and explicitly drives a wedge between human images and the limit-dimension; for this imagination, ultimate reality is what we do *not* possess, what our metaphors and images can *not* express. But the analogical imagination celebrates the metaphors, weaves them, asserting the proportionate (*ana-logos*) relationship between things, the carrying-between (*meta-pherein*) of meaning. This imagination affirms analogies and metaphors, though it is always at least implicitly aware of their partiality, their hypothetical and playful nature, the fact that ultimate reality can be present not directly but only analogically. At their most sophisticated, both forms of imagination possess an awareness that, in Tracy's words, "theological interpretation, like all such interpretations, must always be a highly precarious mode of inquiry," because theological interpretation reflects "on Ultimate Reality, and thereby on the limit questions of our existence. . . . Theologians can never claim certainty but, at best, highly tentative relative adequacy" (*Plurality and Ambiguity* 84–85).

In this study I will examine the ways in which these two orientations—these two imaginative relationships with the absolute, the religious—have shaped much twentieth-century fiction. In the rest of this introduction I will trace the develop-

---

7 Modernity, with its Enlightenment worship of human reason, was as absolutist in its way as the premodern religious worldview. Postmodernity rejects *both* kinds of absolutism.

ment of the two religious imaginations through the Christian theological tradition, and then I will show how they govern two different ways of imagining that mark contemporary fiction. Then, in the chapters that follow, I will provide close readings of a variety of texts in order to sketch out how the two imaginations have unfolded in modern and contemporary English-language narrative literature.

The Dialectical Religious Imagination

David Tracy's dialectical imagination is related to but not identical with what is called "dialectic theology," a specific movement within twentieth-century Protestant theology dominated by Karl Barth and Rudolf Bultmann.[8] The dialectical imagination goes back much further. Its roots are very deep within the Jewish-Christian tradition; in fact, the great Protestant theologians would probably trace them to the beginning of the book of Genesis and the story of the Fall. I will not go back quite that far, but I will suggest that the second Mosaic commandment is one source of this imagination: "You shall not make for yourself an idol, whether in the form of anything that is in heaven above, or that is on the earth beneath, or that is in the water under the earth" (Exodus 20:4, NRSV). Yahweh's command reflects the Hebrew principle—embraced by the Christian dialectical imagination—that the absolute cannot be mediated through any human/worldly image.

The most obvious biblical "classic" expression of dialectical imagining is Paul, especially in a text that has been of particular importance to the Protestant neo-orthodox tradition: the Letter to the Romans. This is the letter in which Paul proclaimed the principle adopted by the Protestant Reformers—that human beings are justified by faith rather than by works—but he founds this principle on a conviction that humans, in their sinfulness, are radically separated from the good and that hence there can be no bridge between the human world and the divine:

> For we know that the law is spiritual; but I am of the flesh, sold into slavery under sin. I do not understand my own actions. For I do not do what I want, but I do the very thing I hate. Now if I do what I do not want, I agree that the law is good. But in fact it is no longer I that do it, but sin that dwells within me. For I know that nothing good dwells within me, that is, in my flesh. (Romans 7:14–18, NRSV)

In analyzing this passage, Karl Barth argues that by "flesh" Paul does not just mean the physical body; Paul is not dichotomizing physical and mental, body and soul. Rather, says Barth, "flesh" for Paul is the entire human self: "We must, of course, bear in mind the meaning of the word *flesh*: unqualified, and finally unqualifiable,

---

8 See James Robinson, ed., *The Beginnings of Dialectic Theology*, 2 vols. (Richmond: John Knox Press, 1968).

worldliness; a worldliness perceived by men, and especially by religious men; relativity, nothingness, non-sense. That is what I am!" (263). Paul, then, establishes the dialectical vision of *nature* as unsound, cut off from the good.

Paul, at least as he is interpreted by much of the Protestant tradition, clearly exemplifies both Tracy's dialectical imagination and his "proclamation" form of religious expression. But I must quickly note that the key New Testament representative of religious "manifestation" (the sacramental orientation), John and the Johannine tradition, also possesses a dialectical dimension. The Gospel of John emphasizes the divine presence—which for the analogical imagination is "always-already," according to Tracy—within worldly image and analogy ("Those who eat my flesh and drink my blood abide in me, and I in them. . . . This is the bread that came down from heaven" [John 6:56, 58, NRSV]). But the Johannine book of Revelation is a key example of apocalyptic literature, a genre that for Tracy is deeply dialectical, emphasizing as it does the deferred presence—the present *absence*—of the divine, what Tracy calls its "not-yet" dimension.

The emphases on human fallenness and on the not-yet of religious reality are the primary marks of the dialectical imagination. In pre-Reformation Christianity, these emphases crop up especially in the negative theology of the mystics. The fourth-century bishop Gregory of Nyssa, for example, in his devotional biography of Moses, specifically stresses the incommensurability of the divine with any representations or analogies. The "divine nature," Gregory says, "transcends all cognitive thought and representation and cannot be likened to anything which is known." Hence Moses, he says, was commanded not to "liken the transcendent nature to any of the things known by comprehension. Rather, he should believe that the Divine exists, and he should not examine it with respect to quality, quantity, origin, and mode of being, since it is unattainable" (43). In addition, Augustine further intensified the Christian church's recognition of the influence and power of sin, and hence of humanity's dialectical separation from God—an issue that the Reformation would eventually address very vigorously.

If they do not alone monopolize the dialectical imagination, the Protestant Reformers and their successors certainly do present it with compelling power. Luther's proclamation of human depravity, and hence of the abyss separating the good from the human, is forceful and uncompromising. "Human works appear attractive outwardly," he says, "but within they are filthy" (43). He argues that human beings are *always sinning*, even "while doing good," because of their radical disconnection from the divine: "That the righteous man also sins while doing good is clear from the following: . . . from the verse Eccles. 7 [:20]: 'Surely there is not a righteous man on earth who does good and never sins'" (60).

It is Luther who first carries out what "death of God" theologian Thomas Altizer would much later define as the key dialectical strategy: an immersion in the profane, which reveals the sacred only by dialectical negation. Because for the dialectical imagination there is no way for humans to approach the divine, no metaphor that can "carry-between," the only available avenue is a descent into the profane world itself, where God is revealed only as an antithesis, an absence. Radical dialectics, Altizer says, demands "existence in the body . . . immanent existence, a total immersion of the self in the immediate moment" (179). Although hardly a Nietzschean "death of God" theologian like Altizer, Luther somewhat similarly immerses humans in the immanent, nontranscendent world: "Thus, you say, 'How do we fulfil the law of God?' I answer, Because you do not fulfil it, therefore we are sinners and disobedient to God" (62). It is this intense awareness of sin that crushes Christians down—impotent, despairing, in need of grace (which is radically other, unmediated by any human act, ritual, or analogy). The purpose of moral law, for Luther, is to drag humans more deeply into an awareness of their own profane nature, accentuating their realization of their hopeless inability to do good: "'Through the law comes knowledge of sin' [Rom. 3:20], through knowledge of sin, however, comes humility, and through humility grace is acquired. Thus an action which is alien to God's nature results in a deed belonging to his very nature: he makes a person a sinner so that he may make him righteous" (51).

Even Christ, from the sternest of Reformation perspectives, is not a positive, incarnational manifestation of God in the human world. Christ is not an image of God's glory, analogically conveyed through the life, death, and resurrection of an admirable human person who is also a revelation of the divine; rather, the Christ image is an image of radical human brokenness—the cross—a veiling rather than a revealing of God's glory: "Now," Luther says, "it is not sufficient for anyone, and it does him no good to recognize God in his glory and majesty, unless he recognizes him in the humility and shame of the cross" (52–53). God can be "recognized" in the cross only dialectically; experiencing the despair of the cross allows a Christian to infer God only as the negation, the dialectical antithesis, of this "humility and shame." Indeed, for John Calvin, all images of God—such as Christ crucified—are anti-images, images that reveal God's absence rather than presence. Calvin echoes Gregory of Nyssa:

> God, indeed, from time to time showed the presence of his divine majesty by signs, so that he might be said to be looked upon face to face. But all the signs that he ever gave forth aptly conformed to his plan of teaching and at the same time clearly told men of his incomprehensible essence. For clouds and smoke and flame [Deut. 4:11], although they were symbols of heavenly glory, restrained the minds of all, like a bridle on them, from attempting to penetrate too deeply. Therefore Moses, to whom, nevertheless, God revealed himself more intimately than to the others [Ex. 33:11], did not succeed by prayers in beholding that face; but he received the answer that man is not able to bear such great brightness [Ex. 33:20]. (102)

On the other side of the descent into impotence and depravity is, for the Reformers, grace—but this grace is radically other, having no analogy with anything human. Kierkegaard later calls it "the absurd" (188).

No discussion of the theological representations of the dialectical imagination would be complete without reference to Karl Barth and Paul Tillich, two of the towering Protestant theologians of the twentieth century. I can hardly do full justice to these men, whose ideas evolved and developed important nuances over the course of their long careers; indeed, for David Tracy the later, softer Barth (who wrote a book called *The Humanity of God*) is more analogical than dialectical, and this could probably be said of the later, gentler Tillich as well. I will just briefly sketch some of the more striking additions they made to the dialectical proclamations of Luther and Calvin.

The Epistle to the Romans is Barth's great, thunderingly poetic embodiment of the dialectical imagination. One of Barth's theses in this work is that even religion is merely human—in fact, it is the most intense awareness of the human, the profane. Religion, Barth claims, is valuable only because by immersing humans in the profane it reveals (*un*reveals?) God in and through God's absence; God is that which dissolves the human, including religion, altogether:

> Religion, as the final human possibility, commands us to halt. Religion brings us to the place where we must wait, in order that God may confront us—on the other side of the frontier of religion. The transformation of the "No" of religion into the divine "Yes" occurs in the dissolution of this last observable human thing. (242)

Any attempt to humanly mediate the wholly other God is futile and even blasphemous, an attempt to "make Him a thing in this world, and set Him in the midst of other things" (244). Genuine, prophetic religion does not bridge the gulf between the human and the divine; it tears the gulf open. It dissolves any "consequently" (an analogical word, a word that tries to draw connections) and replaces it with "nevertheless" (a word stressing incommensurability):

> The righteousness of God is that "nevertheless" by which He associates us with Himself and declares Himself to be our God. This "nevertheless" contradicts every human logical "consequently," and is itself incomprehensible and without cause or occasion, because it is the "nevertheless!" of God. The will of God brooks no questioning: because He is God, He wills. (93)

It is probably Barth, furthermore, who most clearly argues that the radically dialectical version of a "theology of the cross" is founded on a Christ who is an image of human hopelessness rather than of goodness or victory:

> Jesus stands among sinners as a sinner; He sets Himself wholly under the judgement under which the world is set; He takes His place where God can be present only in questioning about Him; He takes the form of a slave; He moves to the cross and to death; His greatest achievement is a negative achievement. He is not a genius, endowed with manifest or even with occult powers; He is not a hero or leader of men;

He is neither poet nor thinker:—*My God, my God, why hast thou forsaken me?* Nevertheless, precisely in this negation, He is the fulfilment of every possibility of human progress, as the Prophets and the Law conceive of progress and evolution, because He sacrifices to the incomparably Greater and to the invisibly Other every claim to genius and every human heroic or aesthetic or psychic possibility. . . of which He did not rid Himself. (97)

Even Jesus, according to Barth, cannot manifest God's goodness and glory but can merely embody human desperation, revealing God only as a negation of this wretched humanness.

Prayer itself is a dialectical act for Barth; far from being a sacramental or even mystical bridge between human and divine, prayer is a descent into human impotence that reveals how radically *other* the divine reality is:

[P]rayer is not at all the "Miracle of miracles, which takes place daily in pious souls": evidently, because the motive of all prayer is not at all the "Striving after the strengthening and consolidating and enhancing of a man's own life": evidently, because the essential element in prayer is not at all "Communion with God, thought of as personal and experienced as present" (Friederich Heiler). But because even the most sincere, most heroic, most powerful prayers . . . do but serve to make clear how little the man of prayer is able to escape from what he himself has thought and experienced, how utterly he—yes, precisely he—is a man and no more, how completely the bravest leaps and the boldest bridge-building activities of so-called "piety" occur within the sphere of this world and have in themselves nothing whatever to do with the incomprehensible and unexperienced but living God. If prayer—and prayer particularly—be thought of as a tangible experience and glorified as such, the objection is justified which Feuerbach brought against all religion: "We do not know." Beyond this "we-not"—in no way related to the technique of "absorption" practised by eastern and western "adepts in prayer," but in vehement protest against so great an ocean of misunderstanding—lies the reality of communion with God. (316)

Barth sums up his dialectical vision with these definitive words:

There is no direct knowledge of God. He decides without the assistance of counsellors. It is impossible to lay hold of Him. Men cannot bind Him, or put Him under an obligation, or enter into some reciprocal relationship with Him. . . . He is God, and God only. (423)

Paul Tillich is less thunderous than Karl Barth. Tillich, in fact, exemplifies much of the softness, the compromise, of the analogical imagination; one of his key concepts for theology is "correlation . . . between concepts denoting the human and those denoting the divine," and "between man's ultimate concern and that about which he is ultimately concerned" (*Systematic Theology* 60). But Tillich does add some important nuances to our picture of the dialectical religious imagination. For example, he extends the doctrine of "justification" to intellectual doubt as well as moral sin; he claims, in other words, that humans are no more justified by their own "right thinking" than by their own good deeds: "You cannot reach God by the work of right thinking or by a sacrifice of the intellect or by a submission to strange authorities, such as the doctrines of the church and the Bible" (*Protestant Era* xi). In both intellectual and moral matters, humans are justified by God alone; hence, it is through God's grace that doubt as well as sin is redeemed: "[J]ust as you are justified as a *sinner* (though unjust, you are just), so in the status of *doubt* you are in the status of truth" (*Protestant Era* xi). The very seriousness of despairing doubt, Tillich says, is "the expression of the meaning in which you still are living," and such despair is a dialectical experience of God: "This unconditional seriousness is the expression of the presence of the divine in the experience of utter separation from it" (*Protestant Era* xi). So the presence of the divine is revealed only in its difference, its absence, from the human (morally sinful, intellectually doubting) world. And Tillich states that it is "this radical and universal interpretation of the doctrine of justification through faith which has made me a conscious Protestant" (*Protestant Era* xi).

Furthermore, Tillich founds his notion of *ultimate concern*, the essence of humans' religious orientation, not on a positive experience of a gracious presence but primarily on a dialectical experience of "nonbeing." Humans, Tillich says, are able to "ask the ontological question"—the question of Being itself, the ultimate concern—because of the "shock of nonbeing" (*Systematic Theology* 186), the human awareness that being is absolutely limited: "Being, limited by nonbeing, is finitude. Nonbeing appears as the 'not yet' of being and as the 'no more' of being. It confronts that which is with a definite end (*finis*). This is true of everything except being-itself—which is not a thing" (*Systematic Theology* 189). Seen in this light, the divine itself is not a being at all, and hence not like worldly beings. Although God is real ("'God' is the answer to the question implied in man's finitude; he is the name for that which concerns man ultimately" [*Systematic Theology* 211]), God does not "exist":

> The ground of being cannot be found within the totality of beings, nor can the ground of essence or existence participate in the tensions and disruptions characteristic of the transition from essence to existence. The scholastics were right when they asserted that in God there is no difference between essence and existence. But they perverted their insight when in spite of this assertion they spoke of the existence of God and tried to argue in favor of it. Actually they did not mean "existence." They meant the reality, the validity, the truth of the idea of God, an idea which did not carry the connotation of some*thing* or some*one* who might or might not exist. . . . It would be a great victory for Christian apologetics if the words "God" and "existence" were very definitely separated except in the paradox of God becoming manifest under the conditions of existence, that is, in the christological paradox. God does not exist. He is being-itself beyond essence and existence. Therefore, to argue that God exists is to deny him. (*Systematic Theology* 205)

That final sentence is a classic example of the kind of paradox that marks the dialectical imagination.

There are, of course, other important theological expressions of the dialectical imagination. I have already mentioned Thomas Altizer, a "theologian" who thoroughly presses home the post-Reformation notion that the only human possibility is a radical negation of the sacred and a descent into the profane; Altizer ends up negating God altogether, proclaiming instead with Nietzschean glee that God is dead. And at the other end of the spectrum from the "proclamation" theologians, who reject what Tracy calls an expression of the religious as sacramental "manifestation," is Mircea Eliade, for whom the only valid religious act is a rejection of the profane/secular and a recovery of the sacred/mythic. In such books as *The Sacred and the Profane*, Eliade says that for the religious person the entire human and natural world is sacrament, overflowing with a manifestation of the divine. Eliade's sacramentalism looks more like a product of the analogical imagination than does the theology of the "proclamation" theologians, and in fact the analogical imagination assimilates much of the myth and mysticism that Eliade venerates. But in his suspicion of the historical/temporal—his vision of a deep abyss between "the sacred and the profane"—Eliade is dialectical. He, like the quintessentially dialectical Kierkegaard, proclaims a radical either/or; the analogical imagination's *ana-logos* and *meta-pherein* are founded on a both/and.

The Analogical Religious Imagination

In describing as "analogical" a religious imagination dominated by image and sacrament rather than by stern negations, David Tracy is indebted to Aquinas and others; the term, however, is now largely associated with Tracy himself.[9] So in this introductory description of the analogical imagination, I will begin not with the early Jewish and Christian tradition but with Tracy's own work: I will describe the analogical theology that Tracy maps out primarily in *Blessed Rage for Order* and *The Analogical Imagination* and secondarily in *Plurality and Ambiguity*, and then I will briefly survey the way other religious writers have exemplified this form of imagining.

In *Blessed Rage for Order* Tracy, as already noted, defines as "religious" those experiences, situations, and questions that make humans confront a *limit*. Tracy says that these experiences take both positive and negative forms:

> The concept itself is mediated by "showing" the implications of certain crucial positive and negative experiential limit-situations. More exactly, limit-situations refer to

---

9 In a later chapter I will discuss William Lynch's use of the term "analogical imagination"—by which he means something very similar to Tracy's concept—in his famous and still valuable literary-critical work *Christ and Apollo*.

two basic kinds of existential situations: either those "boundary" situations of guilt, anxiety, sickness, and the recognition of death as one's own destiny or those situations called "ecstatic experiences"—intense joy, love, reassurance, creation. All genuine limit-situations refer to those experiences, both positive and negative. (*Rage* 105)

Tracy calls the negative experiences, the encounters with a limiting boundary, experiences of a "limit-to," and the positive, ecstatic experiences a recognition of a gracious "limit-of": "we both experience our own human limits (limit-to) as our own as well as recognize, however haltingly, some disclosure of a limit-of our experience" (*Rage* 105). The experiences of a limit-to are quite similar to those immersions in the profane that Luther and the other dialectical theologians speak of. But in saying that humans also experience a limit-*of*, Tracy is adding a slightly different flavor to his analysis of the religious. Tracy claims that inherent in limit-to experiences are disclosures of a "limit-of whose graciousness bears a religious character" (*Rage* 106). The experience of the limit-to is, for Tracy, the "first key" of the religious, but beyond this is another level, a glimpse of a "limit-of the very meaning of existence itself," a gracious grounding reality:

[R]eflection upon limit-questions and limit-situations does disclose the reality of a dimension to our lives other than the more usual dimensions: a dimension whose first key is its reality as limit-to our other everyday, moral, scientific, cultural, and political activities; a dimension which, in my own brief and hazy glimpses, discloses a reality, however named and in whatever manner experienced, which functions as a final, now gracious, now frightening, now trustworthy, now absurd, always uncontrollable limit-of the very meaning of existence itself. I find that, although religiously rather "unmusical" myself, I cannot deny this reality. I also find that reflection upon limit-questions and limit-situations helps me to locate, if not adequately to name, that reality. A neologism does not really seem needed here: that reality is religious. (*Rage* 108–9)

The fact that this religious reality is revealed as *limit* does give it a dialectical dimension; religious limit-language, Tracy says, defamiliarizes, interrupts: "Religious language . . . employs and explodes all our ordinary language forms in order to jar us into a recognition of what, on our own, can seem only a desirable but impossible possible mode-of-being-in-the-world" (*Rage* 135–36). Nonetheless, since for Tracy limit-to experiences also mediate an experience of a grounding reality, a limit-of (however cloudy and mysterious such a ground is), there may at least be bridges (metaphors, "carryings-between") linking the ordinary and the transcendent.

Not surprisingly, the metaphorical picture of God that Tracy paints contains just such a bridge. If "God" is a metaphorical image of the gracious limit-of disclosed through a confrontation with the limit-to, then such a reality could not be utterly removed, distant, sublimely disinterested, and unchangeable. Tracy suggests that the God imaged by analogical Christianity (though in *Blessed Rage for Order* he is not yet using the term "analogical") is "dipolar"—both the "wholly other" God of the Barthians and the immanent, relational God of natural religion. And he constructs this image of God from an analogy with the human self, hence suggesting that such analogies are valid:

> When we affirm that God is dipolar, . . . we affirm that God has both a concrete pole which is eminently social and temporal, an ever-changing, ever-affecting, ever-being-affected actuality, and an abstract pole which is well-defined—if "concretely misplaced"—by traditional Western reflection upon the metaphysical attributes of the Wholly Absolute One. By means of the metaphysical employment of the analogy of the social and temporal self's own dipolar structure, this dipolar understanding of God presents one with what seems to be a coherent and thereby a meaningful concept for the reality of God. For the dipolar concept insists that God alone is both absolute and supremely relative, both ground of all reality and affected by all reality. (*Rage* 183)

Tracy even more explicitly defends the value of analogies and metaphors when he talks about the downright *factual* status of fictions, and builds from this a definition of religious sacrament. Aristotelian actualizations of the possible, he says, are not the only facts. Rather, fiction is also fact insofar as it is a symbolic "re-presentation"—that is, a disclosure of an experience that, although not actualized, *is* already by virtue of its "making present anew, through symbolic expression, a human reality (for example, our basic trust in the worthwhileness of existence) which somehow had become threatened or forgotten" (*Rage* 215). Tracy maintains that fiction, "by redescribing our everyday experience, represents certain imaginative possible modes-of-being-in-the-world that can become actualized for us." The "primordial symbols of our culture," Tracy says, are more than "*mere possibilities.*" Rather, they are "facts: facts, to be sure, not as the actualization of a possibility but facts as ritual, as fictional, as symbolic representations of a real possibility. All genuine re-presentations are not to be assigned to the category 'mere possibility' but the category 'fact'" (*Rage* 215). And sacrament is just such a fact. Without denying the metaphoricity—the as-if dimension—of metaphor, Tracy is able to defend the notion that sacrament makes present the absent and unnameable other: "A Christian sacrament is traditionally believed to be a fact as the re-presentation of a real possibility which God has made present to humanity in Christ Jesus" (*Rage* 215).

Tracy's *Blessed Rage for Order* lays out many of the parameters of the analogical imagination: its image of divine reality as proximate limit-of rather than radically separate; its model of God as dipolar, with a social/immanent as well as unchangeable/transcendent aspect; and its defense of the value of metaphor, analogy, and fiction as re-presentations of the not-actual yet already-real. But it is in his book *The Analogical Imagination* that Tracy most fully sketches out his vision of the analogical alternative to dialectical imagining.

In this later book, Tracy somewhat redefines religion; his new definition does not contradict his earlier notion, in *Blessed Rage for Order*, of religion as encounter with limit, but it does more fully indicate that Tracy's analogical imagination sees things in a quite literally *holistic* way: "[T]he questions which religion addresses," he says, "are the fundamental existential questions of the meaning and truth of individual, communal and historical existence as related to, indeed as both participating in and distanced from, what is sensed as the whole of reality" (*Analogical Imagination* 157–58). A religious *classic*, therefore (and a thesis of my own study is that good secular literature can contain a religiously classic dimension), "may be viewed as an event of disclosure, expressive of the 'limit-of,' 'horizon-to,' 'ground-to' side of religion. . . . [E]xplicitly religious classic expressions will involve a claim to truth as the event of a disclosure-concealment of the whole of reality *by the power of the whole*—as, in some sense, a radical and finally gracious mystery" (*Analogical Imagination* 163). Note that this holistic, analogical description of religion and religious classics contains a dialectical dimension: as mediated by metaphor, religion is *concealment* as well as disclosure. But for Tracy's analogical imagination, religion is at least *partial disclosure* as well as concealment.[10]

Tracy goes on, in *The Analogical Imagination*, to discuss two classic forms of religious expression that I have already mentioned: manifestation and proclamation. "Proclamation" is recognizably dialectical; proclamation theologies are biblical Protestant theologies, which stress the fallenness of the profane world—"radical nonparticipation dominates" (*Analogical Imagination* 203)—into which the divine Word bursts as radically negating, wholly other. In "manifestation," on the other hand, a "radical sense of participation predominates" (*Analogical Imagination* 203), and humans can fully enter into the realm of the primal sacred through myth and ritual. But manifestation in its pure form—the form described and endorsed by Mircea Eliade—is also dialectical rather than analogical; as much as proclamation theologies immerse humanity in the "profane" realm, the realm of the temporal and historical with no natural access to the sacred, extreme manifestation theologies reject the profane and seek immersion in a sacred reality that is nontemporal, nonhistorical.

The analogical, sacramental imagination, however, as usual says not either/or but both/and: a yes to secular history *and* to the primal sacred. "Indeed a sacra-

---

10 In *Plurality and Ambiguity*, as we have seen, Tracy further elaborates on this issue of religious classics' concealment of ultimate reality because all texts are compromised by the plurality of linguistic meaning and the ambiguity of cultural/historical context. But he maintains his belief that classics do disclose, at least partially, through their dialogue with the interpreting subject.

ment," says Tracy, "is nothing other than a decisive re-presentation of both the events of proclaimed history and the manifestation of the sacred cosmos" (*Analogical Imagination* 216). Sacrament yokes together, declares analogous, what dialectics wrenches apart. The dialectical way of describing the human relationship with the whole is a "*not-yet*," imaged by the crucified Christ, "charged with the prophetic, apocalyptic, eschatological sense of a 'great refusal' to the present order of things" (*Analogical Imagination* 312). The analogical way, however, is an "*always-already*"—"the exaltation of a fundamental trust, a wonder at the giftedness of life itself, a radical, universal and finally incomprehensible grace, a pervasive sense of a God of love who is never an 'inference' but an always-present reality to each and to all" (*Analogical Imagination* 311). The analogical imagination entertains a most stunning analogy or simile, even as it is aware of the dialectical "not" enclosed within the "like": "If Jewish, Christian or Islamic, the texts will witness to a faith that the whole is like a who, involved in self-manifestation in the event or events to which these texts bear witness" (*Analogical Imagination* 255).

The analogical imagination is not all sunny optimism. Even this imagination, as I have already noted, contains a dialectical movement; limit experiences include a "No" to the ordinary even if they also affirm a "Yes," and metaphors and analogies link things that are *like*, but *are not*, each other. Tracy warns: "Where analogical theologies lose that sense for the negative, that dialectical sense within analogy itself, they produce not a believable harmony among various likenesses in all reality but the theological equivalent of 'cheap grace': boredom, sterility and an atheological vision of a deadening univocity" (*Analogical Imagination* 413). But Tracy argues that this negative movement operates as a disclosure of the mystery beneath the conventional rather than as an exposure of utter nothingness; he distinguishes this from the negative movement of deconstruction (though what he is referring to is not all of deconstructionist theory but rather the most radically negating strains of postmodernism):

> For most of us, we must be content to allow our present negations of our former negations of "all that" suffice, as we catch a glimpse—no more, but no less—of the astonishing always-already reality that there is anything at all. . . .
> A deconstructionist negative dialectic . . . will "deconstruct" all "meanings" and unravel the thread of every confining web of order. We will do so in order to experience the joyful, life-affirming, self-overcoming vertigo of the underlying, non-grounding nothingness which is the uncanny we should seek and must learn to love. (*Analogical Imagination* 360)

Limit-to/limit-of, secular/sacred, history/myth, actuality/fiction, not-yet/always-already: there are many dialectical antimonies that the analogical imagination holds together—creating metaphor bridges that carry-between. (An important one, as we will see, is the bridge that the analogical imagination builds between *eros*, desiring love, and *agape*, selfless love.) But *The Analogical Imagination* ends by affirming a most modest bridge, that between people: the possibility of conversation. Tracy's analogical pluralism recognizes the extent to which conversation is *not*—the extent to which individuals are trapped in their own experience—and yet it also affirms that analogy allows some communication, some self-transcendence, to occur: "[E]ach of us understands each other through analogies to our own experience or not at all" (*Analogical Imagination* 451). It is precisely our experience of analogies between ourselves and human others that, Tracy says, nudges us (by virtue, perhaps, of what Lonergan calls the transcendental exigence) to imagine analogies between ourselves and the "whole": "Only by analogically reaching out to the hard concreteness of the other and through that expanding conversation to the proleptic concreteness of the whole, will any of us find that we arrive where we began only to know the place for the first time" (*Analogical Imagination* 452). And in his later, explicitly postmodernist *Plurality and Ambiguity*, Tracy states even more emphatically that conversation is the crux of the analogical imagination:

> Conversation in its primary form is an exploration of possibilities in the search for truth. In following the track of any question, we must allow for difference and otherness. At the same time, as the question takes over, we notice that to attend to the other as other, the different as different, is also to understand the different *as* possible. To recognize possibility is to sense some similarity to what we have already experienced or understood. But similarity here must be described as similarity-in-difference, that is, analogy. An imagination trained to that kind of encounter is an analogical imagination. (20)

I will now quickly show how Tracy converses, in a sense, with other theologians; I will indicate how the analogical imagination has evolved within the Christian tradition. And then I will undertake the real conversation that I wish to initiate in this study: that between theology and literature.

If the prophetic and the Pauline traditions are biblical sources of the dialectical imagination, the Wisdom and Johannine traditions are sources of the analogical. The female personification of God in the Wisdom literature is much more immanent, more connected with humanity and nature, than the starkly transcendent God who warns Moses not to image the divine in any way. And John's Gospel's story of the Logos made flesh is a good imaginative presentation of divine reality as always-already, especially for those who eat the flesh and drink the blood of the Christ.

It is foolish to separate the two imaginations altogether, however; that in itself would be extreme dialectical thinking. So I must point out again that the Johannine tradition also produced the biblical book that represents the profoundly dialectical genre of apocalyptic literature: the book of Revelation. The dialectical vision remains enfolded within the analogical, the implicit "not" within each statement of metaphor or analogy. And this is the way the dialectical imagination exists, I think, within the mystical tradition of the early church. Although, as I pointed out, Gregory of Nyssa's retelling of the Moses story contains a dialectical negation, a warning against assuming that images mediate God, much of Gregory's *Life of Moses* is a vivid example of analogical imagining—a fabric of analogies and metaphorical linkages (some of which seem strained and arbitrary to modern tastes). Some classic mysticism *is* quite thoroughly dialectical, a *via negativa* that negates all worldly images and moves into imageless contemplation. But Christianity, probably because of its incarnational and sacramental theology, also possesses a long mystical tradition that makes use of image and analogy as at least a partial and hypothetical approach to the divine.[11]

The most obvious blossoming of the analogical imagination in Christian history is in Thomism. Thomas Aquinas not only writes about the value of analogical thinking itself as a way of approximately understanding the divine nature (always granting the "not," the ultimate incompleteness of this understanding), but he also claims, following Aristotle, that the ideal is enfleshed in the natural world. Thomas's positive view of nature did much to promote an imagining of this world as flawed but basically good. This is quite different, obviously, from the dialectical vision of nature as radically depraved—and the too easy complacency that developed in the late-medieval Catholic imagination is surely one of the things that the dialectical Reformers rose up, prophetically, to deplore.

In the late nineteenth and early twentieth centuries, the Catholic theologian Baron Friedrich von Hügel tried to revitalize the analogical imagination by reintegrating Thomism and mysticism. Later in the twentieth century, Karl Rahner and others like him (including Bernard Lonergan and even, to a degree, Paul Tillich) gave analogical Thomism a phenomenological spin. And most recently, such feminist theologians as Sallie McFague have re-imaged God not as distant, wholly other monarch (a dialectical vision of God) but as mother, lover, and friend.

Stephen Happel and David Tracy describe Baron von Hügel as "a philosopher of religion" who was "the intellectual switchboard for the Modernist conversation" (*Catholic Vision* 133). In the face of post-Reformation Catholic authoritarianism, von Hügel tried to reclaim experience as the key link between the human and the divine. Religion begins with the experiential *Given*, von Hügel says—"with existences, realities, which environ and penetrate us, and which we have always anew to capture and to combine, to fathom and to apprehend . . . as

---

11 Morton Kelsey's popular book *The Other Side of Silence* (New York: Paulist Press, 1997) is a good, practical guide to meditation that explicitly espouses a Western Christian utilization of images as opposed to Eastern imagelessness.

stimulated and sustained by a tenacious conviction that a real, if dim, 'confused' knowledge of reality is with us already prior to all our attempts clearly to analyse or completely to synthesise it" (xiii). Von Hügel claims that the givenness of the religious is similar to the givenness of natural reality. We experience consciousness as transcending itself toward the world and toward the divine, he says; the two movements are analogous (34, 56–57). He similarly defends the analogy of God to a human person; ascribing personhood to the divine is not "rank anthropomorphism," he argues, but rather an analogical imaging of God as possessing the richest reality humans know from the inside: "self-conscious spirit" (50). Hence he protests against the Protestant rejection of images as a failure to recognize the way the imagination can mediate spiritual experience:

> [T]he point specially dear to Luther and his followers, that the act and life of faith have nothing to do, in their generation, with the senses, although, once faith is awakened, there is no harm in expressing this pure spirituality in symbols of sense, is, objectively, a doctrinaire one-sidedness. I kiss my child not only because I love it; I kiss it also in order to love it. A religious picture not only expresses my awakened faith; it is a help to my faith's awakening. And the whole doctrine of the Incarnation, of any and every condescension of God toward man—man so essentially body as well as mind—is against any such "pure" spirituality. (251)

Like the most sophisticated analogical thinkers, Von Hügel understands that a dialectical "not" is curled inside the analogical "like." All "actually lived Religion," he says, is "always simultaneously conscious of two closely interconnected things: *the more than human reality of the Object of its experience*, which Object indeed Itself reveals Itself in, and makes real, this experience, AND *the abiding difference between even this its present experience and the great Reality thus experienced and revealed*" (63).

Karl Rahner, one of the great theologians of the twentieth century, revitalized Thomism by wedding it not only with mysticism but also with modern phenomenology and existentialism. This is hardly the place for a detailed presentation of the complex thought of this prolific theologian, but I do wish to note that Rahner's notion of the divine self-communication as *inherent in human consciousness*—its intentionality, its transcendence of itself—sharply distinguishes Rahner from those who claim that the secular and the sacred are separated by an absolute abyss. Humans by their very nature as conscious beings are, for Rahner, in "the presence of mystery":

> If man really is a subject, that is, a transcendent, responsible and free being who as subject is both entrusted into his own hands and always in the hands of what is beyond his control, then basically this has already said that man is a being oriented towards God. His orientation towards the absolute mystery always continues to be offered to him by this mystery as the ground and content of his being. (44)

Rahner goes on to describe grace not as something radically other but as (to use Tracy's term for the analogical) *always-already*. Having said that humans "are oriented towards God" and that this "original experience is always present" (53), Rahner maintains: "We call this orientation grace, and it is an inescapable existential of man's whole being even when he closes himself to it freely by rejecting it" (57). All of this leads Rahner to his grand analogical both/and—God is *both* incomprehensible *and* self-disclosive:

> [W]hen we say that God is present for us in an absolute self-communication, this says . . . that this self-communication of God is present in the mode of closeness, and not only in the mode of distant presence as the term of transcendence, a closeness in which God does not become a categorical and individual being, but he is nevertheless really present as one communicating himself, and not only as the distant, incomprehensible and asymptotic term of our transcendence. (119)

God's offer of the divine self, Rahner asserts, "belongs to all men and is a characteristic of man's transcendence and his transcendentality." The connection to God is not a dialectical negation of the natural order, but rather "a modality of [humanity's] original and unthematic subjectivity" (129).

This barely scratches the surface of Rahner's theology, and it only hints at how analogies and metaphors might mediate this divine self-communication. It should be clear, however, that Rahner views the human self as possessing a bridge beyond itself, an inherent transcendence. This is quite a different picture of the self from that of the "proclamation" theologians; it is even different from that of a dialectical "manifestation" theologian like Eliade, since Rahner claims that the divine is manifest here and now, in secular human history, rather than only in a primordial past that needs to be recovered through myth and ritual.

But it is feminist theologians such as Sallie McFague who more fully use this Rahnerian insight—that humans are connected, however imperfectly, to the divine—to weave new images and metaphors of God. Interestingly, in her 1982 book *Metaphorical Theology*, McFague, a Protestant, specifically differentiates her "metaphorical sensibility" from David Tracy's analogical imagination. She argues that metaphorical statements, unlike symbolic or analogical ones, "always contain the whisper, 'it is *and it is not*'" (*Metaphorical Theology* 13). She acknowledges that Tracy's post-Enlightenment revival of analogical imagining does take negativity more seriously than medieval figuralism did (*Metaphorical Theology* 198), but she places herself in solidarity with "the iconoclastic tendency in Protestantism, what Paul Tillich calls the 'Protestant Principle,' the fear of idolatry, the concern lest the finite ever be imagined to be capable of the infinite" (*Metaphorical Theology* 13). Still, as a portrayal of a religious imagination, I find McFague's 1987 book *Models of God* to be, in the terms of this study, more "analogical" than "dialectical." Whatever her beliefs about their metaphysical status,

McFague affirms that metaphors can at least hypothetically mediate the reality of God.[12] In addition, she endorses the creation of new metaphors specifically because they reflect what seems to me a very analogical vision: one of connectedness rather than separation.

McFague claims that feminist and ecological studies have made us more aware that the world is an interconnected and interdependent whole, and that previous mechanistic models of the world that represent people and things as atomized individuals need correction. Individuals or entities, McFague says,

> always exist within structures of relationship; process, change, transformation, and openness replace stasis, changelessness, and completeness as basic descriptive concepts. Whereas with the model of the machine, life is patterned on the nonliving, with the organic model the nonliving takes on characteristics of life, . . . and hence the qualities of life—openness, relationship, interdependence, change, novelty, and even mystery—become the basic ones for interpreting all reality. (*Models of God* 10)

Instead of claiming that "laws" and "rights" yoke things together that are inherently separate, as the atomistic/mechanical model does, McFague's model finds "relationships as the most basic given of existence" (*Models of God* 11). And McFague claims that the Christian vision is a vision of precisely such organic wholeness, though this vision has been buried beneath dialectical images of God as ruler over against a world of wretched subjects. She claims that Jesus, in his parables, his table fellowship, and his death on the cross, reveals a loving, inclusive, connected God (*Models of God* 56). And to make imaginatively real such a theological stance, McFague sketches playful (serious, but explicitly metaphorical rather than literal) new images of God's relationship with the world: she imagines the world as God's body, and she describes God as not a distant king but as mother, lover, and friend.

By imagining the world as God's body, McFague pictures God as organically a part of the universe: "If the entire universe, all that is and has been, is God's body, then God acts in and through the incredibly complex physical and historical-cultural evolutionary process that began eons ago" (*Models of God* 73). And imagining God as mother, lover, and friend leads McFague explicitly to reject the classic dialectical disjunction between *agape* and *eros*. In his book *Agape and Eros*, for example, the dialectical theologian Anders Nygren uses an interpretation of Luther to proclaim that divine love (*agape*) is utterly different from desire-driven human love (*eros*), and that God's love is always marked by the radical selflessness of the Cross, the complete emptying of personal desire: "God is

---

12 We saw earlier that this stance separates McFague from those radical postmodernists who would argue that there is nothing outside language, and I think it separates her from the more dialectical branch of her own Protestant tradition as well.

Agape. . . . Only at the Cross do we find God, but there we really find Him. 'Theologia crucis' is the only true theology" (740). But imagining God as mother allows McFague to repersonalize *agape,* not as sublimely disinterested, impersonal love but as deeply concerned parental love: "Parental love wills life and when it comes, exclaims, 'It is good that you exist!'" (*Models of God* 103). And the metaphor of God as lover reclaims *eros;* obviously McFague is aware of the quintessentially dialectical critique of *eros* when she describes divine love as, in a sense, erotic:

> This description of eros—that it is a passionate attraction to the valuable and a desire to be united with it—may initially mark it as a strange candidate, from a traditional Christian perspective, for expressing God's saving love. It implies that the world is valuable, that God needs it, and that salvation is the reunification of the beloved world with its lover, God. (*Models of God* 131)

Finally, the image of God as friend allows McFague to attribute to God friendship-love, *philia*—a kind of love that emphasizes freedom, commonality, inclusiveness, solidarity, hospitality, companionship (*Models of God* 157–80). In each of these cases, McFague is imagining God's loving as analogous to human loving—and hence is imagining human love as a revelation of God.

A Supplement

McFague reminds us again and again that she is not asserting that the world *is* God's body or that God *is* a mother, a lover, or a friend. But I think she is nonetheless in tune with the broadly analogical imagination in suggesting that human imaging can mediate, albeit incompletely, that reality which David Tracy calls limit-of, which Baron von Hügel calls the Given, which Rahner calls mystery. As I have noted several times, both the analogical and the dialectical imaginations possess, in different ways, an awareness of their own metaphoricity. Hence, the postmodern "linguistic turn" is relevant to *both* imaginations, and I must briefly discuss a critic of religion and literature whose theory of the inadequacy of propositional language and of the necessity and value of the Derridean *supplément* strikes me as a nuance that enriches an understanding of both imaginations.

Kevin Hart is a deconstructionist with a deeply religious bent, and in his book *The Trespass of the Sign* he uses postmodern, deconstructive strategies to overthrow classical metaphysics in order to open up space for a truly transcendent, ultimate reality. "Metaphysics," Hart says, invoking Heidegger, "is that discourse which takes Being as the ground of beings" (76), and metaphysics derives this ground from "the principle of sufficient reason," which asserts that "Nothing is without ground" (241). But Heidegger, in examining Being itself, the supposed "ground" of beings, exposed a reality that could have no ground. "Being" is a groundlessness *outside* metaphysics, separated from metaphysics by a leap, revealing metaphysics' inability to totalize, to capture the whole of reality within its system. Derrida would later call this untotalizable excess a *"supplément"*— something *outside* the system that nonetheless emerges from *within* the system, an *addition* to the system that *supplants* the system. And since all systems have a *supplément,* humans never have access to total presence but only to *différance.*

Hart's negative or "non-metaphysical" theology separates God from philosophical concepts in the same way that it separates Being from metaphysics. Such a theology, Hart says, is "one which would show that metaphysics obliges us to take God as a ground; it would uncover a sense in which God could be apprehended as a non-ground; and it would show that the conceptions are systematically related" (104). In other words, the God of faith is the supplement, outside "ontotheology," impossible to totalize, overflowing metaphysical concepts; the God of faith is the addition to rational human philosophy that supplants this philosophy. Not surprisingly, Hart invokes Barth and Kierkegaard to describe this nonphilosophical God, a God who is a shock, a scandal, a God who is *God* rather than some human concept. In this sense, Hart's postmodern, deconstructionist theology sounds deeply dialectical, a proclamation of the bridgeless gulf between the human and the divine. But the notion of a supplement complicates such a reading. *Différance* is an ambiguous relationship, not a dialectical either/or but an analogical both/and: "[A]lthough a supplement adds itself as a surplus, appearing to work for completeness, it is always unequal to the task. That which requires supplementation already has within it a trace of what the supplement brings: just as speech already harbours the difference which marks the supplement of script, so too labour is always already marked from within by play" (Hart 197). The supplement is both outside and inside what it supplements, both not-yet and always-already. This is the way God, for the analogical imagination, is related to the human: as the not-yet who is always-already, as the unnameable who is experienced, imaged, as a person. Indeed, David Tracy himself considers such a deconstructionist insight to be intrinsic to the analogical imagination. Derrida, Tracy says, has demonstrated that presence is never full: "Like a Zen master, Derrida has exposed an illusion, the illusion that we language-sated beings can ever be fully present to ourselves or that any other reality can be fully present to us either" (*Plurality and Ambiguity* 59). So for Tracy knowledge, although real,[13] can only be approximate and hence analogical. Knowledge is always subject to supplementation—especially knowledge of "Ultimate Reality": "There is no classic discourse on Ultimate Reality that can be understood as mastering its own speech. If any human discourse gives true testimony to Ultimate Reality, it must necessarily prove uncontrollable and unmasterable" (*Plurality and Ambiguity* 109).

---

13 Even in his very postmodernist work *Plurality and Ambiguity,* Tracy affirms, "What we know we know with relative adequacy" (61).

Thus, Kevin Hart's discussion of the supplement is relevant to both the dialectical and the analogical imaginations, and to literary texts that lean toward both kinds of imagination; indeed, it suggests the complex interconnection of the two imaginations, each of which supplements the other. I suspect that the analogical imagination tends to stress that the supplement adds to, while the dialectical imagination stresses that it supplants; but both imaginations are aware that images, metaphors, analogies are incomplete and that their supplementation is both outside and inside. And in their treatment of such analogies—their consideration of analogies' power *and* impotence—both the analogical and dialectical theologians have important things to say about the ways human language and especially human fiction-making can mediate significant visions not only of human society but of what Tracy calls "the whole of reality" (*Analogical Imagination* 158).

I will end this introductory presentation of the two imaginations by showing examples of each occurring in two works of contemporary fiction that explicitly deal with religious issues: John Updike's *Roger's Version*, which exemplifies the dialectical imagination, and Andre Dubus's *Voices from the Moon*, which is imbued with an analogical imagination. Then, in the rest of the study, I will show more fully how these two kinds of imagination provide a useful paradigm for describing the ways modern and contemporary fiction writers have presented their visions of humanity, the world, and God.

The Dialectical Imagination in Fiction: Updike's *Roger's Version*

I have already written a rather lengthy piece on John Updike's *Roger's Version*, in which I argued that the novel has a strain of affirmation beneath its negations— that it is, in a sense, analogical as well as dialectical (though I did not use these terms).[14] I still believe that this is the case, and it serves as a warning against too rigidly dividing up the two imaginations. As I have already said, such dichotomizing would itself be an extreme form of dialectical imagining. Nonetheless, Updike is a writer whose Protestant heritage and Christian faith are deeply important to him,[15] and his sense of his vocation as a writer of Christian fiction represents

---

14 See John Neary, *Something and Nothingness: The Fiction of John Updike and John Fowles* (Carbondale: Southern Illinois University Press, 1992). Although in that work I generally describe Updike's vision of God's self-manifestation through the "something" of textured worldly imagery (an analogical way of imagining), I also discuss in some detail Updike's affinity for the work of the deeply dialectical theologian Karl Barth (62–68, 201–12), whom Updike has called "the most prolific, and (it seems to me) persuasive of twentieth-century theologians" (*Assorted Prose* [New York: Knopf, 1965], p. 273).

15 Updike wrote the following in a 1997 issue of *America*, upon being awarded the St. Edmund Campion Award for being a "distinguished Christian person of letters": "I have been a churchgoer in three Protestant denominations—Lutheran, Congregational, Episcopal—and the Christian faith has given me comfort in my life and, I would like to think, courage in my work. For it tells us that truth is holy and truth-telling, a noble and useful profession, that the reality around us is created and worth

a very nuanced and thoughtful articulation of the dialectical imagination: "Is not
Christian fiction, insofar as it exists, a description of the bewilderment and panic,
the sense of hollowness and futility, which afflicts those whose search for God is
not successful? And are we not all, within the churches and temples or not, more
searcher than finder in this regard?" ("Disconcerting Thing" 9). It is with only
slight qualification, then, that I am using *Roger's Version* as a literary demonstration of the dialectical imagination. Indeed, if many of Updike's other novels
are arguably as analogical as they are dialectical, *Roger's Version*—with a protag-
onist/narrator, Roger Lambert, who is a Barthian theologian, and a particularly
severe one at that—seems to me a sharp literary embodiment of the dialectical
way of imagining humans' relationship with what David Tracy calls the "limit-
dimension." Although the novel as a whole may to a degree ironize Roger's fierce
negativity, it is Roger's imagination that dominates the book—and a more dialectical imagination would be difficult to find.

The novel itself is designed dialectically. Virtually every section is organized
around a conflictual or at least tense situation between some pair from among the
major characters: Roger himself, a theologian at a divinity school (which appears
to be Harvard), a glum skeptic who thinks that God, if there is one, is radically
absent from the human world; Dale Kohler, a young Christian computer scientist,
who believes in an immanent God and is determined to prove God's existence sci-
entifically; Esther Lambert, Roger's wife; and Verna, daughter of Roger's half
sister, Edna. There are various dialectical pairings throughout the book (not the
least of which is the pairing between Dale's immanent God and Roger's transcendent one), but I will focus on five that I take to be primary: Roger and Dale, Dale
and Esther, Dale and his computer, Roger and Verna, and Roger and Esther.

Much of the novel is a kind of Platonic dialogue between Roger and Dale. The
action begins with Dale's arrival in Roger's office to discuss the possibility of his
receiving a grant from the divinity school for his research project: an attempt to
prove God's existence, using a computer. Roger agrees to the interview only because Dale is a friend of his half niece, Verna, and he proceeds to tear apart what
he considers Dale's blasphemous view of an immanent God—a self-manifesting
rather than self-concealing God. Dale's God is one who shows a face within
nature, a God who is not separated from the human world by an abyss. "The physi-
cists are getting down to the nitty-gritty," Dale proclaims; "they've really just
about pared things down to the ultimate details, and the last thing they ever expected is happening. God is showing through" (9). This God, Dale says, is not
some safe object for academic study; it is a real, living God—"God as a *fact*, a fact
about to burst upon us, right up out of Nature" (19). And, since Dale imagines God

---

celebrating, that men and women are radically imperfect and radically valuable" ("Disconcerting
Thing" 9).

analogically, he believes that the parts of the universe are microcosmic mirrors of God; thus he proposes to analyze parts of the natural world with a computer to show that God, or God's ordering principle, is contained within these parts.

Of course, the Barthian Roger has no patience with Dale's natural religion, nor with his homey metaphors for the wholly other. Dale describes God as having a "face" which is *"breaking through"*: "They've been scraping away at physical reality all these centuries, and now the layer of the little left we don't understand is so fine God's face is staring right out at us" (20). But Roger sneeringly dismantles this inappropriate metaphor: "Sounds rather grisly, frankly. Like a face through a frosted bathroom door. Or like . . . that poor young sailor from the Franklin expedition they found this past summer up in Canada, nicely preserved by the ice. He was staring right out at us, too" (20). Dale, in other words, employs his metaphors to affirm their at least partial adequacy to reality, but Roger employs his to dialectically expose and explode metaphoricity itself. Similarly, Dale suggests that the vastness of the universe may be "like a demonstration. Of what infinity is" (17). But for Roger the vastness of the natural universe evokes merely a crushing vision of human puniness:

> "I suppose a fundamental question . . . about any modern attempts to relate the observed cosmos to traditional religion becomes the sheer, sickening extravagance of it. If God wished, as Genesis and now you tell us, to make the world as a theatre for Man, why make it so unusably vast, so horribly turbulent, and, ah, crushing to contemplate? . . ." (16)

Roger condemns Dale's theology as "blasphemy" (21), and then reflects on the need to keep God utterly disentangled from nature and the human; in doing so he again plays with, and imaginatively explodes, a metaphor for transcendent imagining: "Barth had been right: *totaliter aliter*. Only by placing God totally on the other side of the humanly understandable can any final safety for Him be secured. . . . All else is mere philosophy, churning the void in the hope of making butter, as it was put by the junior Oliver Wendell Holmes" (32). Holmes's comical metaphor is what the analogical imagination can look like to one who imagines in a sternly dialectical way: soft, buttery, futile.

In a later confrontation, Roger more directly attacks two of Dale's theological strategies that are specifically indicative of the analogical imagination: Dale's claims that subject and object are intrinsically related and that reality is "holistic" rather than a collection of discrete objects. Roger—like Luther, Barth, and Altizer—immerses humanity in a radically fleshly reality, with no analogical bridge to any transcendence, but Dale tries to refute this position, which he considers thoroughgoing materialism. He invokes subjectivity and mental phenomena, and he uses Heisenberg's uncertainty principle to argue that such phenomena are integrally related to physical reality. Quantum physics, Dale claims, tells us that consciousness is "intrinsic to matter: a particle doesn't become actual until it's observed. Until the observation is made, it's a ghost. According to Heisenberg's uncertainty principle—" (180). But at the mention of Heisenberg, Roger rears up angrily: "If there's one thing that makes me intellectually indignant around here it's the constant harping of calf-eyed students on quantum mechanics and the Heisenberg principle as proof of that hoary old philosophical monstrosity Idealism" (180). In place of Heisenberg's principle—which involves analogical imagining, seeing subject and object as inherently analogous, related—Roger offers Tertullian's dialectical affirmation via negation: "*'Certum est,'* I murmured, *'quia impossible est'*" (180). Instead of trying to imagine a reconciliation between seeming incompatibles, Roger yanks them apart and proclaims the dialectical paradox: it is certain because it is impossible. Flesh cannot be reconciled with spirit, nor can God's incarnation in Christ be made understandable through human metaphor. Rather, Roger takes his stand with the "shame, embarrassment" (181) of the fleshly: "Without some huge effort of swallowing shame such as Tertullian outlines, there is no way around matter. It's implacable. It doesn't give a damn about us one way or another. It doesn't even know we're here" (182). And naturally, when Dale goes on to suggest—introducing the kind of ecological theology that Sallie McFague subscribes to—that the modern vision is one of an interconnected cosmos suggested by the word "holistic," Roger is even more outraged. "Next to the indeterminacy principle," he tells Dale, "I have learned in recent years to loathe most the word 'holistic,' a meaningless signifier empowering the muddle of all the useful distinctions human thought has labored at for two thousand years" (183). Roger neatly sums up his attitude about analogical models that attempt to mediate the truth about the absolute: "If it's a faithful model," he says, "it'll plead the Fifth Amendment, just like the real thing" (109).

In describing his interactions with Dale, then, Roger demonstrates a dialectical imagination both in the specific theology he espouses and in the way he attacks any use of metaphor or analogy to mediate an understanding of what Tracy calls the limit-dimension. And Roger also demonstrates his dialectical imagination when he describes the way his thoughts about Dale shape his experience of the world. As he walks through Boston-area streets, for instance, which he knows that Dale himself recently traversed, Roger pictures his surroundings through Dale's eyes; he does this, however, to suggest not a connection between himself and Dale—an analogy between his experience and Dale's—but rather the gap between them. Roger first describes his trek with specific, concrete Updikean detail, and it is a gloomy, empty vision of suburbia that he conveys:

> A supermarket had boarded up the lower portions of its plate-glass windows, making it harder to break them. A drugstore advertised itself with a dead neon sign. . . . There were no more Volvos and Hondas, just Chevies and Plymouths and Mercurys, rusted and nicked, Detroit's old boats being kept afloat by the poor. . . . (54)

In the face of this suburban decay, Roger tries out Dale's analogical tendency to see metaphors of glory, which is exposed as naive if not ridiculous:

> On the asphalt of a gasoline station a puddle of an astonishingly pure green color meant that here a car had been bled of antifreeze; but I sensed that to Dale such utter viridity would have been a marvel, a signifier of another sort, a sign from above. To a believer of his elemental sort glory would have been in the air. . . .
>
> I was seeing with Dale's still-religious eyes. Across the tracks, I saw on the renewed sidewalk a dog turd of extraordinary blackness, a coiled turd black as tar. A certain breed, or an unusual meal? Or an unvarnished wonder, an auspice, like the intensely green puddle? (54–55, 57)

In the context of the entire novel, in which Roger's own irony is at least somewhat ironized, this parody of the analogical imagination may be more affectionate and positive than it here seems. But for our purposes, this is a good example of how the dialectical imagination works: it immerses itself entirely in the profane, secular world, and it spins connective metaphors only to unveil the way they miss the mark.

And this is how Roger narratively presents the relationship—the sexual affair that develops—between Dale and Esther, Roger's wife. Roger uses their affair as a metaphor, an analogy illustrating Tertullian's theological analyses. But he makes it a thoroughly ironic analogy, one that tears itself apart rather than affirming its own validity. Roger accomplishes this by pitting two kinds of discourse against each other: the theological and the pornographic. First he indulges in a sermon— heavily peppered with Latin—on Tertullian's teaching, in *De resurrectione carnis*, that the resurrection of the body is a necessary Christian doctrine because "the flesh cannot be dispensed with by the soul" (160). This would seem to be an opening for the analogical imagination, an imagining of the correspondence between body and soul. But Roger uses these ideas as a way of immersing himself in the disgustingly fleshly: "The thought of all our pale and rancid bodies jostling perpetually in some eternal locker room of a Heaven sickened me" (162). And then he ironizes his entire reflection on this religious limit-dimension by ostensibly illustrating it with pornographic images of Dale and Esther's sexual shenanigans:

> Esther's studious rapt face descends, huge as in a motion picture, to drink the bitter nectar and then to slide her lips as far down the shaft as they will go, again and again, down past the *corpus spongiosum* to the magnificent twin *corpora cavernosa* in their sheath of fibrous tissue and silk-smoothed membrane, their areolar spaces flooded and stuffed stiff by lust; her expert action shows a calculated tenderness, guarding against her teeth grazing, care on one side and trust on another emerging *per carnem*. . . . (163–64)

The ironic play of Latin and the ironic juxtapositions of these comically graphic imitations of pornographic films ("huge as in a motion picture") with learned

theological discourse are a dialectical strategy, disclosing the radical incommensurability of the theological and the human. And it is precisely this incommensurability that is revealed in the novel's two most explicitly religious scenes: the
first, in which Dale sees (but doesn't see) God's face on his computer screen; and
the second, in which Roger and Verna, in an encounter that is shockingly immoral
even by Updikean standards, have a kind of religious epiphany (or anti-epiphany).

Late in the novel, Dale's attempt to prove God's existence has been getting
increasingly desperate. By gnawing away at Dale's beliefs and then essentially engineering Dale's adulterous relationship with Esther, Roger has been progressively
immersing Dale in the profane: "my prayers at night," Dale confesses to Roger,
"—they feel unheard. I've broken some connection" (187). Still, as Dale hovers
over his computer—punching in data, searching for evidence of order within the
micro-model that will prove the existence of an ordering principle in the macro-
universe—his imagination is still hoping for an analogical revelation of the divine
reality through images on his monitor:

> The merged images, as the heaped-on transformations dispassionately work upon
> them, look increasingly like skeins of glutinous polychrome yarn. They look or-
> ganic, as if a certain process of magnification and refinement is bringing up into
> view a core fibrosity in things. There is, Dale supposes, on the analogy of the real
> world, a crystalline level beneath these fibers; but the powers of computer graphics,
> unlike those of the electron microscope, are not yet powerful enough to reach it.
> Dale reasons, however, that the computer world, being man-made, will hold its anal-
> ogous deep structure at a coarser level than the world God has knitted out of quarks.
> He has devised a computer program that applies torque to his chaotic accumulations,
> squeezes them as a giant machine might press layers of shale for a drop, a glistening
> drop, of underlying principle. (261)

And then the "drop" seems to appear: "Out of the instant ionic shuffle a face seems
to stare, a mournful face. A ghost of a face, a matter of milliseconds" (262–63).
The face on the computer monitor, gone in milliseconds, is more an absence than
a presence—but it is an absence that spurs Dale's desire, his passion, to find it
again: "He returns to the terminal and tries again to find that trace, that divine hint"
(264). The text makes it clear that this passion, poignant though it is, is evidence
of idolatry rather than sacramental connection: "[H]e is greedy, spiritually greedy;
he is climbing his Tower of Babel—for a graphic confrontation, a face whose gaze
could be frozen and printed" (265). Feeling more Kierkegaardian "dread" (267)
than hope, Dale desperately tries to pull the image of the face from the computer
again. Instead he finds not a face but a hand, which at first "gives him peace: rap-
ture passes through him" (268). Quickly, though, this hand itself becomes not a
revelation of God but an ironic anti-revelation of the incompatibility of God and
the human; unwittingly parodying the Eucharist, Dale *feeds* God's hand to a computer printer:

> From the other side of the cubicle, near Amy Eubank's lipstick-stained Styrofoam cups, that inhuman shrill chatter of the dot-matrix printer is launched. Imagine being consumed alive by such avid, implacable teeth! Dale is feeding God, that tender shadow on the underside of our minds, to those teeth. (268)

Of course, the "printout is disappointing" (268). Exhausted, Dale asks the computer for a repetition, for a second chance, for a *Deus* who is not *absconditus*. The computer's response, however, is an opaque non-response: "The screen goes a cool gray, saying in unanswerable black letters **Insufficient heap storage**" (270). Dale stares at the blank screen, and then at the empty city windows outside; the episode ends with a painful, dialectical negation of Dale's feverish quest for electronic analogies and sacraments and revelations: "[A]ctually, a row of dead windows, of empty slots, spells words just as well. Zero is information also" (270).

This climactic episode in which Dale confronts God's absence from his computer is one of the novel's two most forceful examples of dialectical imagining; it presents analogies and metaphors for the limit-dimension in order to *un*-present them, to ironically expose their inadequacy and futility. An even more potent example of the dialectical imagination is the episode that immediately follows this one: the episode in which Roger finally has sex with his half niece, Verna. This time the dialectical strategy is not the puncturing of futile analogies but rather the starker narrative presentation of an immersion in a profane world radically devoid of God or the good.

Roger's relationship with Verna has from the start been latent with both a dangerous sexuality and a limit-dimension. As a kind of reincarnation of Roger's half sister, Edna, for whom Roger had distinct but controlled incestuous yearnings, Verna is a repetition for Roger of the possibility of incest. Furthermore, this flirtation with incest has already been linked, within the novel, to that most universal of *limit* realities: death. Roger has been tutoring Verna—a high-school dropout—in American literature, and during an early, sexually charged conversation he has tried to show her the weaknesses of William Cullen Bryant's "Thanatopsis," its failure really to confront the huge limit that is death: the "terror, the really quite radically insupportable terror" (147). Bryant's soft compromises, in other words, are too analogical for Roger's dialectical imagination, which simultaneously perceives both the gulf between life and death *and* that between men and women, the latter of which can be crossed only by sex: "I stood my distance from her, thinking how powerful the sexual impulse is, ever to leap the huge gap between the sexes" (151).

Now, however, near the end of the novel, Roger finally leaps "the huge gap" between himself and Verna, and in doing so he experiences the "quite radically insupportable terror" of death itself. The situation could hardly be seamier. Not only will sex with Verna be adulterous (he leaves Esther in bed, alone, late at night); not only will it be incest. Roger and Verna finally have an occasion to have sex because of an act of child abuse: Verna's illegitimate baby, Paula, has to be hospitalized because Verna has badly struck her, and Roger and Verna will conveniently have Verna's apartment to themselves. Certainly Roger is aware of the sordidness of the situation. He sees Verna, now, not as a revelation of beauty and *eros* but rather of human wretchedness: "I sighed, weary, really, of this half-formed child, of the something half-formed and clumsy about all this abortive to-do we call life" (280). He thinks sadly about the way his Midwestern Protestant tradition has been oppressed by the dark, biblical God, while modern Jews have happily embraced "violin music and clear-eyed, Godless science": "Compared with the Jews we Protestants do indeed dwell in the valley of death" (296). Such thoughts are hardly harbingers of good sex.

When Verna presses Roger to have sex with her, Roger's sharp conviction of the depravity of the act softens, and his language even becomes analogical: "At her attack, the delicious flutter of ambiguity beat its wings, necessarily two, through all my suddenly feminized being. Not either/or but both/and lies at the heart of the cosmos" (301). But the dialectical Kierkegaard called "both/and" the way to hell, and Roger now descends luxuriously into a fleshly hell—literally into Verna's flesh, and in memory into the "musty aroma" of sexually charged hijinks with Edna, Verna's mother, Roger's half sister. And then Roger supplies a paragraph that sums up the dialectical imagination as crisply as any I have seen; he makes it clear that this sexual act was a religious experience—an experience of the sacred, but only through its absence, through a dialectical immersion in the radical profane:

> When I was spent and my niece released, we lay together on a hard floor of the spirit, partners in incest, adultery, and child abuse. We wanted to be rid of each other, to destroy the evidence, yet perversely clung, lovers, miles below the ceiling, our comfort being that we had no further to fall. Lying there with Verna, gazing upward, I saw how much majesty resides in our continuing to love and honor God even as He inflicts blows upon us—as much as resides in the silence He maintains so that we may enjoy and explore our human freedom. That was *my* proof of His existence, I saw— the distance to the impalpable ceiling, the immense distance measuring our abasement. So great a fall proves great heights. Sweet certainty invaded me. "Bless you" was all I could say. (302)

This key passage is not without metaphors and analogies: Roger describes relationship with God in terms of a fall, the distance from a ceiling, and so forth. But these are images and metaphors that dialectically unmake themselves, the kind described by John Calvin: dark, veiled, shadowy images that convey God's "incomprehensible essence" by restraining "the minds of all, like a bridle, from attempting to penetrate too deeply" (Calvin 102). Roger's images, like Calvin's, restrain rather than enlighten. Furthermore, they are images that reveal God not through glory (the word "majesty" here is heavily ironic) but through shame, the kind of shame that for Luther, Calvin, and Barth is the revelation of the divine in the mode of *veiling*—the embarrassing, absurd revelation of the cross. The sacred is revealed only in its absence, only through a radical descent into the profane. The final "Bless you" is a shock, an absurd and unexplainable grace.

This scene is not the be-all and end-all of *Roger's Version*. Roger, in fact, will describe his thoughts as "heresy": "that of committing deliberate abominations so as to widen and deepen the field in which God's forgiveness can magnificently play" (311). (If this is heresy, it is a most dialectical sort.) The book ends with some healing: Verna and Dale return to their Midwest homes, baby Paula moves in temporarily with Roger and Esther, and Roger awaits a renewed, healing contact with his estranged half sister, Edna: "The certainty of this contact, between now and death's certainty, felt to me like money in the bank, earning interest" (353). Most important, the marriage between Roger and Esther seems somewhat healed and enriched. It is Esther who gets the last words of the book; it is she who, I think, somewhat ironizes Roger's fiercely dialectical irony and indirectly introduces an alternative—perhaps graceful and connected—potentiality. The very last exchange in the novel is as follows:

> [Esther] came into the kitchen dressed in a crisp dark suit, with lace at her throat. Her hair was done up in a somewhat triumphant sweep.
> "Where on earth are you going?" I asked her.
> "Obviously," she said, "to church."
> "Why would you do a ridiculous thing like that?"
> "Oh—" She appraised me with her pale green eyes. Whatever emotions had washed through her had left an amused glint, a hint or seed. In her gorgeous rounded woman's voice she pronounced smilingly, "To annoy you." (354)

Esther's fine irony toward her husband the ironist suggests that perhaps there is another—"gorgeous rounded," holistic—way of imagining the human world and the limit-of that grounds the limit-to. In this novel, however, it is Roger's version that dominates, a dialectical version. Any other version is itself hinted at only dialectically, by its absence.

The Analogical Imagination in Fiction:
Dubus's *Voices from the Moon*

Catholic sacramentality is deeply embedded in Andre Dubus's religious imagination. If Protestant Christianity is one of Updike's most important personal and artistic formative influences, Roman Catholicism is equally important in Dubus's development as person and storyteller.[16] Dubus's description of his own reception

---

16 "I grew up," Dubus writes, "in southern Louisiana, in a place of Cajuns and Creoles and Catholics. In the neighborhood where I spent most of my boyhood, only a few girls and boys were Protestants. Most of us came home on Ash Wednesday with dark gray crosses on our foreheads. From the

of the Eucharist is a good reflection on the way, in a sacrament, the transcendent is manifested through the fleshly and mundane:

> This morning I received the sacrament I still believe in: at seven-fifteen the priest elevated the host, then the chalice, and spoke the words of the ritual, and the bread became flesh, the wine became blood, and minutes later I placed on my tongue the taste of forgiveness and love that affirmed, perhaps celebrated, my being alive, my being mortal. This has nothing to do with immortality, with eternity; I love the earth too much to contemplate a life apart from it, although I believe in that life. No, this has to do with mortality and the touch of flesh. (*Broken Vessels* 77)

Dubus here precisely captures the sacramental, analogical imagination as I have been describing it in these pages: a gracious limit-of (forgiveness and love) is experienced through concrete details (host, chalice, words, bread, flesh, wine, blood, tongue, the earth) in a specific, worldly time and place (this morning at seven-fifteen).

Nonetheless, Dubus's *Voices from the Moon* is, in many ways, similar to rather than different from John Updike's *Roger's Version*. Both works have a realistic narrative texture and are set in middle-class, suburban New England; both deal with troubled families who engage in rather seedy (even incestuous) sexual activities; both explicitly grapple with religious issues, with David Tracy's "limit-dimension." Although I will argue that *Voices from the Moon* exemplifies the analogical imagination, there is a lot of dialectical negation in this novella—but Tracy says there should be. Tracy, as we saw, argues that without a "sense for the negative," the analogical imagination leads to "the theological equivalent of 'cheap grace': boredom, sterility and an atheological vision of a deadening univocity" (*Analogical Imagination* 413). The single day portrayed in this novel is an important initiation for the young protagonist, Richie Stowe, in that it moves him from cheap (or at least immature) grace to a more mature joining together of God, self, and world. It is this ultimate *joining together* that makes the book's vision essentially analogical and sacramental.

Voices from the Moon is especially about the joining together of various kinds of love. Unlike dialectical imaginations, which tend to wrench apart forms of love—*agape* from *eros*, sacred from profane—analogical imaginations tend to see them as similar, as like each other, mediated by that synthesis that maintains the reality of each: *caritas*. In *Agape and Eros*, the dialectical theologian Anders Nygren applauds Luther's rejection of this "classical Catholic idea of love, the

---

third through the twelfth grades I learned from Christian Brothers at Cathedral School in Lafayette. The first class of the day was religion, and the Brothers told stories: from the Old and New Testaments and the lives of the saints, and they also told stories to show and dramatize morality. And through the rest of the day, in other classes, they told us stories, in their worthy attempt to teach us about the earth and its people, the living and the dead" (*Broken Vessels* 90).

Caritas-synthesis" (722)—"Luther," Nygren writes, "has observed how the whole Catholic doctrine of love displays an *egocentric perversion*" (683)—and Luther's reestablishment of the disjunction between *eros* and *agape*. David Tracy, however, praises *caritas* as a legitimate bridge between *eros* and *agape*: "As grounded in that gift of trust, *eros* will be transformed but not negated by divine *agape*. That transformation is *caritas*" (*Analogical Imagination* 432). This joining together of the two kinds of love is analogous to the joining together accomplished by sacrament. Most simply, of course, sacrament—as we have just seen in Dubus's brief description—is a linking of the mundane and the transcendent, but Tracy claims that, on a more theological level, sacrament mediates between theologies of mythic immanence and those of historical absence: "Indeed, a sacrament is nothing other than a decisive re-presentation of both the events of proclaimed history [the Word proclaimed in history, the only message from God in this godless universe] and the manifestation of the sacred cosmos [the mythic/sacred, immanent in all of nature, for proponents of full-fledged, often polytheistic, natural religion]" (*Analogical Imagination* 216). *Eros* is like *agape*; history is like eternity—these are the imaginative leaps made by the sacramental, analogical imagination.

Considering Dubus's vivid description of the value of sacrament in his own life and his association of sacrament with love, a love not for eternity but for the earth, it should not be surprising that the action of *Voices from the Moon* deals with sacramentality and love. More specifically, the novella depicts a journey between two sacraments and two forms of love, and it ends with a vision of sacrament that combines the sacred with the ordinary (even the deeply flawed) and of *caritas* that includes more than a touch of (even potentially perverse) *eros*.

The book's main character is twelve-year-old Richie Stowe, a devout Catholic boy who intends to become a priest. At first Richie is a bit of a juvenile Jansenist, and hence his thoughts—though not, I suggest, his imagination—tend to be dominated by a dialectical view of the world. And, indeed, the novella begins with a presentation of Richie's intensified awareness of a rift between the sacred and the profane. The night before the single summer day that the story depicts, Richie overheard something that deeply shocked all his morally idealistic sensibilities: Richie's father, Greg, is going to marry Brenda, the ex-wife of Richie's brother, Larry, and Greg and Larry had a rip-roaring fight about it in Richie's hearing. Over the course of the fight, Richie inferred that Greg has actually been having sex with Brenda (Greg's former daughter-in-law):

> ". . . What do you mean, you started loving her? Are we talking about fucking?"
> "Come on, Larry." (305)

Richie also, perhaps more importantly, inferred that the whole relationship is proof that Catholic optimism about free will is an illusion, that Luther and Calvin were right that humans on their own are incapable of performing moral acts:

". . . You think I chose her?"

"What am I supposed to think?"

"It just happened. It always just happens."

"Beautiful. What happened to will?"

"Don't talk to me about will. Did you will your marriage to end? Did your mother and me? Will is for those bullshit guys to write books about. Out here it's . . . balls and hanging on." (290–91)

In the face of this demonstration of the doctrine of human depravity and the impotence of the will in the face of it, Richie dashes off to morning Mass (which he attends every day) and prays, "Please Jesus Christ Our Lord help me." Thinking about "the temptations that everyone in the family had succumbed to"—the depravity of the Stowe family—Richie says to God, "It will be very hard to be a Catholic in our house" (289).

Richie recognizes that he himself, even at twelve, possesses worldly impulses like those of his family. He remembers that when he listened to his brother and father argue, his heart beat with a kind of fascinated excitement—and, for him, such excitement is a first rush of *eros*, an attraction toward the profane world, precisely the sign of sin in him: "[I]n that beat he recognized another feeling that usually he associated with temptation, with sin, with turning away from Christ: something in him that was aroused, that took pleasure in what he knew, and knew with sadness, to be yet another end of their family" (291). And Richie does not know the whole story of his family's dark *eros*. In a later chapter narrated from the point of view of his brother, Larry, we discover that late in their now-dissolved marriage, Larry and Brenda used to pick up men in bars and bring them home, and then Larry would get vicarious excitement as Brenda had sex with them. The Stowe family *eros* is twisted indeed, an unnerving heritage for a religious boy like Richie.

Interestingly, though, Richie's religious imagination itself has an erotic tinge to it, indicating that beneath his doctrinaire scrupulosity he has imbibed what Andrew Greeley would praise as the Catholic imaginative linking of the erotic and the transcendent. Looking at the ecstatic face of the young priest Father Oberti during the Eucharistic consecration, Richie fabricates a surprising simile: "In movies he had seen faces like it, men or women gazing at a lover, their lips and eyes seeming near both tears and a murmur of love" (291). Though Richie has to deflect this thought—"but they only resembled what he saw in Father Oberti's face, and were not at all the same" (291)—the comparison has established itself, introducing a motif that the entire novella, and especially its ending, will exploit. His feelings about the Eucharist similarly exhibit that linkage between the mundane and the cosmic that for Tracy marks the sacramental/analogical imagination: "Then with his right thumb and forefinger he put it [the host] in his mouth, let it rest on his tongue, then softly chewed as he walked to the pew. He felt that he embraced the universe, and was in the arms of God" (292).

After Mass, Richie goes to talk with Father Oberti about his family, and the wise young priest articulates the message that Richie will have to learn experientially over the course of the book. When Richie says, "I'm afraid I'll lose my faith," the priest tells him, "No. This will strengthen it. You must live like the Lord, with His kindness. Don't think of them as sinful. Don't just think of sex. People don't marry for that. Think of love. They are two people who love each other, and as painful as it is for others, and even if it is wrong, it's still love, and that is always near the grace of God" (293).

As Richie leaves the priest, he has a tiny epiphany of analogical linkage:

> Richie . . . turned and left the sacristy, entered the church near the altar, genuflected, looked up at Christ, and went down the aisle. At the door he turned back to the altar, looked at Christ on the cross, then pushed open the heavy brown door, and stepped into warm sunlight and cool air.
> On the street near his house, in the shadows under the arch of maples, he saw Melissa Donnelly and her golden retriever. (294–95)

Melissa, introduced in this mundane (she is with a "golden retriever") and yet latently mysterious way (he sees her "in the shadows under the arch of maples"), will be the erotic dialectical negation of Richie's agapic love of "Christ on the cross." And yet the prose will ultimately stress the *similarity* as well as the difference between these two kinds of attraction in Richie's life, so that it becomes clear that what Richie is learning today is to connect, not sever, one from the other.

In Richie's first depicted conversation with Melissa, Eucharist is linked, though in a tonally ambiguous way, with smoking. Melissa is envious of Richie's faith—the real, experiential charge he gets from it, and especially from the Eucharist:

> ". . . It's God, so how can I stay home? When He's there every day."
> "I never thought of it like that." The cigarette rose into his vision and she turned in profile to draw from it. "You feel like you have to go?"
> "No. I like it. I love it. It's better than anything. The feeling. Do you think I'm dumb?"
> "No. I wish I felt that way." (296)

Then Melissa shares the thing that gives *her* an experiential "kick":

> "You've never smoked?" she said.
> "No."
> "Here. Try."
> He looked at her, and she held her cigarette to his lips; he drew on it and inhaled bitter heat and waited to cough as he quickly blew out the smoke, but he did not. Then a dizzying nausea moved through him, and was gone. He shook his head.
> "Did you get a kick?"
> "Too much of one." (298)

Finally, with a chaste but suggestive kiss, Melissa initiates Richie into the myster-ies of that other form of intoxication, sex: "Then she leaned over the bicycle and with closed lips quickly kissed his mouth, that was open, his lips stilled by sur-prise, by fear, by excitement" (298). The text—which, bound to Richie's point of view, reflects Richie's own experience and awareness—has so far merely juxta-posed these two kinds of intoxication, the religious and the fleshly; it is unclear whether they are analogous or whether they exist in a dialectical tension with each other. But the linkage has been established.

Later in the day, as Richie is playing softball with friends (he hoped Melissa would join them, but she does not show up), Richie tries to re-present her for him-self, to capture her otherness as a presence even in her absence; he attempts, in other words, to institute a Melissa sacrament. And again the tone is ambiguous; his attempt to reestablish her presence by bathing his senses in various stimuli, mostly drawn from nature, is at least partially comic. Yet the prose has a trace of genuine natural mystery. The attempt to sacramentalize Melissa is leading Richie truly to commune, though not quite with Melissa:

> He tried to taste her, and inhale her, and he smelled grass and his leather glove, the sweat dripping down his naked chest and sides, the summer air that was somehow redolent of freedom: a warm stillness, a green and blue smell of leaves and grass and pines and the sky itself, though he knew that was not truly part of it, but he did be-lieve he could faintly smell something alive: squirrels that moved in the brush and climbed trunks, and the crows and blackbirds and sparrows that surrounded the soft-ball game in trees, and left it on wings, flying across the outfield to the woods where he cross-country skied, or beyond it to the fields where now the corn was tall. (313)

For all Richie's imaginative striving, Melissa remains absent; although this new experience of *eros* has led Richie intensely to experience the outside world, none of these images are Melissa metaphors, Melissa Eucharists. Richie searches and searches his imagination, practicing that act of intentionality that both Lonergan and Rahner consider the inherently transcendent human act: his imagination *in-tends* Melissa, searching for her beyond the images that metaphorically define just Richie's own self. He is trying to make her present by discerning what she, at her home, is thinking about at this moment. And finally he does imaginatively locate her in a small epiphany that is again an uncanny mix of the ridiculous and the truly connected, the sacramental. Richie intuits that Melissa is thinking not of things *he* likes—"chili-dogs, hamburgers, grilled cheese with tomato, Coca-Cola, chocolate milk"—but precisely of that thing that he encountered today as something foreign, other, a Melissa-thing not a Richie-thing. It is the Melissa sacrament:

> Then, picking up a bat and moving to the on-deck circle . . . he saw what her mind saw. The image made him smile, yet what he felt was more loving and sorrowful than amused: she wanted a Marlboro. Her mother was in the house, working with her, and more than anything in her life now, Melissa wanted to smoke a cigarette. (314)

Such a connection, not just with other people but with the natural world, is the foundation of a holistic view that for Sallie McFague is in our time replacing individualistic views of an isolated self over against other selves, the world, and a kingly God. As I argued earlier, McFague's metaphorical approach to theology is analogical, a tapestry of connective metaphors that links the natural, the human, and the divine, rather than a harsh dialectical wedge that separates and then tries to build bridges after the fact. The "organic or evolutionary, ecological model," McFague says,

> is one that unites entities in a way basically different from the mechanistic [individualistic, dialectical] model: instead of bringing entities together by means of common laws that govern all, creating a pattern of external relations, it unites by symbiotic, mutual interdependence, creating a pattern of internal relations. In the organic model, one does not "enter into relations" with others but finds oneself in such relationships as the most basic given of existence. . . . [A]ll entities are considered to be subjects as well as objects. (*Models of God* 11)

Later in the day, as Richie rides and jumps the horse Jenny, he experiences just such a natural holism. This boy, who in his dialectical distrust of all that messy nature that Paul dubbed "the flesh" has feared his connection with his family and their erotic quirks, now feels an integral connection with the natural that is sublime rather than disgusting. He experiences a merging of himself and Jenny and the world through *spiritus*, breath:

> He listened to Jenny's hooves as their striking vibrated through him like drumbeats, listened to her breathing as he felt it against his legs, and listened to his own quick breath too, and the soft motion of air past his ears: a breeze that was not a breeze, for he and Jenny were its sources, speeding through air so still that no dust stirred from the track before them. Then he was in it, in the air, the pine blurring in the distance, and down now, a smooth forward plunge that pulled his body with it, but this time he held, and when Jenny hit, his body did not jerk forward but flowed with hers, in horizontal cantering speed down the track, as he patted her neck, and spoke her praise. (335)

God is mixed in with all this breathy imagery, too: "The two-thirty sun (though one-thirty, really: daylight savings time) warmed his velvet-covered helmet, and shone directly on his shoulders and back, like the hot breath or stare of God" (335–36). Beneath his religious distrust of his own biological nature is a more optimistic—analogical, connected—religious imagination.

I am not suggesting that Richie himself realizes this at his young age. In fact, the chapter ends with Richie pondering on his own rather poignant theology of the cross, which in its innocent, pained way is as condemnatory of the fallen world as Luther's at its most severe. Wounded by a divorce, and now by his father's shocking sexual impropriety and the resultant rift between his father and Larry, Richie concludes with more than a trace of childish condescension that this is the cross that he must bear. But bearing it, he thinks, will take him away from all things of the flesh:

> So it was people. They were the cross, and the sadness they brought you. . . . From Christ he had to receive the strength or goodness or charity or whatever it was to give his father and Brenda more than forgiveness and acceptance. He had to love their days in the house with him, and they had to know he did. . . . He had to love them all, and he could do that only with Christ, and to receive Christ he could not love Melissa. He knew that from her scents this morning, and her voice, and her kiss. (338)

The book never reveals whether Richie will find a way to balance love for Melissa (or someone like her) with love for Christ. But it does end with a scene that suggests that the kind of love—erotic, surely—that he could experience with someone like Melissa is much more similar to that between himself and God than he has yet realized (though his emphasis on encountering God through sacrament—in bread and wine, in the wind that binds him to the horse Jenny, etc.— suggests that his *imagination*, if not his doctrine, has been analogical all along). At the novel's conclusion it is ten o'clock at night; his father is out and Richie, home alone, ventures out into the woods in search of Melissa. He is a juvenile Goodman Brown entering the mysterious Other world to experience a dark *eros*: "clumsily he stepped through the weeds and in and out of ruts, and started to sweat in the warm, close air whose density made him feel he moved through smoke he could neither see nor smell nor taste" (355). But unlike the dialectical Hawthorne's forest, Dubus's woods—though mysterious—are benign, connected to the human world; there are baseball diamonds and dogs and singing cicadas:

> He looked up at the treetops against the stars and sky, then left the trail, and went around the trees and stood beside them, in their shadows, and looked into the infield through the backstop screen, and scanned the outfield.
> First he saw Conroy, the dog, a blond motion, then a halted silhouette in left center field. . . . He saw the brightening glow of her cigarette, then it moved down and away from the small figure that was Melissa, profiled, sitting on the ground. Above her, cicadas sang in the trees. (355–56)

The scene is tender, with a touch of comically melodramatic eroticism: "He was watching her mouth, and he swallowed, and knew he was lost. If only he could be lost without fear" (357). Richie, very aware of the way his feelings are tugging him, looks to the transcendent stars, hoping they will dialectically negate this fleshly experience—though he already suspects that the stars may *side with* this experience: "[I]f only he could look to the stars—and he did: abruptly lifted his face to the sky—and find in them release from what he felt now, or release to feel it" (357).

All that actually happens between Richie and Melissa is that they hold hands and have a conversation: "He watched the stars, and talked" (358). But there is now no gap between the mundane and the cosmic—talking and watching the stars are not in opposition. The entire ambience is one in which everything is linked (not yoked together by force, but in McFague's terms organic, holistic): Richie, Melissa, the night air, the grass, the stars, God; *eros, agape, caritas*. This may mark the beginning of the end of Richie's journey toward the seminary, but it is not an unreligious moment:

> What he felt was the night air starting to cool, and the dew on the grass under his hand holding Melissa's, and under his arms and head and shirt, and only its coolness touching his thick jeans, and the heels of his shoes. He felt Melissa's hand in his, and the beating of his heart she both quickened and soothed, and he smelled the length of her beside him, and heard in the trees the song of cicadas like the distant ringing of a thousand tambourines. He saw in the stars the eyes of God too, and was grateful for them, as he was for the night and the girl he loved. He lay on the grass and the soft summer earth, holding Melissa's hand, and talking to the stars. (358)

Dubus does not achieve this analogical connectedness in an easy, sentimental way. Tracy warns that the analogical must include an awareness of the dialectical—of *negation*—and Dubus's story does so. The Stowe family *eros*, of which Richie is awakening to traces, is very dark indeed; Richie's brother, Larry, in reflecting on the sordid sexual games that he and Brenda used to play, remembers them as a kind of addiction, a proof that Luther and Calvin (and Paul) were right to assert that humans cannot avoid willing the bad:

> [I]t was she [Brenda] who said finally: *There's something dark in us, something evil, and it has to be removed,* and he told her, *We can just stop then; we won't even talk about it again, not ever, it'll be something we did one year.* He kept insisting in the face of her gaze that lasted, it seemed, for days and nights: those unblinking eyes, sorrowful yet firm, looking at him as though they saw not his face but his demons; saw them with pity for both him and herself; and seeing his demons reflected in her eyes, he shrank from them, and from her, and from himself. (320)

There is, in other words, a dark side to the human (and erotic) nature that Richie is being initiated into, one that is profoundly separate from—and self-consciously aware of its absence from—the ordered and the decent. Human nature is hardly ideal in this novel; the closest thing to a "moral" the book has is Larry and Richie's mother's quiet oracular statement to Larry: "[W]e don't have to live great lives, we just have to understand and survive the ones we've got" (355). But despite this revelation of the *limit to* human greatness, a gracious *limit-of* also reveals itself. As John Updike puts it in his review of *Voices from the Moon*, appropriately entitled "Ungreat Lives": "The family and those intimate connections that make families are felt by this author as sharing the importance of our souls, and our homely, awkward movements of familial adjustment and forgiveness as being natural extensions of what Pascal called 'the motions of Grace'" (97). This is the analogical imagination: a vision of the homely and awkward as sacrament, a natural extension of grace. Over the course of *Voices from the Moon*, Richie finds—and the book as a whole affirms—that *eros* is more like *agape* than it sometimes seems to be, and that talking to a girlfriend is like talking to the stars.

Roger's Version and *Voices from the Moon* are somewhat unusual examples of contemporary English-language fiction in that both are explicitly concerned with religious issues. Indeed, the only thing that the two main characters, Roger Lambert and Richie Stowe, have in common is that, for both, the God question is the dominant life question. Some of the modern and contemporary literary artists whom I will examine in this work—James Joyce, say, and Anne Tyler—also deal very explicitly with religious questions, but others do not. But all of them—and, I think, virtually all important writers and thinkers—deal with David Tracy's "limit-dimension," the *limit-to* human experience that is grounded in a *limit-of*. The various ways in which writers of this century have imagined and imaged this limit-dimension can be usefully described as primarily either dialectical or analogical.

2

Conrad and Joyce:
Modernist Imaginations

In many ways, Joseph Conrad and James Joyce are more alike than different. Each was raised Roman Catholic in a deeply Catholic country (Poland and Ireland, respectively); each spent his adulthood in self-chosen exile from his country; and each lapsed from Catholicism. Perhaps most important, Conrad and Joyce are virtually without peer in representing the first and second generations of modernism in English-language fiction. In this study of the imaginations that have dominated English-language fiction in the twentieth century, Conrad and Joyce are very appropriate writers with whom to start.

Literary modernism grew from, but was not identical with, the European intellectual movement that has come to be called "modernity." In his book *Postmodernity*, to which I have already referred, Paul Lakeland defines "modernity" as synonymous with the "Enlightenment project," which he calls "the triumph of reason and the mastery of the human mind over the external world" (13), a replacement of the "authority of both religion and metaphysics . . . by the individual exercise of critical reason" (14). This is consistent with what Lawrence Gamache, in an essay on the "correlation" between religious and literary modernism,[1] calls the "longstanding practice of identifying the time span from the early Renaissance to the present as 'the modern period' . . . to distinguish it from the medieval," a practice "based on an awareness of a shifting focus of attention from the medieval God-centered to a human-centered vision of this world" (67–68). But literary modernism is a shorter and more recent period, "considered most broadly to begin in the last third of the nineteenth century, peaking between 1900 and 1930, and continu-

---

1 Gamache's essay, "Defining Modernism: A Religious and Literary Correlation," uses the lives and careers not of literary writers but of Catholic modernist theologians (Alfred Loisy and George Tyrrell) as exemplars of the modernist movement. Gamache claims that he chose this approach "because religion touches most directly on those facets of human thought and feeling affected by modernism" (68). And Gamache asserts that religious thinkers struggled with these issues *before* literary writers did: "The apparent darkness of modern human horizons became evident to religious searchers sooner than it did to most of their contemporaries, and their perception of that darkness—unlike, for example, Hardy's—was framed by a modernist's sense of place and time and of the general human condition in a modernized world" (78). It is perhaps debatable whether the theologians or the literary artists experienced modernism first; the present study, however, is certainly in agreement with Gamache in finding deep religious issues in the modernist "heart of darkness."

ing to about World War II or shortly thereafter" (Gamache 68). This is really the decline and fall of the Enlightenment period; rather than having an unbridled enthusiasm about human reason freed from religious superstition, modernism is marked by "a distaste for scientific attitudes following the decline of realism" (Gamache 64). By that measure, literary modernism is the last stage of modernity on the way to *post*modernity. If modernity was the breakdown of the medieval synthesis, modernism is the beginning of the breakdown of the breakdown.

The modernist disenchantment with modernity cannot be fully understood without reference to the Victorian Age's last grasp at an Enlightenment synthesis that would be just as airtight as the medieval one. In *A Genealogy of Modernism*, Michael Levenson charts the way the modernist literary movement emerged as the conscious human subject broke off from the attempted (but always fragile) Victorian synthesis between consciousness and authority. Matthew Arnold, Levenson says, acknowledges that transcendent authority for a religious worldview has been fatally undermined by scientific empiricism, but Arnold tries to use this very empiricism to establish a humanistic religion founded not on supernatural but on natural truth. And for Arnold this "natural truth," Levenson says, lies "in the human consciousness of certain psychological experiences, in 'personal experience.' The true meaning of religion implies nothing otherworldly. . . . Religion must be based on human experience" (11). Arnoldian Victorians, Levenson says, felt assured that the loss of transcendent authority was really a gain: "Traditional justifications of value had lapsed, but this was seen less as a cause for regret than as an opportunity. Value will be given a firmer grounding, more in line with inevitable historical development: human subjectivity will become the foundation and support for a range of threatened institutions" (13). Certainty, Levenson says, was now seen to exist "only within the self," but this was "a cause for little distress, since the self was to contain the ground of morality, religion, even the construction of external reality" (17).

Levenson calls this, the brink of modernism's much more thoroughgoing embrace of and limitation to the subjective, "an almost poignant moment in English intellectual history" (13). The Victorian aesthete Walter Pater, Levenson says, saw more clearly than most other Victorians that "to redefine traditional values as phases of the self was to weaken traditional sanctions. Like others, he was intent on restricting attention to the psychologically verifiable, but he had no illusions (or scruples) about rescuing morality, religion or the external world" (17). Gamache claims that in the transition to the modernist era "there has been a progression from the optimistic attempt to discover the real world, studied confidently as the proper object of philosophy and science and as the artist's guide, to people reduced to skepticism and to their own subjectivity" (68).

So the triumph of the subject over the transcendent truth of the past—the survival of the subject as the only foundation of value in the post-Enlightenment world—would become at least as much a problem as a solution, and this problem haunts the twentieth century. As Gamache puts it: "On the whole, Victorians saw the direction of coeval developments in human knowledge positively or, at worst, fearfully; the fearful did not realize the radical effect on their sense of the past and of the present about to invade their basically stable perceptions of the right order of things" (78). Even those Victorians who were fearful of the encroachments of scientific views on a religious sense of value failed, Gamache says, to see the radical skepticism on the horizon, the challenge to a person's "most basic perception of reality" (77). The modernists, however, experienced this challenge profoundly: "The subjectivity and relativity of truth became for religious and literary persons alike a source of deep disquiet, of disillusionment with the heritage they received that was supposed to provide the roots for their understanding and experience of self, society and the universe" (76). Such epistemological relativism will be captured in the increasingly experimental and impressionistic forms of modernist fiction, which inevitably shake the foundations of Enlightenment values.

This struggle between authoritative *values* and highly subjective and unstable *forms*—the emergence of which Levenson finds in the preface and text of Conrad's *The Nigger of the "Narcissus"*[2]—is what Levenson calls "the *agon* of modernism . . . : the struggle between its values and forms, the instability in the forms themselves" (36). This is the context in which the religious imagination finds itself in the early twentieth century, and it is a rich and challenging context, one in which Tracy's two kinds of religious imagination can develop. The dialectical imagination will tend prophetically to call attention to the gaping tension between the "values" (traditional human virtues) and the radically relativized "forms" (subjective, impressionistic); indeed, the subjective forms reveal the *limit to* the traditional values. The analogical imagination, on the other hand, will tend to create bridges and linkages to heal this tension; it will be aware of the modern limit-to but will nonetheless affirm, at least hypothetically and analogically, a grounding limit-of.

In *The Modes of Modern Writing*, a study of modernist and postmodernist fiction, David Lodge examines the experimental narrative techniques, the breaks from conventional literary structures, that literary modernism employed to reflect this severance of subjective forms from traditional values and beliefs. Lodge says that traditional, "realistic" (or "empiricist") fiction—the kind of English-language fiction that by and large preceded twentieth-century modernism, and that reemerged

---

2 Levenson analyzes the tension in the novel's famous preface between, on the one hand, "a rousing rhetorical call for the sensory apprehension of life's surfaces" and, on the other, a demand for "inwardness and depth" (1). And in the novel itself Levenson sees a similar tension—between a thematic sympathy with objective, universal values of "duty, obedience, authority and silence, . . . against individualism, consciousness and loquacity" and a formal commitment "through the person of the narrator . . . to the values of a registering consciousness" (14).

during the world wars, before the advent of postmodernism—is "based on the assumption that there is a common phenomenal world that may be reliably described by the methods of empirical history" (47). Whatever its specific conventions, in other words, traditional realistic fiction is founded on that Enlightenment confidence that humans have fairly direct access to objective reality. But modernist fiction, as I have noted, is marked by the rise of the subject, by the fading of clear and certain objectivity due to the growing skepticism about an objectively ordered cosmos—and also about language's ability to mediate objective truth, to be referential in a one-to-one way, to be a collection of signifiers backed by self-evident signifieds.

In terms of both content and style, this means that modernist fiction will tend to emphasize inner rather than outer reality. In her famous description of the way modern fiction should eschew "the accepted style," Virginia Woolf considers it an unassailable premise that "life" is subjective experience:

> Examine for a moment an ordinary mind on an ordinary day. The mind receives a myriad impressions—trivial, fantastic, evanescent, or engraved with the sharpness of steel. From all sides they come, an incessant shower of innumerable atoms. . . . Life is not a series of gig lamps symmetrically arranged; but a luminous halo, a semi-transparent envelope surrounding us from the beginning of consciousness to the end.
> . . . Let us record the atoms as they fall upon the mind in the order in which they fall, let us trace the pattern, however disconnected and incoherent in appearance, which each sight or incident scores upon the consciousness. (212–13)

The modern novelist, Woolf says, "has to have the courage to say that what interests him is no longer 'this' but 'that,'" and she asserts that "For the moderns 'that,' the point of interest, lies very likely in the dark places of psychology" (215).

David Lodge similarly stresses the inner, subjective orientation of modernist fiction, and he sketches a number of characteristics that emerge from this orientation; the characteristics he lists appear prominently, in varying ways, in the works of both Conrad and Joyce. Modernist fiction, Lodge says, "is experimental or innovatory in form, displaying marked deviations from preexisting modes of discourse, literary and non-literary" (*Modes* 45). Because modernist fiction is "concerned with consciousness, and also with the subconscious and unconscious workings of the human mind," the structure "of external 'objective' events essential to traditional narrative art is diminished in scope and scale, or presented very selectively and obliquely, or is almost completely dissolved, in order to make room for introspection, analysis, reflection and reverie" (*Modes* 45). And because of this subjective and impressionist bent, Lodge claims, a modernist novel tends to lack a traditional, objective form of narration. It "eschews the straight chronological ordering of its material"; it "tends towards a fluid or complex handling of time, involving much cross-reference backwards and forwards across the chronological span of the action"; it "has no real 'beginning,' since it plunges us into a flowing stream of experience with which we gradually familiarize ourselves by a process of inference and association; and its ending is usually 'open' or ambiguous, leaving the reader in doubt as to the final destiny of the characters" (*Modes* 45–46). In place of traditional narrative ordering principles, "alternative methods of aesthetic ordering become more prominent, such as allusion to or imitation of literary models or mythical archetypes, and the repetition-with-variation of motifs, images, symbols" (*Modes* 46). Finally, this deeply subjective orientation leads the modernist novel to forfeit "the use of a reliable, omniscient and intrusive narrator" in favor of "either a single, limited point of view, or a method of multiple points of view, all more or less limited and fallible" (*Modes* 46).

Because of modernism's break from objectivism, Lodge says that "[f]ormalism is the logical aesthetic for modernist art" (*Modes* 48)—in other words, that modernist works are concerned with internal aesthetic structures and not with portraying an objective human or social or cosmic reality. Indeed, Lodge notes that later writers as different as Christopher Isherwood, George Orwell, and Graham Greene reacted against the "subjective novel" for precisely this reason (*Modes* 48–49). But Lodge also remarks that the modernists themselves "often claimed to be representing 'reality' and indeed to be getting closer to it than the realists" (*Modes* 46), and I would suggest that the turn toward the subject represented by modernist writers makes them especially sensitive to the dimension of reality that many modern theologians (themselves largely influenced by phenomenology, philosophy's turn toward the subject) have deemed "religious": "limit" experiences, "ultimate" concerns, the inherently transcendental orientation of human intentionality, and so forth.[3] Lodge notes, in fact, that the materialist drift of much empiricist literature makes it less "religious" than most modernism (*Modes* 51). Virginia Woolf, for example, asserts that the traditional English novelists "have disappointed us" because they "are concerned not with the spirit but with the body," and she claims that the sooner English fiction rejects the traditional for the modern, "the better for its soul" (209). Whatever suspicion some modernist writers, Conrad and Joyce included, may have had about institutional religion, their turn toward subjectivity provides a fine look at early-twentieth-century religious *imaginations*.

So I am using works by Conrad and Joyce to illustrate the forms of these modern religious imaginations. I wish to argue that Conrad's religious imagination tends to be what David Tracy would term "dialectical," while Joyce's tends to be "analogical." I will illustrate Conrad's religious imagination by examining "Youth," *Heart of Darkness*, and *Lord Jim*, the first three works dominated by

---

3 In addition, many modernist fiction writers, Conrad and Joyce among them, forecast the postmodern contextualizing and destabilizing of the subject itself—which, as we saw, leads David Tracy in *Plurality and Ambiguity* to give further nuances to his notion of a "limit-dimension."

Charlie Marlow, the character who perhaps best manifests Conrad's distinctively dialectical narrative voice and worldview—while also embodying the subjective, inward quality of modernist fiction. The Joyce texts that I will examine (albeit incompletely, considering the massiveness and complexity of the latter work) are *A Portrait of the Artist as a Young Man* and *Ulysses*.

Joseph Conrad's Dialectical Imagination

Conrad's "Youth"

"Youth," written in 1897, to a large degree reads like a simple sea yarn rather than like a later, sophisticated Conrad text (though, as I will point out, even the later works retain characteristics of sea-adventure tales). But several elements do make this work a good place to look for the incipient Conradian vision: the story's frame, the eventually familiar device of a monologue delivered by Marlow to a small group of fellow seamen (or former seamen); the frequently repeated thematic motif of "youth," or rather, of the gap between the youthful Marlow within the story and the older, jaded Marlow telling it; the content of the story itself, which deals with the harsh dangers of a sea voyage and the eventual destruction of the ship on which Marlow sailed; and the setting, a juxtaposition of England with the charm and mystery of "the East." Each of these elements portrays a *dialectical* relation between the human subject and what Tracy calls the "whole" or the "limit."

The story's framing creates its dominant sense of irony. An unnamed narrator describes himself and four other men, all sharing "the strong bond of the sea" (93), sitting around a table, drinking claret, and yarning. Then Marlow takes over and begins "the story, or rather the chronicle, of a voyage," his first voyage to "the Eastern seas" (93). And he wryly announces what it is that makes a particular voyage exemplary of universal truth:

> You fellows know there are those voyages that seem ordered for the illustration of life, that might stand for a symbol of existence. You fight, work, sweat, nearly kill yourself, sometimes do kill yourself, trying to accomplish something—and you can't. You simply can do nothing, neither great nor little—not a thing in the world—not even marry an old maid, or get a wretched 600–ton cargo of coal to its port of destination. (94)

So this tale, Marlow says, will be a "symbol of existence" because it is a "not" tale: a tale of not doing, not achieving, not completing. This is the story of the time Marlow did *not* haul a load of coal from Tyne to Bangkok.

Frederick Karl has drawn attention to the story's humor: "the humor," he says, "indicates the distance of an experience which has already been observed, as if the subject were himself outside the sequence of events which were happening to him" (213). But the point, of course, is that Marlow-narrator *is* sagely outside events, while Marlow-character is naively inside them. Much of the ironic humor of the piece lies in the fact that at the time Marlow, who was on his "first voyage as second mate" (94), was blissfully unaware that he was involved in a "not" tale; the present Marlow, however, cannot stop reminding his listeners of his own previous naivete. Within the framed narrative, the young Marlow is always breathlessly exuberant. He says that the day he joined the crew of the *Judea*, the ship hired to haul the coal, was "one of the happiest days of my life! Fancy! Second mate for the first time—a really responsible officer!" (94–95). And he frequently interrupts his story to make such exclamations as the following: "O youth! The strength of it, the faith of it, the imagination of it!" (102). The young Marlow affirms the traditional human values that, according to Michael Levenson, are undermined by subjectivist skepticism in modernist literature. Marlow's present tone, however, is ironic, jaded; exuberant youth is what he and his listeners are now cut off from. Describing the old, battered *Judea*, Marlow says: "She was tired—that old ship. Her youth was where mine is—where yours is—you fellows who listen to this yarn" (107). And he frequently jars his listeners, and us, from the idealistic past to the bleary-eyed present with the words "Pass the bottle."

In itself, this device would merely reflect a conventional gap between youth and age, innocence and experience. The framing text, it seems, is a portrait of age, while the framed narrative, the narrative inside—at the center of—the frame, is a picture of youth. The entire story, then, would seem to be age's reflection on youth, a kind of Eliadean attempt to make present the sacred origin. Such a design might itself reflect a dialectical imagination, separating the secular present from the sacred past and then sacramentally recovering the lost sacred. Conrad's actual dialectic, however, is a bit more complicated, even in this early and rather simple tale. The ironic tone of the narrative makes it clear that the innocence of youth cannot be made present—but the content of the reminiscence indicates, in addition, that it *never* was present. The innocence of "O youth!," even when Marlow was truly young in years, was already a not-yet, or perhaps a nevermore. This is indicated by the fact that the young Marlow is surrounded, within the framed narrative, with representatives of age and deterioration: the elements of the frame, it seems, have leaked into the framed portrait, or perhaps the elements of this picture have leaked out and become the frame. If the framing text is a supplement to the framed tale, we see that the original tale already contained a trace of the supplement; the subjectivity of the older Marlow is needed to bring to consciousness these limits to youthful innocence, but the limits were latently present all along. The boy Marlow is surrounded by worn old men, and their names themselves are nearly allegorical indications of their significance: the ship's captain, though a neophyte (this is his "first command" [94]), is a weathered, bent sixty-year-old named not "smooth-faced boy" but Captain *Beard;* the first mate is the white-bearded Mahon, whose name, Marlow hastens to say, is pronounced *Mann* (95). The pilot, Jermyn, is a cynical old salt who, Marlow says, "mistrusted my youth, my common sense, and my seamanship," and although Marlow still harbors hatred for Jermyn, he now admits that "he was right" (96).

But the most important "leakage" of the aged and jaded tone of the frame into the framed narrative is the portrayal of the leaky old ship itself. The ship is the whole world for Marlow throughout most of the story, and it is a very tired old world indeed. Battered by storms, the *Judea* takes sixteen days just to get from London to Tyne to pick up the coal. Then it gets smashed by a steamer and needs further repairs, and gets storm-battered again and limps back to Tyne. Only after all these mishaps does it truly begin its voyage to Bangkok. And the center of the story, and of the ship, is the coal in the ship's hold, which is literally a very unstable center: the primary plot event is that the coal catches fire and explodes. What had been inside the ship now bursts out, spitting fire and smoke, smashing timber, wreaking devastation. The fire soon burns up the ship, and from their lifeboats the men watch it sink. Marlow links this catastrophe with the inevitable fragility of youth in words that introduce the dark, shadowy language that would become Conrad's hallmark:

> Oh, the glamour of youth! Oh, the fire of it, more dazzling than the flames of the burning ship, throwing a magic light on the wide earth, leaping audaciously to the sky, presently to be quenched by time, more cruel, more pitiless, more bitter than the sea—and like the flames of the burning ship surrounded by an impenetrable night. (120)

So Marlow makes it clear that his story is not a sacramental re-presentation of youth, because youth's light is already "surrounded by an impenetrable night" even when it seems to be blazing. This is not Eliade's dialectic of a return from the meaningless profane back to a sacred past; rather, it is more like Updike's dialectic, in *Roger's Version*, of a necessary immersion in the profane because the innocent sacred is present only in its radical absence. The framed is the frame; the signified is just a shadow of the sign; broken age looks back at hale youth to find—broken age. The story is about not making but breaking connection with the past: youth cannot be reclaimed ritualistically, but only ironically distanced. The title of this short story suggests postmodern writing-under-erasure: the word "Youth" crossed out.

This is, in a sense, the way the East operates in the text: not as a place that in itself mediates a positive, present mystery, but rather just as a dialectical erasure of the West.[4] When the young Marlow first hears that the *Judea* is bound for

---

4 Conrad, therefore, is sometimes criticized for portraying non-Western cultures as a negative projection of the West rather than genuinely attempting to enter into non-Western experience. But I think such criticism overlooks the fact that this tendency to negate is simply how Conrad's dialectical imagination works.

Bangkok, he is delighted: "Bankok! I thrilled. I had been six years at sea, but had only seen Melbourne and Sydney, very good places, charming places in their way—but Bankok!" (96). When he finally reaches Bangkok in his lifeboat, he still feels charmed, but the older Marlow makes it clear that any sense of positive grace was illusory. Rather than encountering what David Tracy calls a gracious limit-of that grounds the limit-to experience he has just had, Marlow encounters a facelessness that immediately and powerfully subverts his naive sense of conquering it:

> The scented obscurity of the shore was grouped into vast masses, a density of colossal clumps of vegetation, probably—mute and fantastic shapes. And at their foot the semicircle of a beach gleamed faintly, like an illusion. There was not a light, not a stir, not a sound. The mysterious East faced me, perfumed like a flower, silent like death, dark like a grave. (128)

This is very similar to the language of negative mysticism, language that is a dialectical self-negation. Even the series of analogies in the final sentence are of the sort that, according to Calvin, appear in the Bible as a way of restraining rather than enabling the imagination: they convey non-images of a vague smell, of silence, of darkness.

And this is, Marlow says at the end of his sea story, the only kind of instruction that the sea ever gives. Rather than revealing, analogically, some presence that transcends the self, all the sea does is dialectically throw the subject back on itself. The sea, Marlow says, is certainly a limit-dimension (and hence, in Tracy's sense, religious): it "could whisper to you and roar at you and knock your breath out of you" (132). But it reveals the transcendent precisely by revealing nothing, by bouncing a person back into immanence, into subjectivity. The sea, the older Marlow says, "gives nothing, except hard knocks—and sometimes a chance to feel your strength—that only" (132).

"Youth," therefore, is a good introduction to the dialectical quality of Conrad's imagination. And the dialectic is produced specifically through Conrad's most modernist device: his focus on Marlow's subjectivity—or rather, on the gap between this subjectivity and the objective adventure story Conrad has to tell. Virginia Woolf describes Conrad as a "compound of two men": a "sea captain" who could celebrate traditionally heroic characters, but also "that subtle, refined, and fastidious analyst whom he called Marlow." In Woolf's view, then, Marlow embodies the modernist, subjectivist voice: "one of those born observers who are happiest in retirement. Marlow liked nothing better than to sit on deck, in some obscure creek of the Thames, smoking and recollecting; smoking and speculating; sending after his smoke beautiful rings of words until all the summer's night became a little clouded with tobacco smoke" (313). Similarly, in *A Genealogy of Modernism*, after describing the tension between objective Victorian virtue and the alternative modernist "value of consciousness" (3) in *The Nigger of the*

"Narcissus,"[5] Michael Levenson locates Conrad's modernist strain most strikingly in the development of the character and voice of Marlow:

> [T]he stratagem of Marlow is paramount. . . . [I]n Paterian terms, he confirms the triumph of "sense of fact" over "fact." He completes what was inchoate in *The Nigger of the "Narcissus"* and embodies the psychologistic premise, namely that the meaning of a phenomenon is its presence to a mind. . . . [H]e is a proprietor of meanings. His first sentence in *Lord Jim* is revealing in its directness: "Oh yes." Not description, not self-identification, no positing of dramatic principles—simply the abrupt contact between subject and world. (20)

Levenson suggests that Conrad's relationship with his own burgeoning modernist strategies is dialectical: "It would distort matters to claim that . . . his sympathies were consistently on the side of consciousness. For every one of Marlow's jibes at unthinking complacency, there is an example . . . where heroism precludes introspection. At the thematic level the conflict between work and consciousness remains persistent and unresolved" (20). Although Levenson does not note any religious dimension to this conflict, I suggest that the subjective consciousness in Conrad's works introduces Tracy's "limit-dimension": an awareness of the dialectical "limit-to" that undermines the complacency of a heroic, enlightened, rational vision of the human world.

Conrad's **Heart of Darkness**

David Tracy, as we have seen, defines the "religious dimension" of human experience as that reality "articulating or implying a limit-experience, a limit-language, or a limit-dimension" (*Blessed Rage for Order* 93), and he states that religious questions are "the fundamental existential questions of the meaning and truth of individual, communal and historical existence as related to, indeed as both participating in and distanced from, what is sensed as the whole of reality" (*Analogical Imagination* 157–58). In these terms *Heart of Darkness*, written shortly after "Youth," is perhaps Conrad's most obviously "religious" work. Marlow's descent into the center of Africa, as well as his narration of this experience in the novella's "frame," is clearly an encounter with and reflection on *limit*, an addressing of questions seemingly related to *the whole of reality*. In his classic study

---

5 "In *The Nigger of the 'Narcissus,'*" Levenson writes, Conrad "makes what amounts to a division of narrative labour. The third-person narrator provides the precision of physical detail but hesitates to penetrate the individual psyche which George Eliot had so remorselessly invaded. Only with the shift to the first person is there a comfortable indulgence in moral and psychological speculation. Where George Eliot maintains the consistency of a single omniscient voice, Conrad here draws upon distinct voices, distinguishable points of view. While he is by no means systematic in his alternation between them, the shifts reveal the pressures upon an omniscience no longer confident that it knows all" (8).

Conrad the Novelist, Albert Guerard describes *Heart of Darkness* as a presentation of a Conradian "night journey"—"the archetypal myth dramatized in much great literature since the Book of Jonah: the story of an essentially solitary journey involving profound spiritual change in the voyager" (15)—and even if the nuances of Guerard's analysis are debatable, his overall placement of the work within a religious "night journey" genre surely has validity. And Conrad's description of the impact of his own Congo experience, the much-documented autobiographical source of Marlow's tale, indicates that such a *limit* encounter with the *whole* was, for him, a defining human event: "Before the Congo," he is said to have told his friend Edward Garnett, "I was just a mere animal" (Sherry 63).

In calling this a "religious" tale, however, I am not suggesting that it narrates some sort of positive encounter with the divine. It presents, rather, the dialectical, Barthian view that even the *religious* is an experience of the absence, within this world, of any divine, providential reality; in Tracy's terms, the text portrays existence as related to "what is sensed as the whole of reality" not as "participating in" but as "distanced from" this whole. For Karl Barth, as we have seen, even religion is merely human, and the religious person is intensely aware of what Tracy calls the limit *to* the human. "Religion," Barth states, "as the final human possibility, commands us to halt" (242). Barth goes on to describe what this religious experience of limit looks like:

> The only world we can know is the world of time, of things, and of men. The final experience to which we have access in this world is summed up in the words—*and I died*, and this is the pre-supposition of all experience. Now, the religious man is bound to encounter this experience, this pre-supposition of all experience, precisely because he is a religious man. . . . There is no escape from this vision or from this undoing. (251)

The Barthian religious is the prophetic "place on the extremest edge of human possibility" (251)—that place "where men are most evidently men, where they are most completely removed from direct union with God, and where human existence is most heavily burdened with its own questionableness" (252). By these dialectical terms, Conrad's Kurtz is a religious prophet. The plot of *Heart of Darkness* is concerned with Marlow's encounter with this prophet of the dialectically religious; in addition, the novella's design and texture are themselves, in the terms of this study, dialectical. I will first examine the novella's framing, then Marlow's narrative of his journey into the Congo and his encounter with Kurtz, to demonstrate the way this work exemplifies the dialectical imagination.

The framing narrative of *Heart of Darkness* is quite similar to that of "Youth," though the frame in the novella is richer, more resonant, than in the short story. Again five men, sharing "the bond of the sea" (135), are together—this time on the Director of Companies' "cruising yawl" (135)—and one of them is the anonymous narrator. Again the situation serves as a frame within which the narrator can convey a long monologue delivered by Marlow, this time describing not a youthful, innocent experience but a later, more troubling one: his journey to the Congo and his encounter with the enigmatic Kurtz. And again one of the text's primary devices is a leakage between the seemingly very dissimilar framing and framed narratives. In "Youth," as we saw, the framing narrative involves jaded middle-aged men while the framed narrative deals with youthful exuberance, but the darker tones of the frame leak into the bright, youthful reminiscence. In *Heart of Darkness*, however, it is the framing narrative that seems peaceful and rational, while the story Marlow tells is dark and troubling—and the darkness of this reminiscence spills out into the seemingly placid present narrative. The effect is dialectical: Marlow's tale pushes the easy conventionality of the framed narrative to the limit, an intense limit-to, an unveiling of the fact that even civil England is a place where, in Barth's words, "human existence is most heavily burdened with its own questionableness" (252).

The narrator's initial description of the scene is serene. It could be called blandly analogical—an easy correspondence between present and distant, and between the earth and the heavens: "The sea-reach of the Thames stretched before us like the beginning of an interminable waterway. In the offing the sea and the sky were welded together without a joint" (135). The narrator goes on to use the image of the Thames to launch a conventional tribute to English history, specifically the history of imperialism, never mentioning that some of the heroes he celebrates were morally questionable at best:

> It [the Thames] had known and served all the men of whom the nation is proud, from Sir Francis Drake to Sir John Franklin, knights all, titled and untitled—the great knights-errant of the sea. . . . Hunters for gold or pursuers of fame, they all had gone out on that stream, bearing the sword, and often the torch, messengers of the might within the land, bearers of a spark from the sacred fire. (137)

But this rather easy, conventional bit of scene-setting and history-retelling is a device to usher in Marlow's narrative, his tale of "savage" Africa that is not after all so different from England. The bright, serene scene darkens—"The sun set; the dusk fell on the stream, and lights began to appear along the shore" (137)—and the darkening present serves to usher in Marlow's dark reminiscence: "'And this [England] also,' said Marlow suddenly, 'has been one of the dark places of the earth'" (138). Marlow's point, of course, is that "civilized" Europe, what we today call "developed" countries, is not essentially different from "primitive" (in today's terms "developing") regions: "I was thinking of very old times, when the Romans first came here, nineteen hundred years ago—the other day" (139). In itself this narrative device—using the familiar (the Thames) to usher in a tale of the exotic (the Congo)—seems more analogical than dialectical. Marlow's fundamental point is that Africa is more *like* than *unlike* England. The framing narrative, then, would appear to operate as a mediator, gently easing the audience into Marlow's story.

I suggest, however, that the effect is precisely opposite. The Thames setting does not familiarize Marlow's Congo story, but rather the Congo story de-familiarizes the framing narrative; the Congo story is the supplement that supplants the Thames narrative. This is because, as already mentioned, Marlow's story acts as a dialectically prophetic unveiling of the Barthian religious, that "extremest edge of human possibility" (251), a dialectical not-yet that underlies cozy comfort as much as "savage" horror. And Marlow accomplishes this because his mode of discourse, the discourse that the first narrator's bland conventionalities usher in, is a kind of non-discourse, a discourse that does not make present but that only suggests what is concealed. It is discourse that J. Hillis Miller describes as both parable and apocalypse, and Miller's description marks this as discourse concerned not with the always-already but with the not-yet:

> [P]arable tends to be oriented toward the future, toward last things, toward the mysteries of the kingdom of heaven and how to get there. . . . Parable, as we can now see, has at least one thing in common with apocalypse: it too is an act of unveiling that which has never been seen or known before. . . . The book of Revelation seeks to unveil a mystery of the future, namely, what will happen at time's ending. ("*Heart of Darkness* Revisited" 210–11)

Miller's analysis of *Heart of Darkness* as parable and apocalypse largely grows from a consideration of one of the novella's most famous passages, the primary narrator's description of Marlow's yarns and their meanings:

> The yarns of seamen have a direct simplicity, the whole meaning of which lies within the shell of a cracked nut. But Marlow was not typical (if his propensity to spin yarns be excepted), and to him the meaning of an episode was not inside like a kernel but outside, enveloping the tale which brought it out only as a glow brings out a haze, in the likeness of one of these misty halos that sometimes are made visible by the spectral illumination of moonshine. (138)

Miller points out that the narrator "here employs two figures to describe two kinds of stories: simple tales and parables" ("*Heart of Darkness* Revisited" 211). The first figure, or analogy, is straightforward, as are the stories it represents; in simple tales, the meaning is neatly contained inside—the narrative is like a nut (a frame) that contains a solid kernel of meaning (the clear, framed moral). But the second analogy, an analogy for Marlow's parables, is a complicated double simile: Marlow's meaning is outside the story (the meaning, then, is the frame rather than the framed?), *like* a glow that brings out a haze *like* a halo around the moon. Miller asserts that this double figure obscures as much as it reveals: "The figure both illuminates its own workings and at the same time obscures or undermines it, since a figure of a figure is an absurdity" ("*Heart of Darkness* Revisited" 212–13). But Miller goes on to explicate the double figure as well as he can, and his explication shows the way the dialectical imagination unmakes rather than makes analogies:

> The story, according to Conrad's analogy, the facts that may be named and seen, is the moonlight, while the halo brought out around the moon by the reflection of the moonlight from the diffused, otherwise invisible droplets of the mist, is the meaning of the tale, or rather, the meaning of the tale is the darkness which is made visible by that halo of twice-reflected light. But of course the halo does nothing of the sort. It only makes visible more light. What can be seen is only what can be seen. In the end this is always more light, direct or reflected. The darkness is in principle invisible and remains invisible. All that can be said is that the halo gives the spectator indirect knowledge that the darkness is there. ("*Heart of Darkness* Revisited" 216)

This indirect image—a nighttime glow reveals not the mist but only the reflected light bouncing off the mist, the mist's limits but not the mist itself—is a kind of analogy for a way of making indirect analogies, and this is precisely how Miller argues religious parables, apocalyptic texts, and *Heart of Darkness* work. It also, of course, explains the complicated way the novella's framing narrative works: not as a shell that contains a kernel but as a halo that is the indirect but sole revelation of darkness. J. Hillis Miller's analysis is a valuable presentation of the mode of Conrad's text—and Miller's linkage of the text with the religious genres of parable and apocalypse is apt and helpful. Miller shows that the narrator's image for the way Marlow's story works is, in the terms we have been using in this study, a dialectical image of the way the dialectical imagination works. Marlow's "halo" of visible imagery reveals the invisible haze indirectly, just as the cross, for Luther and Barth, reveals God's glory negatively, as that-which-is-not-the-cross. This is a use of image that echoes Calvin's biblical "symbols" of God, "clouds and smoke and flame," which, "although they were symbols of heavenly glory, restrained the minds of all, like a bridle on them, from attempting to penetrate too deeply" (102). Such an imagination, as we have seen, is predicated on the conviction that the worldly and any sort of transcendent are radically incommensurable, that the absolute cannot be mediated, even partially, by an analogy.

As with "Youth," then, there is no easy demarcation between the frame and the framed in *Heart of Darkness*. The description of Marlow telling his story, on a dark yawl in the Thames to a group of friends, is like Luther's cross—a revelation via concealment. "Do you see the story?" Marlow suddenly asks his audience, interrupting his tale, inserting a reminder of the Thames scene in the midst of the Congo narrative. He then goes on to remind his listeners, in classic modernist style, that his story is profoundly—even untranslatably—subjective: "Do you see anything? It seems to me I am trying to tell you a dream—making a vain attempt, because no relation of a dream can convey the dream-sensation, that commingling of absurdity, surprise, and bewilderment in a tremor of struggling revolt, that notion of being captured by the incredible which is of the very essence of dreams. . . ." (172). In his biography of Conrad, John Batchelor points out that early in the framed narrative Marlow seems confident that he (unlike naive women, for instance),[6] knows how language and reality relate to each other; in other words, the younger Marlow is a confident, rational Victorian who thinks he *sees*, has clear access to the real. But Marlow's statement in the framing narrative that he feels as if he is "trying to tell you a dream" and that "[w]e live, as we dream—alone" (172) shows, according to Batchelor, that after his Congo experience Marlow has become aware of the instability of the self and of any "reality" that a human self can know: "This knowledge—that the apparently secure and confident self can be experienced as isolated and unstable—. . . becomes the novella's alternative 'reality'" (Batchelor 90). I will try to convey some of the elements of this "dream," this unstable "alternative 'reality,'" that Marlow presents/ conceals—the journey into the Congo and the encounter with Kurtz—and to show how Marlow's narrative employs modernist subjectivity to exemplify a *dialectical* way of imaging the religious "limit-dimension."

Marlow begins the tale of his journey into the Congo by stating that the place where he found Kurtz "was the farthest place of navigation and the culminating point of my experience" (141)—his experience of limit, in other words. And the experience was like the haloed haze—light delineated by darkness, or darkness delineated by light:

> It seemed somehow to throw a kind of light on everything about me—and into my thoughts. It was sombre enough, too—and pitiful—not extraordinary in any way— not very clear either. No, not very clear. And yet it seemed to throw a kind of light. (141)

He was drawn, he says, specifically to the Congo because it was a whiteness (when he was a boy it was uncharted, a blank space on the map) that "had become a place of darkness" (142). Its river, furthermore, looked on the map like a snake, and "[t]he snake had charmed me" (143). When Marlow describes his visit to Brussels ("a city that always makes me think of a whited sepulchre" [145]) to contract with "the Company" to captain a steamboat up the Congo River, he employs rich, nearly Gothic prose filled with details suggestive of an encounter with David

---

6 "It's queer how out of touch with truth women are," Marlow says. "They live in a world of their own, and there had never been anything like it, and never can be. It is too beautiful altogether, and if they were to set it up it would go to pieces before the first sunset. Some confounded fact we men have been living contentedly with ever since the day of creation would start up and knock the whole thing over" (149). But Batchelor states that as Marlow describes the way he was brought to lie by the circumstances of the Congo adventure, his confident—and arrogantly superior—sense of his own grasp on truth begins to crumble "as though that memory of having lied immediately causes Marlow to lose control of his narrative and his sense of self" (89).

Tracy's "limit" or "whole of reality": bizarre women, knitting black wool, usher him into the Company's offices; a strange little doctor measures his cranium and asks him matter-of-factly, "Ever any madness in your family?" (148); and he learns from his aunt that the Company considers him not just a steamboat captain but "an emissary of light" (149) bringing the glories of civilization to the savages. "I felt as though," he remarks, "instead of going to the centre of a continent, I were about to set off for the centre of the earth" (150). Small wonder Guerard has called this an archetypal "night journey."

But it becomes clear that this is a night journey that is religiously revelatory in a dialectical way; the journey's very opacity pushes Marlow back into his own subjectivity and flawed humanity rather than sacramentally unveiling some transcendent sacredness. Traveling down the African coast in a French steamer, Marlow sees a French "man-of-war" firing guns into the impenetrable jungle, which reveals nothing about itself, but only by negation reveals the "touch of insanity" of the Europeans (151–52). Words, similarly, break down in Africa, becoming signs that point to nothing beyond themselves, mere empty sounds. The Africans are called "enemies" (152), "criminals" (154), "workers," and "rebels" (222), but in this context the words have hit their limit, become impotent to signify. The jungle similarly reflects back the absurdity of the accountant in the first Company station, who maintains the starched clothing and precise work habits of Europe, and the moral emptiness of the manager of the Central Station, who survives the harsh dialectical confrontation with Africa because he has "no entrails" (164). And eventually, as Marlow captains the steamer toward the Inner Station that conceals Kurtz, the river and the surrounding jungle—steeped in the thickest of fogs—have become absolutely opaque, a limit that simply outlines the pathetic humans who confront it:

> What we could see was just the steamer we were on, her outlines blurred as though she had been on the point of dissolving, and a misty strip of water, perhaps two feet broad, around her—and that was all. The rest of the world was nowhere, as far as our eyes and ears were concerned. Just nowhere. Gone, disappeared; swept off without leaving a whisper or a shadow behind. (192)

Marlow and his morally shabby cohorts have gone all the way to the limit and found only a reflection of themselves.

This dialectical vision of the jungle as that which says nothing, which just reflects back the depraved humanity of the observer as the invisible mist reflects back the reflected moonlight, has its perfect prophet in Kurtz, whom Marlow calls "[t]his initiated wraith from the back of Nowhere" (207). From early in the text, Kurtz is one who erases discourse more than one who positively reveals anything. Although Kurtz is touted (and secretly hated by the manager and his cronies) as one of the apostles of civilization rather than just a mercenary ivory trader, Marlow is never able to imagine him in any positive way. No metaphors, images, or analogies can convey him; he is the canceling, the erasing, of such images: "I could see a little ivory coming out from there, and I had heard Mr. Kurtz was in there. I had heard enough about it, too—God knows! Yet somehow it didn't bring any image with it—no more than if I had been told an angel or a fiend was in there" (171). Marlow says that right before he met Kurtz he considered him "something altogether without substance." Interestingly, he connected this lack of substance with speaking, with discourse: "I made the strange discovery that I had never imagined him as doing, you know, but as discoursing. . . . The man presented himself as a voice" (203). This may seem to contradict my claim that Kurtz is an opacity rather than a window to some truth; at least he is a voice that speaks, and perhaps he reveals that, even in the dense fog of the heart of darkness, words can pierce through the limit-to and mediate (if only incompletely, analogically) transcendence: "The point was in his being a gifted creature, and that of all his gifts the one that stood out preëminently, that carried with it a sense of real presence, was his ability to talk, his words" (203). Kurtz, with his words, conveys a sense of *real presence*; this is a loaded phrase for the Catholic Conrad—and it sounds more sacramental than dialectical. But Marlow immediately ironizes the phrase, calling Kurtz's gift of expression "the bewildering, the illuminating, the most exalted and the most contemptible, the pulsating stream of light, *or the deceitful flow from the heart of an impenetrable darkness*" (203–4, emphasis added). Discourse that is either a stream of light or a deceitful darkness can convey only a negative, not a positive, presence; it can, in other words, reveal only that words do not clearly reveal.

And this is the way Kurtz's actual discourse works when Marlow finally presents it (or does *not* present it; Marlow quotes few of Kurtz's actual words,[7] just as he describes only vaguely the atrocities Kurtz has been committing among the natives). Kurtz's are words, Marlow tells us, that hide rather than reveal: "Kurtz discoursed. A voice! a voice! It rang deep to the very last. It survived his strength to hide in the magnificent folds of eloquence the barren darkness of his heart" (237). His written discourse contains its own self-cancellation: at the end of his "eloquent" essay on the glorious task of civilizing Africa, Kurtz has scrawled,

---

7 John Batchelor notes that in the original *Heart of Darkness* manuscript Conrad had included more of Kurtz's actual speech: "'I have lived—supremely! What do you want here? I have been dead—and damned.' 'Let me go—I want more of it.' More of what? More blood, more heads on stakes, more adoration, rapine, and murder" (quoted in Batchelor 87). But Batchelor notes that Marlow's "wonderfully laconic statement" in the text's final version ("Mr Kurtz lacked restraint in the gratification of his various lusts") would be "deprived of its effect if Marlow is later to recall Kurtz ranting about blood, heads on stakes, adoration, rapine and murder, and Conrad's artistic instinct clearly served him well when he cut the passage" (87). I suggest that Conrad also cut such passages because they would have made Kurtz too bluntly present rather than dialectically absent-present.

"Exterminate all the brutes!" (208). And his most famous utterance—his last words, "The horror! The horror!" (239)—is an "affirmation" of the most dialectical sort. These are the final, visionary words of a person whose stare is "wide enough to embrace the whole universe, piercing enough to penetrate all the hearts that beat in the darkness" (241), and they are as opaque as the river's fog. Kurtz has reached that "final experience" that Barth says is "summed up in the words— *and I died*" (Barth 251); he has reached that extremity of the human that for Barth *is* the religious, the "place on the extremest edge of human possibility" (Barth 251) where "men are most evidently men, where they are most completely removed from direct union with God, and where human existence is most heavily burdened with its own questionableness" (Barth 252). He has gone to the Barthian religious, the very limit of the human, and he has seen the limit-to—death itself—but no grounding, gracious limit-of:

> This is the reason why I affirm that Kurtz was a remarkable man. He had something to say. He said it. . . . After all, this was the expression of some sort of belief; it had candour, it had conviction, it had a vibrating note of revolt in its whisper, it had the appalling face of a glimpsed truth—a strange commingling of desire and hate. . . . It was an affirmation, a moral victory paid for by innumerable defeats, by abominable terrors, by abominable satisfactions. But it was a victory! (241)

John Batchelor warns us against taking even these words as in any way definitive; Marlow's subjectivity remains the *limit to* what we can know. That Marlow is able to find an affirmative kernel—however ambiguous that affirmation—in Kurtz's proclamation reveals how Marlow has reachieved mental balance after a nervous breakdown,[8] but it reveals nothing about Kurtz and his own indescribable vision: "All we readers, looking over Marlow's shoulder at the dying Kurtz, can say confidently about 'The horror! The horror!' is that we don't know what is going on in Kurtz's mind and therefore we cannot say what his dying words mean. The moral reading of Kurtz's final words is Marlow's invention, authorized by nothing but Marlow's innate moral balance" (Batchelor 92).

So Kurtz's "moral victory"—or rather Marlow's interpretation of it, since the reality itself is inaccessible—is radically dialectical in the sense in which we have

---

8 For Batchelor, this is a primary way in which Marlow is a mirror of Conrad, who himself suffered from deep depression: "Conrad uses the river journey to put Marlow through a process which is like the process undergone by patients who are in psychotherapy. Marlow in his encounter with Kurtz looks into the abyss, Conrad himself is looking at the core of his depression" (95). And Batchelor, perhaps validating my own view of Conrad's dialectical imagination, claims that the "relationship between Conrad the man and Conrad the artist is in a sense adversarial or oppositional": a tension between the outer Conrad trapped by "power-relationships" and a "core of an integrated self" that "counteracts the depression by getting on with the central business of writing" (84–85). That this supposedly integrated "core"-self wrote in such ambiguous ways about an unspeakable heart of darkness adds yet another unsettling dimension to Batchelor's dialectic.

been using the word. Kurtz's final words reflect a full-faced confrontation with the limit-dimension, the whole of reality. But the event has generated no carrying-between of meaning (*meta-pherein*) that can pass over and at least analogically mediate a positive vision of that limit-dimension; rather, all that is revealed is a slamming into the limit, as into a brick wall, and a gasping with pain, with horror. Any further message must be delivered apocalyptically—that is, *not yet.*

Conrad's Lord Jim

Lord Jim, published in 1900 (shortly after *Heart of Darkness*), was the third of Conrad's Marlow narratives, and the last until *Chance* in 1913. The text's narrative structure, along with Marlow's intentionally mystifying discourse, once again serves to drive a wedge between the reader and the tale, to indicate a dialectical incommensurability between language and the content—yet another limit-experience, as we will see—it attempts to make present.

And yet that content, the tale, is also a solid adventure story. Like "Youth" and *Heart of Darkness*, *Lord Jim* demonstrates that Conrad is indeed, as Virginia Woolf says, a "compound" of a Victorian "sea captain" who tells romantic tales and celebrates objective virtue and of a "subtle, refined, and fastidious analyst" whose works are inward, subjective, modern. As John Batchelor puts it:

> Readers of the late twentieth century are accustomed to think of *Lord Jim* as a study of guilt, a psychological study and a work of unprecedented narrative complexity: a novel which belongs with Flaubert, Dostoevsky and Henry James rather than with John Buchan and Robert Louis Stevenson. But it belongs to all the genres that these names evoke: it is both a sophisticated study of private experience and a story of action and adventure. (100)

The novel, Batchelor goes on to say, "is both a masterpiece in a high Victorian tradition (as practiced by Stevenson and Haggard) and a psychodrama in a new form: a work which involves the reader with the narrator and protagonist in unprecedented ways" (109). For Batchelor, this transformation from high Victorian adventure story to modernist psychodrama occurs as we move from a first to a second reading. On first reading, we follow the exciting but complicated plot; once we know the story, however, "we find on a second reading that our attention is pressed back from the content of the tale to the manner of the telling. And, specifically, we find ourselves engaging with Marlow's personality rather than with Jim's and collaborating with Marlow as he tells his tale" (101). In a sense, from first to second reading we encounter the limit to Victorian objectivity and are thrown back upon subjectivity, the subjectivity of the "subtle, refined, and fastidious analyst," Marlow.

Indeed, even on first reading it is impossible not to be struck by the novel's complexity of viewpoints, which itself signals Conrad's concentration on subjective perception rather than objective certainty. The design of *Lord Jim* is very "modernist," in David Lodge's terms, and it is modernist in a dialectical way: as I stated initially, the narrative structure drives a wedge between reader and tale, emphasizing the inadequacy of language to capture the limit-experience being described. In the novel's first four chapters, an anonymous, more or less omniscient narrator tells of Jim, a young seaman who now can only work as a lowly "ship-chandler's water-clerk" in "various Eastern ports" (3) because he abandoned a ship and its passengers. Then this narrator introduces Marlow, who "later on, many times, in distant parts of the world . . . showed himself willing to remember Jim, to remember him at length, in detail and audibly" (33). Marlow now takes over and for the next thirty-one chapters tells Jim's story to nameless, faceless listeners. Then the omniscient narrator takes over again and tells of a "privileged man" (337) who receives a packet containing a letter from Marlow, a brief and aborted note written by Jim, a letter to Jim from his father, and a lengthy text written by Marlow narrating the tragic end of Jim's story (as told to him by Tamb' Itam, Jim's servant, and Jewel, Jim's wife). This time the convoluted form in which we receive the story (the chronology is as mazy as the viewpoints) could never be interpreted—as I have suggested the framing of *Heart of Darkness* might mistakenly be—as a gentle buffer between the familiar and the unfamiliar, as a mediator easing the audience into Marlow's yarn. If anything, the design mystifies what on the surface seems, as Batchelor states, to be a traditional Victorian adventure story about a rather simple but troubled young man.

And mystification is precisely Marlow's intent; when Marlow takes over the story, his hazy discourse deepens the opacity created by the novel's complicated points of view. The omniscient narrator's opening paragraph is a straightforward, objective, formally realistic description of Jim. It suggests that language can make its object present in a plain, unambiguous way, aided by an occasional analogy (Jim has "a fixed from-under stare which made you think of a charging bull" [3]). What Marlow does is undermine such easy signification; in a sense, the rest of the novel is a lengthy erasure of its facile first paragraph. In place of the omniscient narrator's factual clarity, we get Marlow, who considers a "human being" to be just what cannot be mediated by external details:

> My weakness consists in not having a discriminating eye for the incidental—for the externals—no eye for the hod of the rag-picker or the fine linen of the next man. Next man—that's it. I have met so many men . . . met them, too, with a certain—certain— impact, let us say; like this fellow [Jim], for instance—and in each case all I could see was merely the human being. (94)

If *Heart of Darkness* is a parable in which meaning is an invisible haze around the plot, *Lord Jim* is a character study with no details describing the character, or rather, with all the details erased.

Jim, for Marlow, is mystery—that which cannot be understood, that for which every image and analogy is incomplete, in need of supplement. Beneath his rosy-cheeked exterior, Jim is a puzzle: Why did this clergyman's son, who had highly idealistic views of himself and a deep commitment to the "fixed standard of conduct" that binds the "body of men" who go to sea (50), jump from the *Patna* and leave its passengers (presumably) to drown? Why can this rather simple, not terribly reflective young man not shake the memory of what he has done? J. Hillis Miller has argued that the novel, from beginning to end, precisely fails to answer these questions, and that that is the point. In place, Miller says, of the Aristotelian "confidence that some *logos* or underlying cause and ground supports the events," Conrad gives us "the image of a consciousness attempting to grope its way to the hidden cause behind a set of enigmatic facts by moving back and forth over them." And the text, Miller says, "does not permit the reader to decide among alternative possibilities" (*Fiction and Repetition* 35).

Here is Marlow, in a fairly typical passage, conveying (or not conveying) Jim through dialectical pairs of descriptors that cancel each other out:

> I can't explain to you who haven't seen him and who hear his words only at second hand the mixed nature of my feelings. It seemed to me I was being made to comprehend the Inconceivable—and I know of nothing to compare with the discomfort of such a sensation. I was made to look at the convention that lurks in all truth and on the essential sincerity of falsehood. He appealed to all sides at once—to the side turned perpetually to the light of day, and to that side of us which, like the other hemisphere of the moon, exists stealthily in perpetual darkness, with only a fearful ashy light falling at times on the edge. . . . The occasion was obscure, insignificant— what you will: a lost youngster, one in a million—but then he was one of us; an incident as completely devoid of importance as the flooding of an antheap, and yet the mystery of his attitude got hold of me as though he had been an individual in the forefront of his kind, as if the obscure truth involved were momentous enough to affect mankind's conception of itself. (93)

Jim is direct sunlight, indirect moonlight; a trivial particular case, a person of universal significance ("one of us"). Marlow has been "made to look at the convention that lurks in all truth and on the essential sincerity of falsehood": Jim's story has revealed to Marlow that "truth" is just a representation, a sign or image but not a presence, and Marlow is left with the merely emotive ("sincerity of falsehood") rather than with any objective reality. Encountering Jim's story is for Marlow an encounter with "the Inconceivable," and Marlow states outright that he cannot mediate this encounter with words, images, analogies; he knows "of *nothing to compare* with the discomfort of such a sensation" (emphasis added).

So Marlow's is an imagination that must explicitly delineate the inadequacy of images and analogies; it is, as in "Youth" and *Heart of Darkness*, a dialectical imagination. As I have been arguing, however, it is images *of the religious dimension*—of limit-experience, of the whole of reality, of conscious intentionality's transcendental object, and so forth—that the dialectical imagination ultimately crosses out. And in the above passage Marlow indicates that it is this limit-dimension to Jim's story that gives it its urgency: it is, he says, "as if the obscure truth involved" in Jim's story "were momentous enough to affect mankind's conception of itself." This "obscure truth" has to do with the mystery of Jim's act to the passengers of the *Patna*, an immoral act by any accepted human standards.

Ian Watt argues that Jim's act and his remorse for it cannot be seen within a conventional Christian framework of guilt, remorse, and redemption. Jim, Watt says (89), feels not guilt (a sense of transgression against a moral boundary, against the "Super-Ego") but shame (disappointment at not living up to his own self-image, his "Ego-Ideal"). And the novel moves not toward Jim's redemption but toward a tragic vision "of humanity's awed astonishment at the works of fate" (Watt 95). But the elements in Jim's story that Watt discusses, and judges to be specifically non-Christian, actually resonate with the dialectical vision of human inadequacy in the face of moral limits—a vision that, as we have seen, in the Christian tradition extends from Paul down to Luther and Barth. Within this dialectical vision, guilt and shame merge in an intense experience of (and "awed astonishment at") one's inability to do good.

In his Letter to the Romans, as I have previously noted, Paul reports that his own inability to follow the moral law is what has slammed him into that which David Tracy calls the limit-to:

> I do not understand my own actions. For I do not do what I want, but I do the very thing I hate. Now if I do what I do not want, I agree that the law is good. But in fact it is no longer I that do it, but sin that dwells within me. For I know that nothing good dwells within me, that is, in my flesh. (Romans 7:15–18, NRSV)

Luther sees this impotence as humans' necessary immersion in the secular, which reveals the sacred only by its dialectical absence: "Thus, you say, 'How do we fulfil the law of God?' I answer, Because you do not fulfil it, therefore we are sinners and disobedient to God" (62). For Barth, as I said in my discussion of *Heart of Darkness,* this experience of impotence is *the* religious experience—humanity pushed to the very edge. And such moral impotence is exactly what Jim says he experienced when he jumped from the *Patna*. He does not understand his own actions; he did not do what he wanted, but he did the very thing he hated. Though he considered himself wholly moral, and remains certain that "there was nothing in common" between himself and his ethically hollow shipmates (103), he acted exactly as they did. Yet he does not remember choosing to jump, choosing to desert the passengers: at the very last moment he felt "a strange illusion of passiveness, as though he had not acted but had suffered himself to be handled by the infernal powers who had selected him for the victim of their practical joke" (108). And his description to Marlow of this event, the definitive event of his life, is a non-description, the most laconic moment in this very talky novel: "'I had jumped . . .' He checked himself, averted his gaze. . . . 'It seems,' he added" (111). It *seems* he jumped. He cannot even assert this for certain. The only image, therefore, that can convey this experience of the limit is an utterly empty one: "It was as if I had jumped into a well—into an everlasting deep hole. . . ." (111). The ellipses—which are Conrad's, not mine—are probably the most expressive elements in these key passages. Virginia Woolf and John Batchelor are correct to note that Conrad's novels are filled with an interest in and respect for traditional Victorian virtue, but what Jim discovers—or perhaps, what Marlow discovers through Jim—is the modernist *limit to* the Enlightenment picture of a rational, virtuous human self.

This is, of course, only the beginning of the novel. But the story's second half—which presents Jim's seeming rehabilitation as "lord" of Patusan, his mistake in dealing with the evil Gentleman Brown, and his ultimate willingness to confront and be shot by the wronged Doramin (which represents either a brave act of retribution for his earlier sin or just one more escapist "jump")—does not materially change the moral mystery that hangs over Jim's life. Patusan does not supply Jim with a sacramental rebirth; it is, rather, a place of "limit" that more than ever sharply delineates the initial questions, an immersion in the merely human rather than a climb to transcendence. Thomas Altizer, as we saw, claims that a radical dialectical theology demands "existence in the body . . . immanent existence, a total immersion of the self in the immediate moment" (179), and Altizer's mandate here sounds uncannily like that of the oracle of *Lord Jim*, Stein: "In the destructive element immerse," Stein tells Marlow (214). Stein, who creates the Patusan opportunity for Jim, spins for Marlow a dialectical analogy (so to speak) worthy of Luther, Barth, Altizer:

> "A man that is born falls into a dream like a man who falls into the sea. If he tries to climb out into the air as inexperienced people endeavour to do, he drowns—*nicht wahr?* . . . No! I tell you! The way is to the destructive element submit yourself, and with the exertions of your hands and feet in the water make the deep, deep sea keep you up." (214)

Stein suggests, as does the novel, that authentic human life is lived right up against, and is even held up by, the limit-to, but that there is no going beyond (absolutely or even analogically) this unspeakable mystery.

James Joyce's Analogical Imagination

Surely James Joyce's fiction—with its subjective, stream-of-consciousness techniques, which give way to increasingly eccentric formal experimentation—is modernist in the ways I have been describing. Much more than Conrad, Joyce rejects traditional Victorian objectivism and, in David Lodge's words, "is experimental or innovatory in form, displaying marked deviations from preexisting modes of discourse, literary and non-literary" (*Modes* 45). Although Virginia

Woolf cannot rank Joyce's works with the greatest literature because of what she calls "the comparative poverty of the writer's mind," she praises Joyce as a modernist "spiritual" writer who is "concerned at all costs to reveal the flickerings of that innermost flame which flashes its messages through the brain" (214). But over against Conrad's fiction, Joyce's *A Portrait of the Artist as a Young Man* and *Ulysses* embody a form of literary modernism that presents a religious vision—a vision of the relation between the human world and the whole of reality—which is analogical and sacramental rather than dialectical.

I am aware that this is a shaky claim at best. Certainly sacramental images are everywhere in Joyce's fiction; the partly autobiographical Stephen Dedalus's notion of the artist as "a priest of the eternal imagination, transmuting the daily bread of experience into the radiant body of everliving life" (*Portrait* 213), as well as Joyce's adaptation of the religious word "epiphany," reflects a belief that the limit-of can be mediated, analogically, through the worldly. But I realize how arguable it is that Joyce is making fun of sacramentality, parodying it as fully as Buck Mulligan parodies the Mass at the beginning of *Ulysses*. For every William T. Noon, S.J., who in his book *Joyce and Aquinas* describes "the whole Catholic concept of strict sacramentality" behind Joyce's use of language and his developing notion of epiphanies (153), there is a Karen Lawrence, who claims that in *Ulysses* Joyce "parodies the desire for epiphany" and parodies "the search for significance and the creation of symbolism" (201). I wish to argue, however, that over the course of *Portrait* and *Ulysses* Joyce manages to explode the difference between parodic and genuine sacramentality, and that by presenting a vision that ironically includes both the parodic and the genuine he is exercising a very analogical imagination indeed. The very inclusiveness of *Ulysses*—which looks forward to HCE, "Here Comes Everybody," the "hero" of *Finnegans Wake*—involves the ability to linguistically embrace all being while pointing out, laughingly, the inability to do any such thing.

In fact, at the point at which analogy explodes the rational boundaries of language we encounter Noon's Thomistic sacramentality itself, which ends up sounding uncannily like Karen Lawrence's postmodernist radical inconclusiveness. Noon describes sacramental language as signifiers that point not toward concrete, external signifieds but rather toward themselves:

> Crucial to the whole Catholic concept of strict sacramentality is the notion that the Sacraments are not merely signs but practical and efficacious *instruments* which effect what they signify, the conferring of grace. The theological formula insists upon the causality as *ex opere operato* rather than as *ex opere operantis*, two phrases in medieval Latin which are hard to render in English. They are a kind of ecclesiastical shorthand which represents the sacramental rites as working effectively from their own intrinsic causality (as energized, of course, by God) rather than as signs manifest only of God's action or of man's reaction to the conferring of grace. (153)

Ex opere operato: this is self-referentiality squared. Sacramental language, Noon is saying, does not point toward some grace that is somewhere else; it *is* the grace itself. Such a notion is nonsense for the dialectical imagination, which needs to maintain clear distinctions between the merely human representation and the graciousness beyond the limit-to. For the dialectical imagination, a word either means nothing or points toward some thing—and when we realize that the word is always at a distance from that *thing*, modernist and postmodernist skepticism is born. But Noon suggests that Joyce embraces another alternative, a kind of poetic sacramentality, a use of signs comically aware of their distance from any absolute, external signifieds and yet nonetheless mediating a kind of grace not through referentiality but through an inherent sacramental analogy:

> [The poetic word] effects within a structure of analogies some more or less natural modification of being-as-realized, some change in the situation or object which the language *re-presents*. When Aquinas refers to a word as a *similitudo varia, repraesentatio*, or image of an object, there is no reason to believe that he conceives of the object as something which *must* exist ontologically separate from the word and outside the mind. The object, of which the spoken or written word is the image[,] may, as very often happens in poetry, have no other existence than as a creative construction of the mind itself. (154)

If, for Noon's and Aquinas's sacramental imaginations, the "object" of literary language does not necessarily and absolutely exist outside the "creative construction of the mind itself" (or, in these postmodern times, we would say it does not exist outside the text), then this imagination is cut off from any external conclusiveness; this is an imagination deeply at odds with Enlightenment objectivism and rationalism, and hence it is in its own way quite compatible with the modernist (and, eventually, postmodernist) critique of such rational and objective confidence. Linguistic epiphanies, for this imagination, are inadequate "signatures" of the material world, and are hence laughable—and this is just what Karen Lawrence says of Leopold Bloom's famous meditation on water near the end of *Ulysses*:

> In one sense, the catalogue of Bloom's thoughts on the "potency of water as a symbol" can be seen as a projection of his desire to mean something to somebody. But the catalogue also represents a "reading" of water—the book, in this instance, like Stephen in "Proteus," attempts to read a "signature" in the material world. We recognize in this kind of reading a parody of the basic activity of symbol making and deciphering, the kind of activities engaged in by everyone, but by writers and readers especially. (200)

But then Lawrence concedes that the effect of this parodying of conventional signification is not a cancellation of meaning but rather an expansion of it, a suggestion of surplus, overflow: "The leveling of experience that derives from the form and style of 'Ithaca' ultimately does not feel like an aggressive cancellation of possibilities or a ruthless satire of belief but imparts instead a sense of the various possibilities that exist in life" (201). This is not to suggest that Lawrence herself endorses a Thomistic, sacramental reading of Joyce (she explicitly asserts that the "final meaning" of *Ulysses* is *not* "the affirmation of life" [201]). It is rather to show that the postmodernist Lawrence, who sees Joyce as a parodist, ends up as much as Noon endorsing a view of Joyce's imagination as widely and wildly inclusive. I am going to say the same, but I will go further. I wish to show that over the course of *Portrait* and *Ulysses*, a vision of images and words evolves that—while admitting the limitation of language and the incompleteness of the human ability to imagine the whole, the Ultimate—comically mediates a vision of the analogical interconnectedness of the human subject, the other, and even the divine.

Joyce's Portrait

A Portrait of the Artist as a Young Man initially dramatizes the evolution of Stephen Dedalus's natural, untroubled (and obviously naive) analogical imagination, an imagination that finds images that are entirely adequate to mediate the world and even the divine. At first Stephen's experience is not even a collection of analogies but is pure unity; there are no gaps, so there is no need of mediation at all. When Stephen's hairy-faced father tells the story of the moocow who "met a nicens little boy named baby tuckoo," Stephen "was baby tuckoo" (3). This uncomplicated oneness does already give way to slight distinctions on the novel's first page—Uncle Charles and Dante "were older than his father and mother but uncle Charles was older than Dante" (3)—but still there is an easy connectedness among things. Even politics and religion coexist easily, as the religious Dante happily keeps a maroon brush in honor of Michael Davitt and a green one in honor of Parnell. And "Dante gave [Stephen] a cachou every time he brought her a piece of tissue paper" (3).

When he goes away, at age six, to Conglowes Wood College, Stephen begins to get glimpses of the dialectical gaps between images, especially word images, and reality; the analogies begin to tremble a bit. Nasty Roche questions the validity of the signifiers "Stephen Dedalus" ("What kind of a name is that?" [5]), and "Stephen had not been able to answer" (5). Furthermore, Stephen discovers that linguistic sounds do not stay put:

> That was a belt round his jacket. And belt was also to give a fellow a belt. . . .
>   Suck was a queer word. The fellow called Simon Moonan that name because Simon Moonan used to tie the prefect's false sleeves behind his back and the prefect used to let on to be angry. But the sound was ugly. Once he had washed his hands in the lavatory of the Wicklow Hotel and his father pulled the stopper up by the chain

after and the dirty water went down through the hole in the basin. And when it had all gone down slowly the hole in the basin had made a sound like that: suck. Only louder. (5, 7)

Already Stephen is discovering that words are not unambiguously referential; some words are puns. But that, Noon argues (invoking W. H. Auden's article "Notes on the Comic"), is very much a development of an analogical imagination:

[A] good pun . . . is apparently never unrelated to analogy. . . . Always [a pun] must appear to be (and be) a quite deliberate exploitation of a providential similarity in the sound or in the appearance of words, which reflects or captures an unexpected similarity in the manner in which two or more beings indicated in the words exist. . . . [A] successful pun unexpectedly calls attention to some affinity, however remote and unconventional, in the facts of being. (149)

So for the young Stephen, words—though increasingly volatile—analogically mediate the mystery of being itself. Words place Stephen in the cosmos:

He turned to the flyleaf of the geography and read what he had written there: himself, his name and where he was.

Stephen Dedalus
Class of Elements
Clongowes Wood College
Sallins
County Kildare
Ireland
Europe
The World
The Universe (11)

Words even place God:

God was God's name just as his name was Stephen. *Dieu* was the French for God and that was God's name too; and when anyone prayed to God and said *Dieu* then God knew at once that it was a French person that was praying. But though there were different names for God in all the different languages in the world and God understood what all the people who prayed said in their different languages still God remained always the same God and God's real name was God. (12)

Whatever slight nuances Stephen is learning about the instability of signs and signifiers (puns, different languages), the very young Stephen's faith rests on a naive and rather bland Catholic notion that human truth and divine truth are benignly mediated by words and symbols. "That was the meaning of *Tower of Ivory*," Stephen reflects, relating his friend Eileen's "cool white hands" to this designation for the Virgin; "but protestants could not understand it and made fun of it. . . . *Tower of Ivory. House of Gold*. By thinking about things you could understand them" (38).

But the primary action of the first chapter of *Portrait* is the erosion of Stephen's analogical confidence. When we first see Stephen at Conglowes, he has had an early dialectical experience of disgust with human carnality: he has been pushed into the sewage of the school's "square ditch" by Wells. Stephen is learning that there is perhaps something inherently rancid, decidedly undivine, about the human condition. And it is Wells who poses the first potent challenge to Stephen's faith in analogical mediation of meaning. When Stephen answers first "I do" and then "I do not" to Wells's query about whether Stephen kisses his mother before going to bed, Wells laughs at both answers, leaving Stephen confused by the discovery that every declaration has a supplement that supplants it, and that all declarations are equally laughable: "What was the right answer to the question? He had given two and still Wells laughed" (10). Most important, the seeming compatibility of politics (the governance of the human) and religion (the governance of the divine) breaks down in this chapter. Both politics and religion have become limit-realities that Stephen feels woefully incapable of grasping: "It pained him that he did not know well what politics meant and that he did not know where the universe ended. He felt small and weak" (12–13). And at the disastrous Christmas dinner, at which the politically minded men clash irreconcilably with the religious Dante, Stephen fully realizes that human and divine governance have been wrenched apart as violently as Dante has ripped the Parnellian green velvet from her brush (12). Dante proudly proclaims, "God and religion before everything! . . . God and religion before the world!" and Mr Casey shouts back, "No God for Ireland! . . . We have had too much God in Ireland. Away with God!" (34). The analogical seams are tearing rapidly.

The rest of *Portrait* can be read as Stephen's steady loss of faith in the analogical adequacy of human symbols to mediate David Tracy's "whole" or "limit" reality. Stephen's imagination remains at root analogical, especially his verbal imagination ("Words which he did not understand he said over and over to himself till he had learned them by heart: and through them he had glimpses of the real world about him" [57]). Hence the second chapter of *Portrait* does have a smattering of little Joycean epiphanies, clear snippets of external observation of Stephen's aunt in her kitchen (62) or of the "feeble creature" in "the old darkwindowed house" who mistakes Stephen for "Josephine" (62–63). But these epiphanies are archly minimalist, cut off from any larger reality—and certainly from any analogical vision of a "whole." Indeed, in these epiphanies Stephen is already dramatizing himself to himself as absolutely detached, an image of the dialectically detached God/artist he will describe much later in the novel: "He chronicled with patience what he saw, detaching himself from it and tasting its mortifying flavour in secret" (62). It is arguable that these epiphanies are already not about a mediation of the real but rather about paralysis, the human impotence to find any metaphor that can "carry-between" the self and the cosmos; linguistic statements of larger meaning have become, for Stephen, "hollowsounding voices" (78). Hence Stephen's epiphanies ape the sacramental poetic described by Noon—language *ex opere operato*, with an object that has "no other existence than as a creative construction of the mind itself" (Noon 154). But the operation effected seems to be not the kinetic mediation of grace but the static mediation of the absence of grace. It is interesting to note that one of Stephen's Jesuit teachers accuses him of heresy precisely for writing an essay espousing what I have been calling, in these pages, a dialectical vision of the radical impotence of the human to effect any kind of approach to the transcendent:

> Mr Tate withdrew his delving hand and spread out the essay.
> —Here. It's about the Creator and the soul. Rrm . . . rrm. . . . rrm . . . Ah! *without a possibility of ever approaching nearer.* That's heresy.
> Stephen murmured:
> —I meant *without a possibility of ever reaching.* (74)

Stephen's halfhearted qualification notwithstanding, this sounds uncannily like the Karl Barth who proclaims that there "is no direct knowledge of God. . . . It is impossible to lay hold of Him. Men cannot bind Him, or put Him under an obligation, or enter into some reciprocal relationship with Him" (423).

As Stephen's vision of humanity's relation to the Good becomes increasingly dialectical, his growing disgust with depraved human reality (soon to include the reality of his own sexuality) drives him deeper and deeper into a romantic inwardness that does not even partially, hypothetically, analogically mediate anything transcending the self. At first he thinks his inner vision of a lover can be adequately mediated by the outer world: "He wanted to meet in the real world the unsubstantial image which his soul so constantly beheld" (60). But this dream lover represents everything that is not worldly—"He would fade into something impalpable under her eyes and then, in a moment, he would be transfigured" (60)—and the overall movement of chapter 2 of *Portrait* is to parodically undermine Stephen's attempt to find an incarnate analogy for his transcendent vision. When he finds a real woman and encounters the "vague speech" of her lips, "darker than the swoon of sin, softer than sound or odour," the woman is merely a nighttown prostitute (95). Stephen's experience of the dialectical split between sacred and secular has manifested itself in the clichéd Jansenist-Catholic sexual disjunction of virgin/whore.

Portrait's third chapter—the great portrayal of the fire-and-brimstone Jesuit retreat, which frightens Stephen into repentance, confession, and even deeper self-disgust with his own physical humanity—clinches his move from an analogical/sacramental Catholic imagination (founded on a vision of the natural world as oozing with God's grandeur) to a dialectical/Jansenist Catholic imagination (founded on a vision of natural depravity and transcendent judgment). This chap-

ter demonstrates that, despite Andrew Greeley's linking of the dialectical imagination with Protestantism and the analogical with Catholicism, there exists a very
Catholic version of extreme dialectical thinking. Father Arnall's retreat sermons
are steeped in Catholic imagery, and in that sense seemingly analogical: founded
on the assumption that the transcendent can be mediated through worldly images.
Arnall's lavish poetic descriptions and especially his Ignatian "composition of
place" (120) in his evocation of hell are identifiably Catholic, different in poetic
flavor from, say, the equally fierce but poetically sparer writings of a Cotton
Mather. The effect of this imagery, however, is to intensify even further Stephen's
sense of the gulf between his humanity and anything good or graced. The dialectical imagination has never been at a loss to present images of evil; it is worldly
symbols that can mediate images of *God* that the dialectical imagination lacks.
And this is a way in which Arnall and Cotton Mather do resemble one another:
both present vivid images of the devil (though Arnall's appear rather Dantesque
while Mather's look more like spunky New England women), while the divine is
unimaginably beyond the puny human person.

And Stephen does indeed leave the retreat with an excruciating sense of his
own depravity, of the inherently evil will of his own body:

> He was in mortal sin. Even once was a mortal sin. It could happen in an instant. . . .
> But does that part of the body understand or what? The serpent, the most subtle beast
> of the field. It must understand when it desires in one instant and then prolongs its
> own desire instant after instant, sinfully. It feels and understands and desires. What a
> horrible thing! Who made it to be like that, a bestial part of the body able to under-
> stand bestially and desire bestially? (133)

Such a passage has an obvious affinity with that great bit of dialectical imagining
in Paul's Letter to the Romans: "I do not do what I want, but I do the very thing I
hate. . . . For I know that nothing good dwells within me, that is, in my flesh."
(Romans 7:15, 18, NRSV)

The fact that Stephen is saved from this horror not by some predestined,
unearned, transcendent grace but rather by a gentle old Franciscan priest in a
confessional may prefigure the later softening of this dialectical vision in *Ulysses*,
but it hardly softens Stephen for now. The newly pious Stephen of *Portrait*'s chapter 4 is simply the other side of the self-hating young man who visited prostitutes
and wallowed in the interconnectedness of the seven deadly sins (100). Yes, he
has now found analogues that seem to mediate a vision of the transcendent—"he
seemed to feel his soul in devotion pressing like fingers the keyboard of a great
cash register and to see the amount of his purchase start forth immediately in
heaven not as a number but as a frail column of incense or as a slender flower"
(142)—but this is parodic analogical imagery that cancels itself out. Stephen's
imagination is still imbued with a sense of the depravity of the human condition.

He is able temporarily to hold off fleshly human depravity, an approaching sexual thought, by (and the pun is surely intentional) "a sudden act of the will or a sudden ejaculation" (146), but the depravity is all around him because, as Barth would remind him, flesh is what he *is*.

It is precisely a realization that he is a fleshly, lust-filled human being that leads Stephen eventually to reject an invitation to join the Jesuit priesthood and instead to embrace a priesthood of poetry. This seems to be the foundation of a truly sacramental imagination, an imaging of the Good as pouring through the worldly and fleshly; as I have already noted, this artist as a young man defines himself as "a priest of the eternal imagination, transmuting the daily bread of experience into the radiant body of everliving life" (213). Indeed, in *Joyce's Catholic Comedy of Language* Beryl Schlossman asserts that in *Portrait* "Stephen rejects the Church in order to become, theologically, Catholic. He will be a writer rather than a priest" (xv). And Stephen says his first poetic Mass, so to speak, when he imaginatively transforms a girl wading into the water into the poetic image of a bird:

> A girl stood before him in midstream: alone and still, gazing out to sea. She seemed like one whom magic had changed into the likeness of a strange and beautiful seabird. Her long slender bare legs were delicate as a crane's and pure save where an emerald trail of seaweed had fashioned itself as a sign upon the flesh. Her thighs, fuller and softhued as ivory, were bared almost to the hips where the white fringes of her drawers were like featherings of soft white down. (164)

But (*pace* Schlossman) this act of Eucharistic poetry is, as many critics have pointed out, ambiguous: it is at best immature and perhaps even a parody of itself, dialectically pointing toward Stephen's inability to transmute ordinary reality into anything but the ridiculous. J. Mitchell Morse puts it this way: "[Stephen's] incipient naturalistic tendency is overwhelmed by an adolescent mysticism personified in the girl: Dedalus's chosen artistic medium, unlike Joyce's, is a stale poetic prose like that of Oscar Wilde's fairy tales" (32).

In any case, Stephen's reason for turning to this new poetic "priesthood" so far seems less motivated by a new hopefulness about human images' ability to mediate reality—to celebrate the proportionate (*ana-logos*) relationship between things, the carrying-between (*meta-pherein*) of meaning—than by a kind of hopelessness:

> The snares of the world were its ways of sin. He would fall. He had not yet fallen but he would fall silently, in an instant. Not to fall was too hard, too hard: and he felt the silent lapse of his soul, as it would be at some instant to come, falling, falling but not yet fallen, still unfallen but about to fall. (155–56)

Poetry, then, for Stephen cannot be that analogical experience described by David Tracy of "a dimension which, in my own brief and hazy glimpses, discloses a reality, however named and in whatever manner experienced, which functions as a final, now gracious, now frightening, now trustworthy, now absurd, always uncontrollable limit-of the very meaning of existence itself" (*Rage* 108–9). It is, rather, more like Thomas Altizer's dialectical "existence in the body . . . immanent existence, a total immersion in the immediate moment" (179)—similar, as we saw, to Stein's mandate in Conrad's *Lord Jim*.

It is no wonder that Stephen's motto, as *Portrait* approaches its conclusion, is Satan's "*non serviam*," which is not unlike Paul Tillich's entirely unsatanic Protestant principle, "the divine and human protest against any absolute claim made for a relative reality" (*Protestant Era* 163). I will end my discussion of *Portrait* by indicating the way Stephen's dialectical protest (always with a Catholic flavor, of course) issues in a poetic theory embedded explicitly in a dialectical image of God. It is this image of God, too often discussed as if it were endorsed not just by Stephen Dedalus but by Joyce himself, that *Ulysses* moves from, enlarges, even supplants—indicating, I think, that the dialectical and analogical imaginations depend on and complement each other.

Despite his apparent dependence on Thomas Aquinas's philosophical realism, Stephen's lengthy theorizing in *Portrait*'s final chapter indicates that he remains self-enclosed, cut off from analogical otherness. For example, he defines truth and beauty, for him the bases of aesthetics, not as manifestations (epiphanies?) of a grounding presence (or even of its absent presence) but only as psychological realities. They are qualities that exist only in the intellect of the apprehending subject:

—. . . The first step in the direction of truth is to understand the frame and scope of the intellect itself, to comprehend the act itself of intellection. . . .

—To finish what I was saying about beauty, . . . the most satisfying relations of the sensible must therefore correspond to the necessary phases of artistic apprehension. (200, 204)

For Stephen, furthermore, the most crucial element in an object's aesthetic beauty is, in Thomistic terms, its radiance (*claritas*), but this again he defines not as genuinely epiphanic but as private, psychological:

The radiance of which [Aquinas] speaks is the scholastic *quidditas*, the *whatness* of a thing. This supreme quality is felt by the artist when the esthetic image is first conceived in his imagination. The mind in that mysterious instant Shelley likened beautifully to a fading coal. The instant wherein that supreme quality of beauty, the clear radiance of the esthetic image, is apprehended luminously by the mind which has been arrested by its wholeness and fascinated by its harmony is the luminous silent stasis of esthetic pleasure, a spiritual state . . . which the Italian physiologist Luigi Galvani, using a phrase almost as beautiful as Shelley's, called the enchantment of the heart. (205–6)

This may seem to be a description of the very action of *meta-pherein*, the carrying-between of meaning (in this case, from aesthetic object to perceiving mind) that I have been describing as essential to the analogical imagination. It certainly carries a trace of this meaning, which will blossom into the fully sacramental/analogical vision of *Ulysses*. But so far this is only a trace, much distorted by Stephen's dialectical suspicion of deeply rooted links and analogies. As Don Gifford points out, what Stephen is saying here is a significant distortion of Aquinas, who grants a supreme status to the aesthetic object itself and its genuine self-revelation; Stephen, Gifford notes, virtually ignores the actual, substantial object, emphasizing a dialectically cut-off, self-stimulating mind:

> [I]n his discussion of the term *claritas*, Stephen seriously distorts the meaning of St. Thomas. Aquinas defines *claritas*, the radiance of the beautiful object, as *resplendentia formae*, the splendor of the form of the object itself. Stephen echoes Thomas's *resplendentia formae* when he speaks of the "clear radiance of the esthetic *image*," but he finds the source of this in the mind. In this way the objective and realist view of Aquinas is transformed by Stephen into something very like the subjective and idealist theories of Shelley. (168)

A comparison of this passage in *Portrait* with the corresponding passage in *Stephen Hero*, Joyce's earlier version of the Stephen Dedalus story, more precisely indicates the way *Portrait*'s Stephen is distorting Aquinas's analogical aesthetic theory, giving it a dialectical spin. In *Stephen Hero*, Stephen defines the Thomistic concept of *claritas* much as he would define it in *Portrait*; in *Stephen Hero*, however, he adds an important element to his definition—the famous notion of "epiphanies":

> For a long time I couldn't make out what Aquinas meant. He uses a figurative word (a very unusual thing for him) but I have solved it. *Claritas* is *quidditas*. . . . This is the moment which I call epiphany. First we recognize that the object is *one* integral thing, then we recognize that it is an organized composite structure, a *thing* in fact: finally, when the relation of the parts is exquisite, when the parts are adjusted to the special point, we recognize that it is *that* thing which it is. Its soul, its whatness, leaps to us from the vestment of its appearance. The soul of the commonest object, the structure of which is so adjusted, seems to us radiant. The object achieves its epiphany. (*Stephen Hero* 213)

Imagining that soul can leap from the "vestment" of appearance is clearly *analogical* in the terms of this study—an at least partial and hypothetical crossing over to ground or essence or being, located not just in the mind of the subject but *out there*, in the beautiful object itself: "The object," says Stephen in his earlier incarnation, "achieves its epiphany." For Hugh Kenner, the crucial omission of the doctrine of epiphanies indicates that "by the time he came to write the *Portrait*

Joyce had decided to make its central figure a futile *alter ego* rather than a self-image." Kenner continues:

> In the *Portrait* the exposition [of the aesthetic doctrine], correct so far as it goes, has omissions dangerous for the reader interested in Aquinas rather than in Stephen. The absence of the crucial doctrine of epiphanies, and the soft-pedalling of the location of *pulchram* in *ens*, emphasize Stephen's highly subjective bent. (137)

For our purposes, however, the even more crucial part of Stephen's aesthetic doctrine comes when he demands that the artist abscond from the work; it is here that he invokes a theological framework that is distinctly dialectical, not Thomistic at all. Stephen explicitly suggests that the artist/artwork dynamic is revelatory of the whole of reality, an image of the relation of God (the principle of the whole) to the world. So far this sounds like a very analogical vision of art: even if the institutional church is too oppressive to mediate a fair vision of the whole, perhaps art can do so. But the vision or structure that art mediates is, in his famous formulation, one of transcendent absence, not of analogical presence. As art moves toward its highest form, the dramatic, the artist withdraws, a God more Barthian than even Barth imagines:

> —. . . The artist, like the God of creation, remains within or behind or beyond or above his handiwork, invisible, refined out of existence, indifferent, paring his fingernails.
>
> —Trying to refine them also out of existence, said Lynch. (207)

Lynch's sarcastic touch, which gives Stephen's God a quirky personality, supplements Stephen's formulation with a comically analogical footnote; the supplement reveals, however, just how starkly *im*personal, dialectical, Stephen's image of the artist/God is on its own. Stephen's annihilation of both the human *logos* of art and the divine *logos* of reality, which used to be quoted as a forthright statement of James Joyce's own aesthetic, is the climax of Stephen's rejection of the too-easy Catholic analogical imagination of his boyhood and his embrace instead of a radically dialectical vision. According to William Noon, Joyce plainly intends this climax to be ironic, founded as it is on a misreading of Aquinas:

> Stephen misses the clue, as Joyce intends he should, which is not annihilation of the artist's personality, but the symbolic presentation of reality, be it the artist's personality or the personality of others or "the signatures of things." The comparison of the artist with the God of creation, who "remains within or behind or beyond or above his handiwork, invisible, refined out of existence, indifferent, paring his fingernails," is the climax of Joyce's ironic development of the Dedalan aesthetic. (66–67)

But we need not invoke extratextual authorial intention to claim that Stephen's dialectical formulation is undermined. Lynch's jokey thickening of Stephen's image of God—"Trying to refine them [God's fingernails] also out of existence"—

is only the beginning of Joyce's analogical supplementing of Stephen's dialectical image. The rest of the supplement, which thickens Stephen's formulations in ways that Lynch could never dream, is *Ulysses*.

Joyce's Ulysses

In his dialectical rejection of fallen, human Dublin, Stephen Dedalus flies, Daedalus-like, from Ireland at the end of *A Portrait of the Artist as a Young Man*:

> I will not serve that in which I no longer believe whether it call itself my home, my fatherland or my church: and I will try to express myself in some mode of life or art as freely as I can and as wholly as I can, using for my defence the only arms I allow myself to use, silence, exile and cunning. (238)

But now, in *Ulysses*, he has crashed, Icarus-like, against the painful human fact of his mother's death, and he has returned from the Continent to Dublin. On the single day depicted by the novel, June 16, 1904, Stephen is confronted with the same problems that plagued him before; he needs friends, but he also needs to remain aloof and superior—and Buck Mulligan, with whom he shares living quarters in a Martello tower (one of the military towers on the Irish coast), is hardly a genuine friend anyway. Most important, Stephen is troubled by the same metaphysical and theological doubts as before: having rejected Roman Catholicism, and having adopted a self-inflating but also self-annihilating aestheticism, he has lost all his ontological foundations. His now-entrenched dialectical sense that his humanity cuts him off from the whole of reality—from the limit-of that grounds the limit-to (which his Catholic imagination symbolizes as God, whether he is a propositional believer or not)—has him flailing around in search of new connections and analogies. But *Ulysses* is hardly a sentimental or nostalgic novel; a naive return to Catholicism is as impossible for Stephen as an embrace of Irish nationalism. And yet the novel does trace, in a sense, Joyce's retrieval of an orthodox image of God. The action of *Ulysses* can be described as a replacement of the earnest dialectical Deism of Stephen's aesthetic theory in *Portrait* with a highly qualified, comic, parodic—yet ironically genuine—analogical Trinitarianism.

The third chapter of *Ulysses*, the chapter in which Stephen walks on Sandymount Strand and ties himself in Protean epistemological knots, shows him struggling against his dialectical imagination, establishes the Trinitarian underpinnings of the issues he is struggling with, and demonstrates that solitary cognition cannot resolve his problems. "Ineluctable modality of the visible: at least that if no more, thought through my eyes" (37).[9] It now matters to Stephen that his

---

9 *Ulysses* has a complicated publication history, and there are a number of editions of the novel with some textual differences. At the insistence of the Estate of James Joyce, I am using Oxford University Press's facsimile of the original 1922 edition. My quotations, therefore, include apparent misprints contained in this historically significant but imperfect edition of *Ulysses*.

perceptions are tied to something outside himself, and he is trying to establish the real presence of the outside world rationally, intellectually. Perhaps he has no analogical connection with some larger limit-of, but "at least that" (that is, the visible) truly is present. He invokes Jacob Boehme's concept of *Signatura Rerum*, though Boehme's theosophy must generally be at odds with Stephen's Aristotelianism: "Signatures of all things I am here to read, seaspawn and seawrack, the nearing tide, that rusty boot" (37). But of course he is not reading signatures (signifiers) of indubitable things (signifieds); he is only experiencing the sensation of color: "Snotgreen, bluesilver, rust: coloured signs" (37). Yes, Aristotle (whom Stephen conflates with Samuel Johnson) knocked "his sconce" against things and hence was "aware of them bodies before of them coloured" (37), but this only defers the issue of presence. The reality of the world is still mediated through the five senses; hence, in its essence it is absent from the conscious subject. Stephen's experiment with blindness—he walks with his eyes closed, feeling and hearing rather than seeing his surroundings—does end with an affirmation of presence, but the affirmation is not a statement of rational certainty but rather a prayer, a statement of comical/hopeful faith: "See now. There all the time without you: and ever shall be, world without end" (38).

So perhaps it is theology, not epistemology, that is at issue for Stephen. The appearance of two midwives leads him to a humorous but very serious consideration of limit: of humanity's origins and connections to ultimate reality. It is here, appropriately, that he first reflects on the Christian tradition's doctrines of—and heresies about—the Trinity.

Stephen first observes the midwives with an almost objective precision— "They came down the steps from Leahy's terrace prudently, *Frauenzimmer:* and down the shelving shore flabbily their splayed feet sinking in the silted sand" (38)—but he quickly uses their profession as a vehicle for reflecting on limit reality. Through birth, he thinks (with a Joycean mix of humor and seriousness), all humans are linked back umbilically, through their navels, to the Ultimate:

> What has she in the bag? A misbirth with a trailing navelcord, hushed in ruddy wool. The cords of all link back, strandentwining cable of all flesh. That is why mystic monks. Will you be as gods? Gaze in your omphalos. Hello. Kinch here. Put me on to Edenville. Aleph, alpha: nought, nought, one. (38)

This would seem to be a comic *analogical* image of humans' connection to ultimacy: the fleshly (the navel) is connected to the transcendent. A developing sense of humor, it seems, is curbing and softening Stephen's dialectical harshness. Indeed, S. L. Goldberg considers Stephen's development of a sense of humor to be a sign of his growing maturity: "The humourless and priggish aesthete appears much less certain about his poses; he has, after all, we discover, some sense of the ridiculous and some glimmerings of maturer values" (158). As Stephen goes on to reflect jokily about theosophy's attempt to cancel out Eve's fleshliness by claiming she "had no navel . . . Belly without blemish" (38), he seems to be laughing at his own former disgust with the human and fleshly.

Still, his reflections take a sour turn, leaving an image of a profound dialectical gap between the fleshly and the Good. "Wombed in sin darkness I was too, made not begotten" (38): reversing the Nicene Creed's descriptions of Christ's origins ("begotten, not made, consubstantial with the Father"), Stephen is proclaiming the baseness of his own wombed-in-sin beginnings. He is not a "begotten" person, but merely a "made" thing. Indeed, he is setting himself up as a sort of flesh-bound anti-Christ, born not of some divine dispensation but rather of a degraded act performed by his all-too-human parents: "By them, the man with my voice and my eyes and a ghostwoman with ashes on her breath. They clasped and sundered, did the coupler's will" (38). Stephen's own debased birth—"made not begotten"—leads him then to debase all reality, even anything puny humans might call "God." Having willed Stephen's existence, the creator can be nothing but a meaningless mechanical force: "From before the ages He willed me and now may not will me away or ever. A *lex eterna* stays about Him" (38). If "God" is really bound by a *lex eterna*, then this reality is bound by the limit-to as much as humans are; a gracious limit-of, a ground of being, is only inferred by dialectical antithesis as that-which-is-not. Stephen's bitter reflections leave even God on the debased side of the dialectical gulf; like a much more pessimistic Thomas Altizer, Stephen is suggesting that the *truly* divine (as opposed to some limited force bound by a *lex eterna*) is at a transcendent distance from the secular—and that this gracious limit-of is nonexistent.

So Stephen here sketches the first of the images of the Trinity that wind through *Ulysses*, and it is a paradoxical blend of the orthodox and the heretical. Fittingly, he invokes "poor dear Arius" (38), the heretic who argued that Christ, being human, was limited and hence not divine; Stephen is agreeing with Arius, reflecting that the human is too deeply depraved to coexist with or analogically manifest the divine. But ironically Stephen is also siding with the Council of Nicaea, which designed its Creed as an explicit rebuttal to the Arian heresy by declaring the consubstantiality of Father and Son. The Father and Christ and presumably all creation, Stephen is suggesting, *are* consubstantial, sharing one limited *inferior* substance: "Is that then the divine substance wherein Father and Son are consubstantial?" (38). Poor Arius never managed to defend his stance, but the story of his death nicely reflects the degradation in which Stephen is reveling:

Where is poor dear Arius to try conclusions? Warring his life long upon the contransmagnificandjewbangtantiality. Illstarred heresiarch. In a Greek watercloset he breathed his last: euthanasia. With beaded mitre and with crozier, stalled upon his throne, widower of a widowed see, with upstiffed omophorion, with clotted hinderparts. (38)

Stephen here sinks into a dialectical vision of the world that makes Luther, Calvin, Barth, et al., seem like giddy optimists: he, humanity, the universe, even God, all are sullied.

The chapter as a whole does offer hints, as I suggested, that a newfound sense of humor may be softening Stephen's pessimism. And there are other indications that some providential otherness is about to leak into Stephen's consubstantially airtight, depraved world. For one thing, despite all his inner musings, Stephen seems more clearly, precisely aware of the concrete external world than he has seemed for a long time; the chapter is filled with minor epiphanies—including a witty vignette about what he would encounter if he were to visit his uncle, Richie Goulding—that reveal language's ability to reach beyond the confines of the merely subjective. In addition, Stephen remembers having had a dream last night of someone who pressed on him a vision of the physical world as lush and lovely rather than sinful:

> After he woke me up last night same dream or was it? Wait. Open hallway. Street of harlots. Remember. Haroun al Raschid. I am almosting it. That man led me, spoke. I was not afraid. The melon he had he held against my face. Smiled: creamfruit smell. That was the rule, said. In. Come. Red carpet spread. You will see who. (46)

Of course, Stephen *will* "see who" by the end of the novel. And this upcoming encounter with some other (Leopold Bloom) is rather explicitly linked, in the last sentences of the chapter, with an image of the Trinity. After urinating and picking his nose, Stephen has an intuition that someone is watching him, and he turns and sees the "high spars of a threemaster" with its sails on "the crosstrees":

> Behind. Perhaps there is someone.
> He turned his face over a shoulder, rere regardant. Moving through the air high spars of a threemaster, her sails brailed up on the crosstrees, homing, upstream, silently moving, a silent ship. (50)

Perhaps a new image of the Trinity—the relation of God's transcendent, human, and enlivening persons—is coming over the horizon. In the third chapter of *Ulysses*, however, Stephen's dominant Trinitarian image remains primarily pessimistic, dialectical: Nicene consubstantiality is a cover for Arian human depravity.

"But Stephen is no Arian," says William Noon:

> However much he may deplore the sordid ending of the "illstarred heresiarch," as he calls Arius, Stephen has little sympathy for a theology which would take away the basis of Fatherhood in God. Nor is there any hesitation in Stephen's preference for the Nicene over the Arian formulation. (109–10)

In *Portrait*, as we saw, Stephen spins an aesthetic theory about art and its relationship with the artist that is founded on an image of the relationship (or non-relationship) between God and creation. In the ninth chapter of *Ulysses*, the presentation of Stephen's lecture on Shakespeare in Dublin's National Library, Stephen revises his aesthetic theory, founding it this time not on an image of God as detached but rather on one of God as Father. Hence, he argues that Shakespeare inheres in *Hamlet* not as Prince Hamlet the son, as conventional biographical critiques would have it, but as King Hamlet the father. Adapting orthodox Catholic doctrine to his argument, Stephen ultimately declares that the two are consubstantial: Shakespeare the artist/father embodied himself in *Hamlet*, his artwork/son— "and," Stephen adds laughingly, "in all the other plays which I have not read" (204). John Eglinton, one of Stephen's Platonist listeners, sums up Stephen's argument neatly: "The truth is midway. . . . He is the ghost and the prince. He is all in all" (204).

Stephen has revised his image of the whole of reality, of the relation of the grounding reality (God) with the world. He has imaged God not as a detached, impersonal entity "within or behind or beyond or above his handiwork, invisible, refined out of existence, indifferent, paring his fingernails" but as a parent. And this is a parent who is consubstantial with the offspring: Shakespeare is consubstantial with his works, as the Father is consubstantial with the Son. This *seems* to be an analogical vision, a vision of the sacramental epiphany of the whole of reality in each of its parts, the individual self always epiphanizing itself and God always epiphanizing God:

> [Shakespeare] found in the world without as actual what was in his world within as possible. Maeterlinck says: *If Socrates leave his house today he will find the sage seated on his doorstep, If Judas go forth tonight it is to Judas his steps will tend.* Every life is many days, day after day. We walk through ourselves, meeting robbers, ghosts, giants, old men, young men, wives, widows, brothers-in-love. But always meeting ourselves. The playwright who wrote the folio of this world and wrote it badly (He gave us light first and the sun two days later), the lord of things as they are whom the most Roman of catholics calls *dio boia*, hangman god, is doubtless all in all in all of us. . . . (204)

This formulation is more or less where many critics leave Joyce: he is all in all in all of *Ulysses*. Joyce-Stephen goes out of his house today and finds the sage Joyce-Bloom seated on his doorstep. In *Reading Joyce's Ulysses*, Daniel Schwarz asserts this position fairly definitively: "That Stephen's discussion of Shakespeare is an expressive theory of art which views the works of an artist as an expression of the author's life defines Joyce's own aesthetic assumptions in *Ulysses*. The theory, located in the ninth of the eighteen sections, educates the reader on how to read the novel" (149). But aside from the fact that such a definitive statement of Joyce's "aesthetic theory of art" seems far too absolute for this most mercurial of novels (Schwarz's claim is as one-eyed in its way as the simplistic propositions skewered in the novel's Cyclopean twelfth chapter set in Barney Kiernan's pub), such a reading of *Ulysses* collapses the analogical vision that I think the book moves toward. Although the description of consubstantiality that emerges from Stephen's lecture may seem analogical—Shakespeare shines through the plays, God shines through Christ and the creation—it really is not. Analogy, as we have seen, implies difference: the sacred *imaged within* the worldly, the limit-of *gracing* the ordinary. Stephen's imagery in the library remains dialectical; lacking the carrying-over of metaphor or the proportionality of analogy, all Stephen can assert is identity. This, I think, is why his image of God remains that of the *dio boia*, the hangman god. He still cannot imagine any God that could be immanent in nature without sacrificing godly graciousness.

Stephen is still, in Trinitarian terms, a heretic. After acknowledging that Stephen is no Arian, William Noon goes on to say, "[T]hat is mainly because Stephen in his thinking cannot free himself from the other principal Trinitarian heresy, Sabellianism, a far subtler, more rationalistic, and quite modernistic heresy" (110). In brief, whereas Arius argued that the Father could not be consubstantial with the Son because the Son's humanity drove an absolute wedge between himself and divinity, Sabellius granted the Son's consubstantiality with the Father by claiming that the Son was not really human—not really a separate person from the Father at all—but merely a ghostly mode or manifestation of God. As Noon puts it:

> Sabellianism is sometimes called Modalism, since it conceives of the divine Persons as being no more than *modes* or *modalities* of the Divine Essence. Sometimes too it is called *Monarchianism*, since it was to save the "divine monarchy," as they said, that the Sabellians denied the real distinctions between the Persons of the Trinity. It is in Sabellianism as Monarchianism that Stephen finds the link for tying together the story of the murdered king of Denmark and the dialectical rationalism of a theology that makes the Son no more than a specter of the Father. (110–11)

For our purposes, the issue at stake is whether Stephen has found a way to analogically connect the human with the ultimate. And it still seems that he has not. In his life as a paralyzed poet, only able so far to squeeze out a few overwrought lyrics, Stephen has found no bridge out of his isolation.[10] And his theoretical position is equally lacking in fruitful analogical connections. He seems to be trying, in the National Library, to work out a theory of analogies—of how the word mediates the real and how the Word mediates the Whole. And he does arrive at a theory of the artist more fully involved with the work than the earlier theory that he proposed in *Portrait*. But there is still no bridge between genuine *others*, no

---

10 Of course, for the likes of Luther or Kierkegaard or Barth or Paul, this dialectical impotence is itself its own solution, placing the subject at the hopeless limit-to from beyond which amazing grace pours. But no absurd burst of grace has leaped, unmediated, across the chasm of Stephen's limit-to.

"like" amid difference: no child is born who is truly different from the parent. All Stephen's theory ends up describing is mechanical repetition in which the creation simply is the creator, a romantic emanationism that absorbs all back into the same (the author, or God). The dialectical gulf remains unbridgeable: God touches nothing that is not-God, artist touches nothing that is not-artist, self touches nothing that is not-self.

Indeed, in *Ulysses and Justice* James McMichael claims that Stephen's lecture (which McMichael definitely distinguishes from Joyce's own vision) draws the harshest of dialectical lines between the realm of pure, transcendent, self-enclosed artistic "postcreation" and the messy human world of lovemaking and parenting:

> The program itself is as follows. As the father is "himself His Own Son" in the meaningful substance of His Word, so is the writer Himself His Own Reader. Writing is to meaning as father is to son: unless daughters are prepared to undergo a sex change, they need not apply to Stephen's word. If the program stopped there, it would negate natural generation by eliminating mothers. But it is more extravagant still. As father and son are to the number one, so also are writing and meaning: no reader of either sex need apply unless prepared to concede that "the postcreation" Stephen writes into being is meaningful without readers ever finding it so. Their natural progenitors will have done Stephen and the race no favor by having sinfully conceived, given birth to, and nurtured mortal readers whom he later redeems as his spiritual progeny. For while readers live and die in need of its redemptive power, the meaning of Stephen's word does not need them. Since "in the economy of heaven, foretold by Hamlet, there are no more marriages, glorified man, an androgynous angel, being a wife unto himself" [205], the more people there are who both need and atone with Stephen's meaning, the fewer people there will be. If Stephen has his way, they will eventually get it right. (100–101)

To "get it right" would mean to halt reproduction, to put a stop to the human species altogether. This is hardly a view of the human world as sacramental, as oozing, in Gerard Manley Hopkins's terms, with "the grandeur of God."

And yet, when John Eglinton asks Stephen whether he believes his own theory, we are told, "—No, Stephen said promptly" (205). There is an alternate movement within the chapter that suggests that encounters with real others, not just with modalities of the self, are important to Stephen and to the novel. For example, while ostensibly criticizing Ann Hathaway, the truly other person who touched, seduced, and procreated with Shakespeare, and whom Shakespeare had to escape so he could become an artistic/heavenly Father, Stephen thinks to himself, "And my turn? When?" (183). Apparently Stephen *wants* to be touched; he wants genuine communion with not-self. Wound through his theoretical portrayal of Shakespeare as spectre and text, as all in all, are images of fleshly human relationships—lover to lover (Shakespeare and Ann Hathaway), parent to child (Shakespeare and

Hamnet, Lear and Cordelia, Pericles and Marina, Simon and Stephen)—that undercut the wispy emanationist/expressivist theory that Stephen is weaving.

And then the chapter ends with Stephen's first encounter with Leopold Bloom, which provides Stephen with a tiny epiphany that undercuts his self-enclosed Father-Son paradigm. Buck Mulligan is walking out of the library, reading aloud his new play about masturbation (a parody, apparently, of the aesthetic theory Stephen has just been defending); Bloom comes up behind them:

> About to pass through the doorway, feeling one behind, [Stephen] stood aside.
> Part. The moment is now. Where then? If Socrates leave his house today, if Judas go forth tonight. Why? That lies in space which I in time must come to, ineluctably. . . .
> A man [Bloom] passed out between them, bowing, greeting.
> —Good day again, Buck Mulligan said. (209)

The simple matter-of-factness of Bloom's passage between Stephen and Buck counters the airy abstraction of Stephen's reflections ("If Socrates . . ."). And the event, so small in itself, leads him to remember his dream: "Last night I flew. Easily flew. Men wondered. Street of harlots after. A creamfruit melon he held to me. In. You will see" (209). And it is this insignificant encounter with an *other*, the unintellectual Jew Bloom, rather than any resolution to the library argument about Shakespeare, that gives the end of the episode, both for Stephen and for the reader, the sacramental serenity of the end of Shakespeare's *Cymbeline*:

> Kind air defined the coigns of houses in Kildare street. No birds. Frail from the housetops two plumes of smoke ascended, pluming, and in a flaw of softness softly were blown.
> Cease to strive. Peace of the druid priests of Cymbeline, hierophantic: from wide earth an altar.
>
> *Laud we the gods*
> *And let our crooked smokes climb to their nostrils*
> *From our bless'd altars.* (209)

Noon explains what is missing from Stephen's theory of the Trinity so far, and it is precisely the dimension that I am arguing creeps into the edges of the library chapter: *relationship*. Stephen's Trinitarian imagery, Noon argues, for all its adoption of the word "consubstantial," is Sabellian rather than Nicene:

> Trinitarian theology is a theology of relationships. Aquinas calls the Three Divine Persons three Subsistent Relations. How could Stephen, whose own sense of relationship was so dim, be expected to follow? One works from analogy back to God. Stephen had lost the analogues. He could not see that relationship is an *ens reale*.
> Unless you see this you will, in Trinitarian theology, end in Sabellianism. The Father becomes the Son; the Son, the Father. So the relationship perishes, and without these relations there can be no Holy Spirit. (95)

Noon goes on to argue that the essential relationality of the Christian God is precisely analogical; the analogical "procession" of the divine through three persons is the very basis of relationality:

> In virtue of an analogical rather than univocal predication, Aquinas sets out to establish that procession in God implies simply a relationship of origin between two: for example, the Son is He Who proceeds from the Father, the Father is He from Whom the Son proceeds. So when Aquinas says that there are processions in God, he means simply that there are real relations of origin in God. (111)

Obviously for this study both in general and in relation to *Ulysses*, the issue is not a propositional espousal of a Thomistic Trinitarianism; the issue is the way literary classics, such as *Ulysses*, present *images* of the relation of the human with limit reality. What Noon makes clear is that the analogical way of imagining this relation is founded on relationality (not disjunction) itself. Although Stephen began *Portrait* with an easy sense of the connectedness of each to each and himself to all, we have watched that analogical trust crumble. His flirtations with the Arian and the Sabellian pictures of the Trinity reveal Stephen's continuing attempt to weave for himself a new, more mature, image of the whole. So far, though, as Noon, McMichael, and others make clear, this image is as harshly univocal and dialectical as the darkest aspects of Conrad's vision. I believe, however, that the dialectical negativity is, in *Ulysses*, gathered up into a larger analogical imaging of the world, leading ultimately to an analogical vision that truly acknowledges and contains the dialectical (as David Tracy says all but the most bland and naive analogical imaginations must do).[11]

If Stephen Dedalus's story is to achieve true analogical epiphanies, it will have to reach beyond Stephen himself. Throughout *Portrait*, and in the Stephen chapters of *Ulysses* (until, as we saw, Bloom intrudes in chapter 9), Stephen is all in all in all; the novels embody modernist subjectivism even more profoundly than Conrad's works, with no analogical bridge to anything outside the subject, Stephen. It is, therefore, an amusing jolt to encounter the first sentences of the fourth chapter of *Ulysses*:

> Mr Leopold Bloom ate with relish the inner organs of beasts and fowls. He liked thick giblet soup, nutty gizzards, a stuffed roast heart, liver slices fried with crustcrumbs, fried hencods' roes. Most of all he liked grilled mutton kidneys which gave to his palate a fine tang of faintly scented urine. (53)

---

11 Tracy, as I have already noted, claims that a fully developed analogical imagination must possess a dialectical dimension: "Where analogical theologies lose that sense for the negative, that dialectical sense within analogy itself, they produce not a believable harmony among various likenesses in all reality but the theological equivalent of 'cheap grace': boredom, sterility and an atheological vision of a deadening univocity" (*Analogical Imagination* 413).

Bloom is the supplement that will supplant Stephen as the Joycean hero. A full discussion of Bloom would require its own book (and quite a few have been written), but his otherness from Stephen and his rich comic earthiness are already apparent from those first sentences that Joyce wrote about him. And if those sentences are not an obvious dislodging of Stephen's headiness, consider the end of this first Bloom chapter, in which Bloom reads not a serious philosophical or literary text but a light magazine story—while defecating in his outhouse:

> Quietly he read, restraining himself, the first column and, yielding but resisting, began the second. Midway, his last resistance yielding, he allowed his bowels to ease themselves quietly as he read, reading still patiently that slight constipation of yesterday quite gone. Hope it's not too big bring on piles again. No, just right. So. Ah! Costive one tabloid of cascara sagrada. Life might be so. It did not move or touch him but it was something quick and neat. Print anything now. (66)

"Print anything now"? Indeed. And of course Bloom's encounter with literature ends this way: "He tore away half the prize story sharply and wiped himself with it" (67).

In a discussion of *Ulysses* as comic novel, Zack Bowen describes the way in which such prose supplements Joyce's presentation of Stephen:

> If Bloom can't take satisfaction in either traditional societal approbation or financial remuneration for his talent, and if he is no longer the sole or even infrequent proprietor of [his wife] Molly's body, he nevertheless follows the comic tradition by achieving a measure of satisfaction from his own, more basic bodily functions such as taste, flatulence, and elimination. . . . In doing so Bloom has in a serious but comic way become more independent, more able to survive in the often inhospitable environs of dear dirty Dublin.
>
> While Stephen's all-encompassing theories about life and art and Hamlet are trivialized in the library scene, Bloom's mundane philosophy and rationality gain importance as natural functions of survival and vitality for the common man. The pretensions of Stephen's vision cannot stand the light of comic reality because they lack vitality, whereas although Bloom's unique if zany solutions to both his and society's problems seem ridiculous, they nevertheless possess the vital energy that transcends traditional morality and informs a comic vision that reduces the greatest epic in Western civilization [the Odyssey] to a set of domestic circumstances. (5)

In the terms of Kevin Hart's postmodern theological/literary analysis, Bloom is a truly *other* supplement to Stephen's "all-encompassing theories" (if he were not truly other, he would not be outside the all in all in all), and yet he is not a dialectical cancellation of Stephen but rather an analogical enlargement of him: "That which requires supplementation," Hart says, "already has within it a trace of what the supplement brings" (197). Bloom is other, yet the eating, defecating, comic human reality he adds to the novel is simply the fleshly reality that Stephen has had—but suppressed—all along.

This is not to say that Bloom is some sort of crass slob. Like Stephen, Bloom is sensitive, lonely, alienated from Dublin. Bloom's loneliness, however, springs not from abstract cosmic rebelliousness but from very specific personal issues: the prejudice that he experiences as a Jew in Catholic Dublin; the lingering sadness he feels because of the death ten years ago of his infant son, Rudy, which has caused a ten-year lapse in Bloom's sexual relationship with Molly, his wife; the anxiety he undergoes knowing that today Molly is planning to commence an adulterous affair with the revolting Blazes Boylan. Bloom's very specific personal concerns add a thick texture to his chapters that Stephen's never seem to have.

The eighth chapter, in which Bloom eats lunch in Davy Byrne's pub after leaving the Burton restaurant in disgust, is clearly a counterpart to the third chapter, in which Stephen broods on Sandymount Strand; like Stephen on the strand, Bloom closes his eyes to see what it would be like to be blind, encounters a dog, composes bad poetry, reflects on rotten teeth.[12] But the differences are more interesting than the similarities. Bloom has his own bout with solipsism in this moody chapter, but he still seems stunningly in touch with his surroundings. His impressions of the Burton restaurant, for instance, although they might support a dialectical vision of the human, fleshly world as disgusting, seem nonetheless remarkably *true:*

> Stink gripped his trembling breath: pungent meatjuice, slop of greens. See the animals feed.
> Men, men, men.
> Perched on high stools by the bar, hats shoved back, at the tables calling for more bread no charge, swilling, wolfing gobfuls of sloppy food, their eyes bulging, wiping wetted moustaches. A pallid suetfaced young man polished his tumbler knife fork and spoon with his napkin. New set of microbes. A man with an infant's saucestained napkin tucked round him shovelled gurgling soup down his gullet. A man spitting back on his plate: halfmasticated gristle: no teeth to chewchewchew it. Chump chop from the grill. Bolting to get it over. Sad booser's eyes. (161)

For all its sense of disgust, this is a lavish epiphany that Stephen ought to envy, not least of all because for all its negative tone it remains wonderfully funny. And it ends with a note of compassion that, again, we rarely encounter in Stephen: Bloom notices that the "booser's eyes" are "sad." In fact, there are compassionate moments all through this lunch chapter, from Bloom's feeding of "Those poor birds" (146) early in the chapter to his gentle guiding of the blind stripling near the end ("Say something to him. Better not do the condescending" [172]).

In addition, where Stephen has been trying to halt relationality—to encompass the world within art, the Father within the Son, reality within his own

---

12 Erwin R. Steinberg presents an impressive list of the parallels between the two chapters. See *The Stream of Consciousness and Beyond in Ulysses* (Pittsburgh: University of Pittsburgh Press, 1973), 65–88.

subjectivity—Bloom shows himself in this chapter (and throughout *Ulysses*) to be deeply concerned with personal relationships. When Bloom thinks about his sexual problems with Molly—"Could never like it again after Rudy" (160)—he suppresses the key pronoun, as McMichael points out: "Which of them could never like it again?" (173). McMichael suggests that Bloom suppresses the pronoun out of neurotic avoidance, so he will not have to fully explain the situation to himself and face the fact "that he owes Molly a good turn in bed" (174), and this is undoubtedly true. But Bloom's ability so easily to elide the subject of this sentence indicates his marital closeness to this woman; it is unlikely that Stephen could speak or think a sentence that so implicitly links himself with another. Similarly, Bloom's very concrete memories of Molly at a choir picnic ("Molly had that elephantgrey dress with the braided frogs. Mantailored with selcovered buttons" [148]) reveal that his sense of his own life story is grounded in its connection to another. And his memory of himself and Molly making love on Howth hill has fairly explicit Eucharistic overtones; Molly offers Bloom food that symbolizes and mediates life: "Softly she gave me in my mouth the seedcake warm and chewed. Mawkish pulp her mouth had mumbled sweet and sour with spittle. Joy: I ate it: joy. Young life, her lips that gave me pouting" (167).

The word that haunts Bloom's imagination in this lunchtime chapter is "parallax," which Don Gifford and Robert Seidman define as "the apparent displacement (or the difference in apparent direction) of an object as seen from two different points of view" (28). The word "parallax" is a kind of scientific reflection on the very notion of relatedness and compassion: it acknowledges that others have different perspectives on reality from one's own, and that these perspectives should be acknowledged but cannot and should not be appropriated. It is Bloom's parallactic, analogical vision that supplements (and at least potentially heals) Stephen's univocal vision.

Even before Bloom introduces the word into *Ulysses*, the text itself begins to behave in a parallactic way. With the abrupt intrusion of newspaper headlines in the seventh chapter, set in a newspaper office, the book's style-shifting begins. A chapter written as a musical fugue gives way to the Cyclopean chapter's barrage of overblown (one-eyed, not parallactic) interpolations, which is followed by the girlishly romantic prose of Gertie MacDowell's chapter, and then by the laborious progression of literary styles in the maternity-hospital chapter, in which Mina Purefoy gives birth while Stephen and his friends carouse and Bloom becomes paternally concerned about Stephen's welfare. It seems clear that this eruption of styles operates on a textual level in the way that Bloom operates on a narrative level: to undermine and subvert the univocal stream-of-consciousness style, closely identified with Stephen Dedalus, that had become the hallmark of both *Portrait* and the first half of *Ulysses*. And I suggest that this is all part of a strategy to retrieve an analogical way of imagining the world and the whole of reality, a way that acknowledges and celebrates parallax, genuine multiplicity, a heavenly Father and a human Son who are both consubstantial and distinct.

Certainly it is possible to describe the style-shifting in an alternate way, just as it is possible to describe supplementation not—as Kevin Hart does—as an enlargement of vision but rather as a radical annihilation of all vision. For example, Karen Lawrence's fine study of the book's "Odyssey of style" seems to describe *Ulysses* as an antinovel that undermines the possibility of saying anything about anything:

> Ulysses is a set of fictions that reveals the inconclusiveness of all "fictions," a compendium of schemes of order that implies that there is no absolute way to order experience, either in life or in literature. . . . The excess of details and styles makes us pare away what we cannot assimilate to our critical statements about the book, but the surplus remains to remind us of what cannot be incorporated in one scheme or interpretation. . . .
>
> In abandoning the norm with which the book begins and substituting instead a succession of stylistic experiments, Joyce reveals how style is always an interpretation of reality, a choice among many possibilities. In the direction of the style, from the breakdown of narrative, to the borrowing of styles, to the new mode of parody that he created in "Ithaca," Joyce signaled the end and the reconstitution of the form of the novel. (208)

Yet even Lawrence marvels at how much survives Joyce's "reconstitution" of the novel form. She asserts, as we saw, that the deep parody of the penultimate chapter ("Ithaca") "ultimately does not feel like an aggressive cancellation of possibilities or a ruthless satire of belief but imparts instead a sense of the various possibilities that exist in life" (201). The inconclusiveness of the book, she says, "does not lead to a sense of a dead end" but rather "leads to a picture of a survivor and an appreciation of the stamina it takes to get through the excesses of even one day's experience" (209). I agree, but I go further. I suggest that over the course of this long literary day Joyce actually retrieves, or shows the potential of retrieving, the analogical, sacramental vision that Stephen Dedalus lost in *Portrait*. And Joyce does this in a new, mature, comic form—a form that, far from retreating from modernism back to empiricism, rather pushes modernist experimentation to a higher and more complex level. I have been suggesting ways in which Joyce retrieves the analogical imagination throughout *Ulysses*, but it is time to skip to the final few chapters to see the comic epiphany—and the new vision of the Trinity—that the novel mediates.

The epiphany is preceded by the darkest material in the novel. Stephen and Bloom must both confront the deepest negativity—the absolute limit-to—before receiving a glimpse of the gracious limit-of. At the drunken party in the maternity hospital, Stephen expresses the most vigorous blasphemy we have heard from him yet. The young revelers are wondering why young, seemingly healthy children sometimes suddenly die (a question that has certainly plagued Bloom—and not just academically). Stephen, to whom the parodic nineteenth-century narrator grants the degree "Div. Scep." (Sceptic of Divinity), proposes an explanation:

> Mr S. Dedalus' (Div. Scep.) remark (or should it be called an interruption?) that an omnivorous being which can masticate, deglute, digest and apparently pass through the ordinary channel with pluterperfect imperturbability such multifarious aliments as cancrenous femoules [females] emaciated by parturition, corpulent professional gentlemen, not to speak of jaundiced politicians and chlorotic nuns might possibly find gastric relief in an innocent collation of staggering bob, reveals as nought else could and in a very unsavoury light the tendency above alluded to [i.e., Stephen's "perverted transcendentalism"]. For the enlightenment of those who are not so intimately acquainted with the minutiae of the municipal abattoir as this morbidminded esthete and embryo philosopher who for all his overweening bumptiousness in things scientific can scarcely distinguish an acid from an alkali prides himself on being, it should perhaps be stated that staggering bob in the vile parlance of our lower class licensed victuallers signifies the cookable and eatable flesh of a calf newly dropped from its mother. (399)

Babies die, Stephen is saying, because the *dio boia* nibbles young flesh to cleanse his palate after eating "cancrenous" women, tough old professional gentlemen, politicians, and nuns. This comic but serious passage reveals the hopeless limit-to that Stephen has slammed against.

Bloom's limit-to takes longer to present. The book's fifteenth chapter ("Circe"), set in Dublin's nighttown, is a lengthy surreal play that uncovers the sludge—the very bottom—of primarily Bloom's but also Stephen's psyches. A series of wild fantasies inflates and then deflates Bloom, ultimately transforming him into a cringing woman dominated by the overbearing whorehouse madam Bella, who herself has been transformed into the fiercely macho Bello. I can think of no literary hero who is debased as deeply as Bella/Bello debases Bloom in this scene:

> You will make the beds, get my tub ready, empty the pisspots in the different rooms, including old Mrs Keogh's the cook's, a sandy one. Ay, and rinse the seven of them well, mind, or lap it up like champagne. Drink me piping hot. Hop! . . . Swell the bust. Smile. Droop shoulders. What offers? (*He [Bello] points.*) For that lot trained by owner to fetch and carry, basket in mouth. (*He bares his arm and plunges it elbowdeep in Bloom's vulva.*) There's fine depth for you! What, boys? That give you a hardon? (*He shoves his arm in a bidder's face.*) Here wet the deck and wipe it round! (505)

Is such a passage funny or intolerable? In the context of *Ulysses* as a whole, it is both at once: Joyce must explore even the most deeply intolerable and make it comic—and not blackly, satirically comic, but movingly, humanly so—if he is really to embrace the whole.

Still, this is arguably still not an analogical acceptance of the whole as oozing with grandeur (though it is oozing with something). It looks as much like a dialectical immersion in the grossly secular to reveal the *absence* of grandeur. And it is Stephen who brings the book to just this immersion—though ironically, analogically, his immersion in grimly profane alienation will actually usher in a comic all-inclusiveness. After Bloom breaks free of the degrading Bella/Bello fantasy (comically, the snapping of a trouser button—"Bip!" [516]—brings him back to himself), Stephen has his own terrifying hallucination of his dead mother, drawing him to death. *"[B]reathing upon him softly her breath of wetted ashes,"* she urges him, "All must go through it, Stephen. More women than men in the world. You too. Time will come" (540). Stephen asks her to tell him the secret of the gracious limit-of: "Tell me the word, mother," he begs her, "if you know now. The word known to all men" (540). But rather than mediate an analogical vision of ultimate reality,[13] she merely berates him for falling short: "Prayer for the suffering souls in the Ursuline manual, and forty days indulgence. Repent, Stephen" (540). The experience brings all of Stephen's dialectical protestations, which we have seen accumulating throughout both *Portrait* and *Ulysses*, to a head: "The corpsechewer!" he shouts. "Raw head and bloody bones! . . . *Ah non, par exemple!* The intellectual imagination! With me all or not at all. *Non serviam!*" (541). And then he yells—or rather, in his best Wagnerian tenor voice, sings—his ultimate word of defiance: *"Nothung!"* (542). Invoking Siegfried's magic sword, which ushers in the Twilight of the Gods at the end of Wagner's Ring Cycle, Stephen smashes the whorehouse lamp with his ashplant and runs out into the street. He has exercised to the maximum degree Paul Tillich's "Protestant principle": "the divine and human protest against any absolute claim made for a relative reality" (*Protestant Era* 163).

But Bloom has a more modest principle to attend to: the principle of paying a just price. While Stephen is raving and smashing lamps, Bloom is quietly making sure that Bella and her prostitutes do not overcharge Stephen either for their favors or for the broken lamp. "Why pay more?" Bloom asks, though the head-in-the-

---

13 The recent "Corrected Text" of *Ulysses*, edited by Hans Walter Gabler, reveals that this "word known to all men" is *love*: "Love, yes. Word known to all men" (*Ulysses* by James Joyce, ed. Hans Gabler with Wolfhard Steppe and Claus Melchior [New York: Vintage, 1986], 161). (The passage did not appear in earlier editions of the novel.) It is debatable whether Joyce would have approved of reinserting the passage into the text, but the addition is nonetheless illuminating. The Joyce critic and biographer Richard Ellmann says this about the restoration of the word "love": "It is extremely helpful to have Joyce confirm that the word known to all men is *love*, and Gabler must be commended for unearthing this passage. But there are reasons for arguing that, however much it may clarify Joyce's outlook, it should not be included in the final text. . . . No doubt the debate about this emendation in the new edition will continue. Whether accepted or not, it confirms that Joyce wished to present Stephen and Bloom as in accord about love, the nature of which is anatomized in several chapters" ("The New *Ulysses*," *Georgia Review* 40 [1986]: 554, 555).

clouds Stephen says, "Doesn't matter a rambling damn" (521). And it is common-sensical Bloom (who circumvented his own fiercest encounter with psychic darkness by popping a trouser button) who turns Stephen's most terrible existential crisis into a merry chase in which "Here Comes Everybody":

> *He hurries out through the hall. . . . Incog Haroun al Raschid, he flits behind the silent lechers and hastens on by the railings with fleet step of a pard strewing the drag behind him, torn envelopes drenched in aniseed. The ashplant marks his stride. A pack of bloodhounds led by Hornblower of Trinity brandishing a dogwhip in tallyho cap, and an old pair of grey trousers, follows from far, picking up the scent, nearer, baying, panting, at fault, breaking away, throwing their tongues, biting his heels, leaping at his tail. He walks, runs, zigzags, gallops, lugs laid back. He is pelted with gravel, cabbagestumps, biscuitboxes, eggs, potatoes, dead codfish, woman's slipperslappers. After him, freshfound, the hue and cry zigzag gallops in hot pursuit of follow my leader: 65 C 66 C night watch, John Henry Menton, Wisdom Hely, V. B. Dillon, Councillor Nannetti, Alexander Keyes, Larry O'Rourke, Joe Cuffe, Mrs O'Dowd, Pisser Burke, The Nameless One, Mrs Riordan, The Citizen, Garryowen, Whatdoyoucallhim, Strangeface, Fellowthatslike, Sawhimbefore, Chapwith, Chris Callinan, sir Charles Cameron, Benjamin Dollard, Lenehan, Bartell d'Arcy, Joe Hynes, red Murray, editor Brayden, T. M. Healy, Mr Justice Fitzgibbon, John Howard Parnell, the reverend Tinned Salmon, Professor Joly, Mrs Breen, Denis Breen, Theodore Purefoy, Mina Purefoy, the Westland Row postmistress, C. P. McCoy, friend of Lyons, Hoppy Holohan, man in the street, other man in the street. . . .* (544–45)

Out in the street, Bloom breaks up a fight between Stephen and two British soldiers, while apocalypse rages all around: "*Brimstone fires spring up. Dense clouds roll past. Heavy Gatling guns boom. Pandemonium*" (555). The novel's climax has become an over-the-top comic parody of literary climaxes, and it is fittingly capped with nothing less than a Black Mass: "*Introibo ad altare diaboli. . . . Htengier Lnetopinmo Dog Drol eht rof, Aiulella!*" (556). But as Bloom saves Stephen from the soldiers, the Mass reverses. "THE VOICE OF ALL THE BLESSED" proclaim, "Alleluia, for the Lord God Omnipotent reigneth!"; nothing less than "*the voice of Adonai*" calls out, "Goooooooooood!"; and "*In strident discord peasants and townsmen of Orange and Green factions sing* Kick the Pope *and* Daily, daily sing to Mary" (557). The ordinary has become transcendent and the transcendent ordinary and ridiculous: the chapter has exploded into a comic chaos in which it no longer makes sense to distinguish the serious and the parodic. Clearly we are in territory that differs from the familiar dialectical rebellion of the Stephen who vows "*Non serviam.*" It is this strange paradoxical territory that marks the minor epiphany that concludes the nighttown chapter and the major epiphany that concludes the encounter between Stephen and Bloom.

In the final two pages of the nighttown chapter, after many pages of surreal fantasies and personal climaxes, Bloom stands over Stephen, who lies in the street, in the fetal position, rendered unconscious by both alcohol and a soldier's punch (or, as young Stephen would say, his "belt"). Bloom "*brings his mouth near the face of the prostrate form*" and for the first time speaks Stephen's name: "Stephen! (*There is no answer. He calls again.*) Stephen!" (564). And then this man, who has been sadly mourning his dead son for more than ten years and has obviously been looking for a surrogate to help him reestablish a connectedness to the world, has a vision of "*a fairy boy of eleven, a changeling, kidnapped, dressed in an Eton suit with glass shoes and a little bronze helmet, holding a book in his hand. He reads from right to left inaudibly, smiling, kissing the page*" (565). Bloom is "*Wonderstruck,*" and he "*calls inaudibly*": "Rudy!" (565). It would be easy to dismiss this as a Joycean parody of shameless sentimentalism, but the novel has been breaking down those easy dialectical dividers between the sentimental and the coolly detached. The moment is truly moving; as Anthony Burgess, hardly a sentimentalist, puts it, "Only the hardest-hearted of readers will withhold his tears" (164).

So Bloom and Stephen are finally together. They achieve a grand integration of their opposite human temperaments ("The scientific. The artistic" [635])—by drinking hot cocoa together. The chapter in which Bloom briefly brings Stephen home to sober up and then go on his way—the seventeenth chapter ("Ithaca," i.e., "Home"), which this entire, enormous novel has been leading up to—is easily one of the most striking anticlimaxes in all of literature.

For one thing, the narrator of the chapter is as unemotional and abstract as a narrator can be; the chapter is designed as a Catholic catechism, with a cold, tedious series of questions and answers. Stanley Sultan claims that, of all the strange narrative manners created in the novel, this alone "does not seem to have any special fictional work to do; it neither makes a point about the theme nor implements the unfolding action of the chapter" (383). Sultan concludes that the chapter is designed as it is to complete a tendency that he feels has developed throughout *Ulysses*; the progression of the novel, he thinks, has tended "to remove the author's voice from [the] respective chapters, to make the work more dramatic" (383). The catechetical form, in other words, so depersonalizes the narrator that, in effect, he disappears. In the words of Stephen in *Portrait*, the narrator remains "within or behind or beyond or above his handiwork, invisible, refined out of existence, indifferent, paring his fingernails."

But I have been arguing throughout this discussion that Joyce does not authorize Stephen's program (which, as McMichael points out, has as its dialectical goal the elimination of the biological human race [100–101]). It seems much more likely that this voice is yet another Joycean parody, this time of Stephen's own program of artistic detachment, pressed to its limit.

As usual, however, the parody overflows itself and becomes its opposite. Perhaps the most-discussed of all the catechism answers is the 450-word answer to the question "What in water did Bloom, waterlover, drawer of water, watercarrier, returning to the range, admire?" (624). Each of the details contained in this huge answer is, in itself, nothing more than a bald, cold fact; the answer, then, seems to parody authoritative answers of any kind to anything. Accumulated, however, the details are awesome in a comical but ultimately sublime way. A. Walton Litz says that the catechism format "relies on the epic impact of overmastering fact" (387), and this passage seems especially to raise the chapter to an epic level—while simultaneously parodying that very effort. Litz describes the way the chapter eludes any clear dialectical categories that readers try to impose on it; he criticizes "the attempts of so many readers to press *Ulysses*—and especially the 'Ithaca' chapter—into some easy equation of 'either/or.'" Litz goes on to list the inappropriate dichotomies that readers create:

> Either Joyce's method is a satire on the naturalistic writer's preoccupation with detail, or it is a humourless exercise in the manner of classic naturalism. Either it is *reductio ad absurdum* of naive nineteenth-century faith in science, or a serious application of scientific theories to human psychology. "Ithaca" is either a final celebration of Bloom's heroic qualities as Everyman, or a cold revelation of his essential pettiness. . . . But the genius of Joyce and of *Ulysses* lies in the indisputable fact that the form is both epic and ironic, Bloom both heroic and commonplace. (391)

Both/and, as we have repeatedly seen, is the very fabric of the analogical imagination, as either/or is the fabric of the dialectical. In any case, calling this homage to water a "both/and" passage is an understatement; it is an "and/and/and . . ." passage. We are told that Bloom admires such a vast array of water's properties—"Its universality: its democratic equality . . . its imperturbability . . . its violence . . . its secrecy . . . its buoyancy . . . its metamorphoses . . ." (624–25)—that a description of water becomes a comic celebration of nothing less than the analogy of being. If the episodes of this novel and the aspects of physical reality are all analogically contained—even if only comically, as a kind of absent presence, a not-yet that is always-already—within a saucepan of water, then ultimate reality is graciously, sacramentally self-disclosive.

Indeed, Stanley Sultan very seriously describes the coming together of Stephen and Bloom over hot cocoa as a sacramental, Eucharistic event. Although he misses the parodic elements—which, I would suggest, actually add to rather than subtract from the sacramentality of the episode, highlighting as they do the extraordinary *ordinariness* of this communion—Sultan wisely notes the Eucharistic paradigm of Bloom and Stephen's interaction. Bloom and Stephen, Sultan claims, truly unite. Stephen really receives Holy Communion from Bloom the Father in the form of "Epps's massproduct," cocoa:

> Not only Stephen and the narrator but also Joyce himself insist that Stephen has in this episode accepted the sacrament proffered by God's emissary. The conjunction of details confirms this, and the preceding action carefully prepares for it. Receiving

Holy Communion, Stephen is returning to what in the fourteenth chapter was called "Holiness," reverence of, and acceptance by, God. (389)

The event begins with a stress not on Stephen and Bloom's union (this is not a Sabellian dissolving of son into father) but on their *parallelism*, a more analogical word that echoes Bloom's word "parallax":

> What parallel courses did Bloom and Stephen follow returning?
> Starting united both at normal walking pace from Beresford Place they followed . . . (619)

Stanley Sultan points out that "the term 'parallel' injects the suggestion that the courses Bloom and Stephen follow to Bloom's house, being parallel, shall never meet" (384). This communion, in other words, is ultimately partial; a dialectical gulf will always separate Bloom and Stephen. Analogy is not union. And yet the chapter insists on the analogy, the proportionality, the *meta-pherein* that carries-between. Stephen and Bloom do walk parallel, deliberating on

> Music, literature, Ireland, Dublin, Paris, friendship, woman, prostitution, diet, the influence of gaslight or the light of arc and glowlamps on the growth of adjoining paraheliotropic trees, exposed corporation emergency dustbuckets, the Roman catholic church, ecclesiastical celibacy, the Irish nation, jesuit education, careers, the study of medicine, the past day, the maleficent influence of the presabbath, Stephen's collapse. (619)

Showing that the narrator, along with Bloom, is aware of the tragic dialectic contained within a comic analogical vision, the novel quickly confronts us with catechism questions that stress Bloom's aloneness, his failure to connect with a parallel other. Bloom's experiences of intimate conversations have progressively diminished over the course of his adult life:

> Had Bloom discussed similar subjects during nocturnal perambulations in the past?
> In 1884 with Owen Goldberg and Cecil Turnbull. . . . In 1885 with Percy Apjohn. . . . In 1886 occ[a]sionally. . . . In 1888 frequently with major Brian Tweedy and his daughter Miss Marion Tweedy. . . . Once in 1892 and once in 1893 with Julius Mastiansky. . . .
> What reflection concerning the irregular sequence of dates 1884, 1885, 1886, 1888, 1892, 1893, 1904 did Bloom make before their arrival at their destination?
> He reflected that the progressive extension of the field of individual development and experience was regressively accompanied by a restriction of the converse domain of interindividual relations. (620–21)

So the fact of communication is immediately juxtaposed, in Bloom's mind, with the fact of aloneness, which in turn immediately gives rise to the realization of the ultimate experience of aloneness, death:

As in what ways [was the progressive extension of the field of individual development and experience regressively accompanied by a restriction of the converse
domain of interindividual relations]?
     From inexistence to existence he came to many and was as one received: exis-
tence with existence he was with any as any with any: from existence to nonexistence
gone he would be by all as none perceived. (621)

Far from being always-already, connection, it seems, is a not-yet—or rather, as
humans age it becomes a nevermore. And yet, the novel finds some analogy, some
parallelism, between Bloom and Stephen right at the heart of this nevermore. A
short while later Bloom's private thoughts—"from existence to nonexistence"—
are echoed by Stephen, who affirms "his significance as a conscious rational
animal proceeding syllogistically *from the known to the unknown*" (650, emphasis
added). Even in their awareness of "the incertitude of the void" (650), Bloom and
Stephen do, after all, possess some kinship, and Bloom is at least subliminally
aware of this:

Was [Stephen's] affirmation apprehended by Bloom?
Not verbally. Substantially. (650)

So Bloom and Stephen's sharing of hot cocoa in the Blooms' kitchen—for all
the limitation, qualification, and irony that the text insists on—is a sacramental
event. Using that marvelously universal water, Bloom prepares the cocoa with
ritualistic care:

How did Bloom prepare a collation for a gentile?
He poured into two teacups two level spoonfuls, four in all, of Epps's soluble
cocoa and proceeded according to the directions for use printed on the label, to each
adding after sufficient time for infusion the prescribed ingredients for diffusion in
the manner and in the quantity prescribed. (629)

To be hospitable, Bloom drinks from an ordinary cup rather from his special
"moustache cup of imitation Crown Derby presented to him by his only daughter,
Millicent (Milly)," and he serves Stephen an inordinate amount of "the viscous
cream ordinarily reserved for the breakfast of his wife Marion (Molly)" (629).
And all of these little acts add up to a "jocoserious" liturgy:

Was the guest conscious of and did he acknowledge these marks of hospitality?
His attention was directed to them by his host jocosely and he accepted them
seriously as they drank in jocoserious silence Epps's massproduct, the creature
cocoa. (629)

At this point—although Bloom notes "four separating forces between his tem-
porary guest and him," i.e., "Name, age, race, creed" (630)—the analogies and

linkages between Stephen and Bloom begin to proliferate. And as is the case throughout the novel, the connections are *both* ridiculous *and* genuine. One elaborate catechism question, for instance, asks, "What relation existed between their ages?" (632), and the answer regales us with an elaborate set of mathematical proportions comparing their ages. This is the analogical imagination at its most playful. We also learn that when Stephen was five years old, he invited Bloom to dinner, just as Bloom now invites Stephen to spend the night. The responses are touchingly analogous:

> Did Bloom accept the invitation to dinner given then by the son [Stephen] . . . ?
> Very gratefully, with grateful appreciation, with sincere appreciative gratitude, in appreciatively grateful sincerity of regret, he declined. (633)
> Was [Bloom's] proposal of asylum [to Stephen] accepted?
> Promptly, inexplicably, with amicability, gratefully it was declined. (648)

We learn that Bloom knew "Mrs Riordan, a widow of independent means" (633), and even remembers the very "green and maroon brushes for Charles Stewart Parnell and for Michael Davitt" (634) which were among Stephen's earliest observations in *Portrait*; that Bloom and Stephen were both baptized by the same priest ("the reverend Charles Malone C.C., in the church of the Three Patrons, Rathgar" [635]); and even that, with regard to Bloom's Jewishness, they seem able reciprocally to read each other's minds:

> What, reduced to their simplest reciprocal form, were Bloom's thoughts about Stephen's thoughts about Bloom [and] . . . Stephen's thoughts about Bloom's thoughts about Stephen?
> He thought that he thought that he was a jew whereas he knew that he knew that he knew that he was not. (634)

And in a discussion of the two men's "educational careers," the narrator playfully merges—creates a kind of proportion between—their names: "Substituting Stephen for Bloom Stoom . . . Substituting Bloom for Stephen Blephen" (635). No longer do we have one isolated monad named Stephen and another named Bloom; we have, rather, Stoom/Blephen.

The most substantial linkage that occurs over this comic Eucharist is that both Stephen and Bloom recite to each other Irish and Hebrew, respectively:

> What fragment of verse from the ancient Hebrew and ancient Irish languages were cited with modulations of voice and translation of texts by guest to host and by host to guest?
> By Stephen: *suil, suil, suil arun, suil go siocair agus suil go cuin* (walk, walk, walk your way, walk in safety, walk with care).
> By Bloom: *Kifeloch, harimon rakatejch m'baad l'zamatejch* (thy temple amid thy hair is as a slice of pomegranate). (640)

Like other sacramental moments, this is on the surface trivial. And yet, considering Stephen's conflicted relationship with his Irishness and Bloom's with his Jewishness, the comfort with which they share their ethnic heritages here is quite striking. In addition, the narrative insists on an analogy between their ancestral languages, as Stephen and Bloom perform a "glyphic comparison of the phonic symbols of both languages" (640) by writing and comparing Irish and Hebrew letters. We are even told the "points of contact" that "existed between these languages and between the peoples who spoke them" (641), and these "points" include a comic yet serious summary of the stories of Stephen and Bloom: "their dispersal, persecution, survival and revival" (641).

The sharing of each other's ancestral languages climaxes in an epiphany for each of them—a momentary analogical experience of resolution to the ultimate issues that have haunted them. Stephen, who has been oppressed by the past ("History . . . is a nightmare from which I am trying to awake" [34]), experiences the past redeemed: listening to Bloom chanting Hebrew, Stephen "heard in a profound ancient male unfamiliar melody the accumulation of the past" (642). Bloom, on the other hand, in losing his son, Rudy, has lost his progeny, his future; looking at Stephen, however, Bloom "saw in a quick young male familiar form the predestination of a future" (642). And then they truly *know* each other in a funny but profound way, penetrating to each other's limits, their "concealed identities"; Stephen sees Bloom as an image of Christ as the intersection of the human and the divine ("The traditional figure of hypostasis"), and Bloom hears Stephen as prophetic poet ("The Traditionnal accent af the ecstasy of catastrophe") (642).

These analogies between Stephen and Bloom, along with their glimpses into a kind of essential truth about each other, are in keeping with the inherently relational nature of the sacramental imagination. As Stephen sang at the end of the previous chapter, gaps have been healed, *"Und alle Schiffe brücken"* (618)—"And all ships are bridged." It is in this context that the larger religious analogies dear to analogical theologians are possible. The analogical imagination sees connections, bridges, woven tapestries, and God emerges merely (merely?) as the whole of the tapestry; it is such a large, relational image of God that, as William Noon argues, is symbolized by the Christian Trinity. So it is appropriate that only now, after the institution of the hot-cocoa sacrament, does *Ulysses* truly leap from Arian and Sabellian heresies—which cannot abide the irrational melding of the human and the divine—to a fully Trinitarian vision of the whole, of ultimate reality. This is not to say that the novel ends with pious orthodoxy. The Trinitarian insight is presented through the image of two men urinating in a garden while a woman who has just reveled in adulterous sex looms over them.

The two men are, of course, Stephen and Bloom. Stephen having "gratefully" declined Bloom's offer of "asylum" (mixed as it was with Bloom's cloudy but certainly unseemly plans for making Stephen Molly Bloom's new lover—the analogical imagination intertwines the sacred with the very profane), Stephen and

Bloom leave the Blooms' house with "intonation *secreto*" of Psalm 113, "*In exitu Israël de Egypto . . .*" (651). In the Blooms' garden, Stephen and Bloom confront a cosmic "spectacle"—"The heaventree of stars hung with humid nightblue fruit" (651)—which leads Bloom to meditate, in a way that links his own scientific speculations with the kind of theological, "limit" reflections that have long occupied Stephen, on "the parallax or parallactic drift of socalled fixed stars, in reality evermoving from immeasurably remote eons to infinitely remote futures in comparison with which the years, thre[e]score and ten, of allotted human life formed a parenthesis of infinitesimal brevity" (651). Bloom's cosmic speculations go on at great length, embracing everything from the universe's size and evolution to extraterrestrial life to astrology. The text is clearly—in a way that, as is typical in *Ulysses*, thoroughly blends the ironic and the sublime—putting this event in relation to the whole of reality, a relation that David Tracy would call religious: "[T]he questions which religion addresses," Tracy says in *The Analogical Imagination*, "are the fundamental existential questions of the meaning and truth of individual, communal and historical existence *as related to, indeed as both participating in and distanced from, what is sensed as the whole of reality*" (157–58, emphasis added).

And it is in this context that the novel's image of the Trinity emerges. As we saw, Stephen has struggled, on Sandymount Strand and in the National Library, with Arian and Sabellian views of the Trinity, both of which are predicated on the impossibility of a full incarnation of the divine in the human; as William Noon points out, what is missing from both Arius's and Sabellius's notions of the Trinity is an awareness of the centrality of *relationship* to the nature of God. But Joyce's final image of Trinity as a manifestation of deep reality—an image, we must remember, not a doctrine—is deeply relational, as relational as the partnership of a husband and wife, of a parent and child.

First Molly Bloom makes her presence known, a quietly sublime light shining over the garden. The text implies the sublimity of the light, but also attests to its empirical ordinariness. This is the light of the Holy Spirit as it shines through a Dublin-made window blind:

> What visible luminous sign attracted Bloom's, who attracted Stephen's gaze?
> In the second storey (rere) of his (Bloom's) house the light of a paraffin oil lamp with oblique shade projected on a screen of roller blind supplied by Frank O'Hara, window blind, curtain pole and revolving shutter manufacturer, 16 Aungier Street. (655)

But the trivially empirical quickly becomes relational:

> How did he [Bloom] elucidate the mystery of an invisible person, his wife Marion (Molly) Bloom, denoted by a visible splendid sign, a lamp?
> With indirect and direct verbal allusions or affirmations: with subdued affection and admiration: with description; with impediment; with suggestion. (655)

Bathed in the splendid, trivial, loving, adulterous light of this unorthodox orthodox Holy Spirit, Stephen and Bloom become an image of the relation of the Father
and Son that Aquinas himself could applaud:

> Both then were silent?
> Silent, each contemplating the other in both mirrors of the reciprocal flesh of
> theirhisnothis fellowfaces. (655)

Whether Aquinas would applaud the novel's next image of this Father and
Son—as they urinate together (the text with hilarious solemnity compares the "tra-
jectories of their, first sequent, then simultaneous, urinations" [655]) and then
think about each other's "invisible audible collateral organ" (Bloom thinks bio-
logically, while Stephen reflects on "the divine prepuce, the carnal bridal ring
of the holy Roman catholic apostolic church" [655–56])—is more doubtful. And
yet if the analogical religious imagination is a bridge between the human and the
divine, an obliterating of the gulf between the sacred and the profane, I can think
of no more analogically religious scene in all of literature. When a shooting star
flies overhead, drawing a line from the constellation Lyra (the lyre of Orpheus—
the constellation of the poet), above the "Tress of Berenice" (the constellation
of the Penelope-like Berenice, who "pledged her hair to Aphrodite on the condition that her husband, Ptolemy III, return safely from a military expedition; when
he did return, she sacrificed her beautiful head of hair and it was translated into the
heavens to commemorate the intensity of her love" [Gifford and Seidman 480]),
and "towards the zodiacal sign of Leo" (or Leopold?), the star acts as a visual
meta-phor or bridge-between, linking this somewhat shabby but genuine trinity
(656). The worldly is the transcendent; the farcical is the profound. An analogical
both/and has replaced the dialectical either/or.

    This is a grand scene—but also, importantly, a funny one. A labored analysis of
this and other scenes in *Ulysses* can tend to obscure the book's comedy, which is
perhaps the key way in which Joyce's massive and important novel exemplifies
the analogical imagination. I have taught *Ulysses* to undergraduates on a number
of occasions, and although they usually feel somewhat oppressed by the book's
difficulty, it often makes them laugh very, very hard. Joyce's ability to explore
every nook and cranny of human quirkiness—and even of human desolation and
outright horror and evil—and still broadly and unmaliciously laugh is precisely
the curative power of this great book. The characters are plagued by artistic, emotional, sexual, and relational sterility (Stephen cannot write, Bloom and Molly
cannot have sex, Dublin cannot establish a fruitful political life), and the book
ends with no real resolution. Bloom crawls into bed with Molly, but they do not
have sex; at best fertility is potential but not-yet. Through laughter, however, the
dialectical not-yet is transformed into an analogical always-already, as Catholic
theologian Karl-Josef Kuschel says in *Laughter: A Theological Reflection:*

[I]n myth and poetry the time of renewal, of fertility, of birth and rebirth, is at the same time a time of laughter. Thus in the famous Fourth Eclogue of the Roman poet Virgil (70–19 BCE), a century before Luke, there is mention of a child of God whose birth similarly [like Jesus'] ushers in a new age. This newborn child laughs, and in so doing betrays "his supernatural descent: he is from the family of Helios, the smiling god (of the sun)" [quoted from E. Norden]. This terminology has lasted down to the present day, when we talk of the "smiling sun." It refers to a mythical origin and associates with the sun new life, new creation, new time.

Laughter and new life: we again know this connection from the apocryphal writings of early Christianity. These not only tell of a laughing mother but also say of the newborn Jesus that he did not cry like other children, but "laughed," and "smiled with the most sweet smile" [Pseudo Gospel of Matthew]. . . .

There are also parallels to this in fairy tales and folksongs: laughter as an expression of fertility, of the fullness of life, of resistance against death. (70–71)

Molly and Bloom may not have fertile sex in the early morning of June 17, 1904. But Molly, invoking Kuschel's smiling sun ("as for them saying theres no God . . . they might as well try to stop the sun from rising tomorrow" [731]), remembers that Bloom said "the sun shines for you" the day they "were lying among the rhododendrons on Howth head": "the day I got him to propose to me yes first I gave him the bit of seedcake out of my mouth" (731). Remembering, she exuberantly and repeatedly says, "Yes." And Stephen goes off to become James Joyce and, laughing, write *Ulysses*, which is read by laughing readers. The not-yet of present sterility has become the always-already of laughter. And skeptical, subjective modernism has found an analogical linkage—a carrying-between (*metapherein*)—with the grounding limit-of, with ultimate reality.

3

Three Christian Critics:
Nathan Scott, William Lynch, and Cesáreo Bandera

So far I have established my theological paradigm—a comparison of the dialectical and the analogical imaginations—and have discussed this paradigm briefly in relation to two contemporary fiction writers (John Updike, Andre Dubus) and more thoroughly in relation to two significant modernists (Joseph Conrad, James Joyce). And in the next chapter I will go on to show how these theological imaginations have evolved in later twentieth-century English-language fiction. I would be remiss, however, to imply that I am the only literary critic who has taken a theological approach to literature, and in my introduction I did at least allude to connections between contemporary literary theory—especially the "postmodern context" of our time—and theological concerns. But I wish now to look somewhat more closely at three literary critics whose work seems to me especially apropos to my theme here; not only do these critics deserve tribute in their own right, but they also will supply further insight into the religious imaginations of the novelists with whom this study is primarily concerned. Of the critics to whom I wish to pay tribute, two—Nathan Scott and William Lynch, S.J.—espouse religious ways of imagining that are roughly equivalent to David Tracy's "analogical" imagination, and one—Cesáreo Bandera, a follower of René Girard—is a fine contemporary representative of the dialectical imagination.

Scott and Lynch seemed to me from the outset inevitable literary critics to examine, since Scott's sacramental imagination and Lynch's analogical imagination both resonate with David Tracy's theology. I was aware, however, that neither critic is a darling of the current, postmodern literary academy. It was interesting, then, to read Nathan Scott's own 1997 tribute to William Lynch, in which Scott expresses dismay that Lynch has not received the credit due him. Lynch's most famous work, *Christ and Apollo*, "received virtually no attention at all" when it was published in 1960, and Scott attributes this to "the immensity of the distance that separates those granting hospitality to theological perspectives from the general intellectual and literary life of our period" ("Theology, Poetics, Psychotherapy" 60). And now, as a study of the imagination "has at last begun to captivate contemporary theologians," Scott "is again astonished to remark how much for them Lynch is as if he had never been, for nowhere does one find Julian Hartt, John Coulson, David Tracy, Gordon Kaufman, John McIntyre, Garrett Green, and various others reckoning with his work at all" ("Theology, Poetics, Psychotherapy" 61). Furthermore, those "under the influence of such French savants as Barthes and Foucault and Derrida" ("Theology, Poetics, Psychotherapy" 68)— who, Scott says, assert that imagination, meaning, and the self have no substantive reality[1]—have no interest in Lynch's substantive theory of the imagination. Nonetheless, says Scott, "'Radical *chic*' of the present time . . . has by no means suddenly condemned his whole project to irrelevance" ("Theology, Poetics, Psychotherapy" 69). Scott is inclined "to feel that not since Coleridge has any thinker in the English-speaking world made his way toward so high a doctrine of the imagination as Lynch developed" ("Theology, Poetics, Psychotherapy" 75) and that "he was an 'original' whom we ought to try to recover from the obscurity into which his career has been allowed to descend" ("Theology, Poetics, Psychotherapy" 75–76). I agree that Lynch's theory of an analogical imagination is significant and well worth recovering, and I hope to do it some justice in the pages that follow. I also would observe that Scott's tribute to Lynch is at least as much an explication of his own literary and theological ideas; Scott's sacramental imagination is not identical to Lynch's analogical imagination, but the concepts harmonize with each other in ways that highlight aspects of David Tracy's theological concepts, on which the present study is built.

So Scott and Lynch are fitting critics to examine in this discussion of theological imaginations in modern literature. But both critics, despite traces of dialectical thinking, exemplify aspects of the *analogical* imagination, and I would be remiss if I did not balance my presentation of their works with an examination of a literary critic whose theological imagination is decidedly *dialectical*. An analysis of the theory of Cesáreo Bandera seems to me a necessary supplement to my discussion of Scott and Lynch; what Bandera introduces into contemporary literary theory is a prophetic voice—one that focuses not on sacrament (as Scott does) or on incarnation (as Lynch does) but on the dialectical *theology of the cross*.

Scott, Lynch, and Bandera together demonstrate how vital a theological imagination can be to a discussion of literature that takes seriously the ultimate questions and limit realities that underlie literature—specifically modern and contemporary fiction. I will discuss each critic's particular image of God (or, in Bandera's case, "the sacred") and conception of what God (or the sacred) is, then his overall philosophical position, and finally the literary theory that emerges from these ideas.

---

1 Scott, as I will discuss at greater length in my analysis of his thought, places all postmodernists in the "radical historicist" camp described by Paul Lakeland (16). Obviously, such religious postmodernists as Kevin Hart and even David Tracy do not fit Scott's extreme stereotype.

Nathan Scott's Sacramental Imagination

During his long, distinguished career at the University of Chicago's Divinity School and now at the University of Virginia, Nathan A. Scott, Jr., an Anglican priest, has actively accomplished the very integration that this study has largely been about. He is neither a literary critic who dabbles in theology nor a theologian who toys with literature; he is, rather, a scholar of religion *and* literature. As such he is conscious of running against the grain of what he calls "this late time at the end of the modern age" (*Visions of Presence* 5), and yet he is hardly a reactionary traditionalist. He thoroughly takes account of modern skepticism about traditional theism; he acknowledges the extent to which conventional Christianity's anthropomorphic "God" is dead, and he refuses to revive personal images of God—even of the revisionist sort that such theologians as Sallie McFague propose. As such, his theological stance is, in our terms, sternly dialectical in a very contemporary, even postmodern, way. And yet his vision of the world, and of humans' relationship with it, is deeply sacramental, analogical: Scott posits at least hypothetically an analogy of being that makes the other truly *present*—integrally, reciprocally connected—to the human subject, and hence allows the other to be not opaque but sacramentally revelatory of deep mystery. In this short examination of Scott's religious and literary vision, then, I will begin with his seemingly dialectical picture (or non-picture) of God, and then go on to describe his sacramental vision of the world and of literature.

Andrew Greeley, remember, in his explanation of David Tracy's typology, claims that the cornerstone of the dialectical and analogical imaginations is the underlying picture of God: "The central symbol is God. One's 'picture' of God is in fact a metaphorical narrative of God's relationship with the world and the self as part of the world" (*Catholic Myth* 45). The analogical imagination, Greeley maintains, pictures an involved, interactive God—"a God who is present in the world, disclosing Himself in and through creation. The world and all its events, objects, and people tend to be somewhat like God" (*Catholic Myth* 45). The dialectical imagination, on the other hand, assumes a God wholly unlike the world and its events, objects, and people—"a God who is radically absent from the world and who discloses Herself only on rare occasions (especially in Jesus Christ and Him crucified)" (*Catholic Myth* 45). And although, as we will see, Scott ultimately does not consider God to be "radically absent from the world," God's being and hence God's presence is for Scott a deeply dialectical affair. Nathan Scott's divine reality is profoundly *unlike* the world and its events, objects, and people.

In perhaps his most systematic religious statement, his 1971 book *The Wild Prayer of Longing: Poetry and the Sacred*, Scott specifically states that the old figural interpretation of history and of literary (primarily scriptural) texts is no longer tenable in modern times because it was founded on an outmoded theology. Figuralism saw all worldly events as part of a cosmic drama overseen by a kind of supernatural dramatist-God. All human history is connected for the figural imagination because, "given its providential supervision by the divine Sovereign, history has such a unity as makes all persons and events belong essentially to one continuum"; because everything issues from the same Creator, there is "some significant analogical relationship" between any two persons or events (xv). But such images of a Sovereign God are, for Scott, mere "supernaturalist projections of traditional piety" (xiii), part of an outmoded, myth-ridden system of religious imagery that modern thought has exploded: "a system of supernaturalism, the doctrine of the two realms, the God of the stopgap, the interpretation of transcendence in metaphysical terms, the spatialization of the Divine, the projection into the skies of a heavenly *Pantokrator*" (*Negative Capability* 155). Adopting the demythologizing stance of that most dialectical of theologians, Rudolf Bultmann, Scott tries to strip away mythic accretions to religion—which turn out to be any elements that, in Greeley's words, imagine that "[t]he world and all its events, objects, and people tend to be somewhat like God." Scott states his demythologizing premise in this way:

> For men breathing the atmosphere of the modern world the theistic hypothesis, let us quickly grant, may be an utterly superfluous piece of intellectual baggage, insofar as it posits the "existence" of some impalpable entity standing over against and yet somehow being also pervasive throughout the space-time universe. This is what Bonhoeffer called the God of the "stop-gap," Who is brought forward as a cosmological principle wherewith the incoherences of nature and history may be theoretically resolved. But this, as Rudolf Bultmann would say, is to think "mythologically," whereas the whole emphasis of modern science commits the people of our age to the supposition that the events of nature and history are understandable only in terms of factors immanent in the events themselves. (*Wild Prayer* 55)

In place of this "God-thing," this "divine pantokrator" that is "felt to be an unmanageable piece of metaphysical lumber which is without any 'cash value' in the human life-world" and even "a morally intolerable conception which invites an attitude of reverence before a frigid monstrosity" (*Wild Prayer* 53), Scott does not offer Sallie McFague's alternate images of God as mother, lover, and friend, or even David Tracy's more general analogical suggestion that "the whole is like a who, involved in self-manifestation" (*Analogical Imagination* 255). Rather, Scott prefers a theology that dialectically negates *all* images of the divine, the theology of the *via negativa*, which he calls

> a great tradition which has steadily resisted the tendency of the *philosophia perennis* to conceive what is ultimate in reality as *a* Being above and among other beings, or as *a* Person. . . . Indeed, it is precisely this fear of all anthropomorphic representa-

tions of the Transcendent which has recurrently led the religious imagination to embrace some sort of *via negationis*; and in Eckhart, Ruysbroeck, and Boehme we get classic statements of an enduring conviction that the only adequate approach to the Divine Dark is by way of the disclamations of negative theology. (*Wild Prayer* 56–57)

Scott stresses here the extent to which the *via negativa* has been predicated not just on an affirmation of unspeakable mystical experience but also on a *resistance* to images of God as a being or a person and on a *fear* of "all anthropomorphic representations of the Transcendent." A commitment to the negative way, then, is for Scott a commitment to Paul Tillich's very dialectical "Protestant principle"—"the divine and human protest against any absolute claim made for a relative reality" (*Protestant Era* 163).

In place of the personal *pantokrator*, Scott may not suggest alternate personal pictures of God, but he does posit a divine reality; this reality, however, can be described only in dialectical ways. It is Heidegger who supplies Scott with the most helpful dialectical discourse for discussing the divine. Although Scott agrees with Heidegger that "Being" is not *God*, blemished as the word "God" has been by an "onto-theo-logy" that cannot resist reducing "God" to "*an* entity or object, a particular being, albeit the Highest or the Supreme Being" (*Wild Prayer* 68–69), Heideggerian Being gives Scott a conceptual framework for affirming a divine reality.

Scott begins his discussion of Heideggerian Being with, again, a dialectical strategy. He acknowledges that for "the reigning schools of contemporary philosophy" the concept of Being is nonsense, founded on a foolish reification of what is only a word: "We have the noun *being* in our inherited language, and thus we mistakenly suppose that there is some discriminable entity to which the word refers—but, as recent analytic philosophy reminds us, in point of hard fact no such entity exists" (*Wild Prayer* 60). Scott answers this critique, however, by pointing out not what Heidegger's Being is but what it is *not*: it does not belong to "the category of 'things'" (*Wild Prayer* 61). Rather, Being "is that which is constantly present in all the things of this world, enabling them to be whatever it is for which they are destined by their inner constitution" (*Wild Prayer* 61). But even this affirmation must be dialectically negated, since Being is no more an attribute than it is an object: "To say that a thing *is*, is not to have specified one of its distinguishing properties" (*Wild Prayer* 61). Being, for Heidegger, is neither object nor attribute, but is "a transcendental," which Scott can define only dialectically as "a reality which is to be reached only, as it were, by moving through the contingent realities of nature and history and which is therefore 'above' the ordinary categories of reflection" (*Wild Prayer* 62). Being, Scott says, ends up for Heidegger emerging from an experience of what deconstructionists would later call a *supplément*, that which is left over "once the established sciences have launched all their various inquiries into the nature of the existing world": "'nothing' is left over. But, then, in a brilliant tour de force, [Heidegger] declared that very nothingness to be the ultimate subject of philosophy" (*Wild Prayer* 64).

Being is like Nothing in that it is "not *a* being" and is "*absolutely* different from all beings" (*Wild Prayer* 65). This, as we have seen, is why Heidegger and Scott resist equating Being with 'God,' a word that connotes a specific being. And it even gives Scott room to claim that he is no more a pantheist than he is a traditional theist. Pantheism, says Scott, asserts "that the world and God are coterminous and that the multiplicity of finite existence is wholly absorbed in some impersonal Absolute" (*Wild Prayer* 58), but Heideggerian Being is *not* "the totality of all beings" (*Wild Prayer* 69) any more than it is a being: "Being is . . . that *transcendens* which, as the enabling condition of everything that exists, is 'wholly other' than and distinct from all particular beings, even in their totality" (*Poetics of Belief* 143). It sounds, though, as if this *totaliter aliter* is nothingness itself: "Indeed, when thought of in relation to the world of particular beings, it must be considered to be 'that-which-is-not,' or Nothing" (*Wild Prayer* 69).

But the Wholly Other—Being—*is*, for Scott. Being is not, finally, a nothingness (although nothingness is its best analogy, since Being is neither object nor attribute): "the metaphysic of Nothingness," Scott says, "was intended by Heidegger "only to be a propaedeutic looking forward to a metaphysic of Being" (*Wild Prayer* 65). The "threatening specter of Nothing," Scott says, "awakens in us that ontological shock wherewith we notice that, indeed, we face not Nothing but *something*" (*Wild Prayer* 65). Jarred by the specter of Nothing—an existential experience of "the final certitude of death," of "radical finitude," which causes the world to sink "into a profound kind of insignificance, and the only thing that remains is the primordial Nothingness" (*Wild Prayer* 64)—humans are shocked out of a bland, manipulative and acquisitive attitude toward the world and into a surprised awareness of the *something* that surrounds them. They become aware that reality is not flat but is deeply mysterious: they experience "the dimension of *presence*—and, here, the decisive experience is a presentiment at once of the rich inexhaustibility and of the vital responsiveness of the world that presses in upon me" (*Broken Center* 173). Those who have this experience hear "the 'voice' of Being" (*Wild Prayer* 67).

Scott does eventually get around to describing this Being, this divine reality, that he has been approaching with such dialectical caution. Nathan Scott's Heideggerian Being is very much like what David Tracy, as we have seen, calls a gracious limit-*of* that we encounter as a grounding of the limit *to* human reality:

> [I]t is the mission of Being to establish the possibility of *presence* for all particular beings. Being is that primal energy which gathers things into themselves and so keeps them thus assembled that they can stand out before the gaze of intelligence. *A* being might be said to be simply that-which-is-present, that-which-is-in-the-open;

whereas Being itself *is* that Openness which lights up the things of earth, which enables us to behold them in their radical actuality, and which is never itself, therefore, conceivable as a being. (*Wild Prayer* 70–71)

This, then, is Scott's religious credo:

> To affirm God's "existence," in other words, is not to assert that a particular being—the Supreme Being—dwells in some invisible realm behind or beyond the phenomenal world. It is, rather, to declare, as a matter of radical faith, that Being is steadfast, reliable, gracious, and deserves our trust. To say that God "exists" is, in short, to say that the Wholly Other, the uncreated Rock of reality, is *for* us, not against us. (*Wild Prayer* 72–73)

Being, then, is "hidden and far away because it is the source (*Ursprung*) of all reality" (*Wild Prayer* 71). Being is a *Deus absconditus*, a hidden God, precisely the kind of God imagined—or, rather, *not* imagined—by the dialectical imagination. And yet Scott's dialectical strategy—establishing a concept of a God who is radically non-personal, who is neither a being nor an attribute but is Being itself, the very presence of the other opening itself to the experiencing subject—actually attempts to undermine the distant God of dialectical theology. Scott's Heideggerian Being is hidden but also generously self-manifesting, much like Rahner's self-communicating (and deeply analogical) God. Scott believes that analogically imagining God as a person has, ironically, in practice served what Greeley and Tracy would call a *dialectical* function; it has turned God into a distant King, uninvolved in human affairs:

> For what we are offered is the conception of a supreme Being Who, being eternally immutable and impassive, is forever unaffected by and consequently indifferent to all the endeavors and vicissitudes which make up the human story. For such a God man's earthly pilgrimage is, ultimately, of no account, since nothing that we do or fail to do can augment or detract from the static perfection that this God enjoys. (*Wild Prayer* 54)

This is the same complaint that Sallie McFague registers against traditional personifications of God as king and ruler. But whereas McFague tries to retrieve the analogical vision of a God who is like the world, manifested within the world, by developing new, warmly personal images of God as mother, lover, and friend, Scott believes that such a "personalist"—and hence analogical, immanentist—vision of divine presence can be best achieved by the dialectical strategy of the *via negativa*:

> In those traditions of mystical and philosophical theology which have resisted the anthropomorphic fallacy, the controlling motive . . . has not been that of any sort of aposiopesis. The basic intention, rather, has been that of affirming the coinherence in

the world of the human creature of that encompassing reality which meets us in the terms of grace and demand and which, precisely because it is (as Eckhart said) the *Is-ness* of everything that exists, is inexpressible in the imagery of anthropomorphism. What is witnessed to is not a supernatural Person but "the dearest freshness deep down things" [Gerard Manley Hopkins, "God's Grandeur"] that flows out toward the farthest peripheries of the universe and invades the most intimate neighborhood of our experience. (*Wild Prayer* 57)

Being, for all its transcendence, is intimately a part of human experience: "Being is not that which man stands out from or over against. On the contrary, it is that in which he most deeply participates, that by which he is most deeply grasped" (*Wild Prayer* 62). Present within the human person and within all the rest of reality—indeed, the glue that connects the self to the other—Scott's God is profoundly immanent, not dialectically distant or absent at all. It is, in fact, this view of an immanent God that leads Scott to endorse Archbishop William Temple's description of the *materialistic* character of Christianity: "The Christian imagination," Scott says, "does not shrink from the tangibility and gross concreteness of our life in time. . . . It is, indeed, affirmative—radically affirmative—in its attitude toward nature and time and history. It does not spend its time looking about for an elevator that will whisk it up out of the world into eternity, for it is committed to the world" (*Broken Center* 115).

So the vision of the world that Scott is trying to found with his very dialectical concept of God turns out, after all, to be analogical and sacramental in David Tracy's terms. Perhaps Scott has truly plumbed the dialectic enfolded within the analogical imagination, what Tracy calls "that sense for the negative, that dialectical sense within analogy itself" (*Analogical Imagination* 413). In the remainder of this discussion of Nathan Scott, let us look more closely at the sacramental orientation that Scott espouses, and then see how it shapes his literary theory and his attitude about other contemporary literary theories.

Using the Anglican Catechism's definition of sacrament—"an outward and visible sign of an inward and spiritual grace" (*Wild Prayer* 49)—Scott formulates what he calls "the sacramental principle": "that certain objects or actions or words or places belonging to the ordinary spheres of life may convey to us a unique illumination of the whole mystery of our existence, because in these actions and realities (to use Rudolf Otto's famous term) something 'numinous' is resident, something holy and gracious" (*Wild Prayer* 49). Scott claims that such a sacramental attitude flows directly from an awareness of the graciousness of Being: "[W]hen that which is transcendent of every particular being, yet present in every being as the power whereby it is enabled to be—when this *Mysterium Tremendum* is declared to be holy, then the world is by way of being envisaged as a truly sacramental universe, as an outward and visible expression of an inward and spiritual grace" (*Wild Prayer* 73). This is precisely the way the world looks to the analogical imagination, according to David Tracy:

[T]he distinct but related principles of order grounded in the focal meaning of the extraordinariness of the ordinary and the reality of the paradigmatic yield, in a genuinely theological-analogical imagination, their own patterns of ordered relationships. . . . The entire world, the ordinary in all its variety, is now theologically envisioned as sacrament. (*Analogical Imagination* 413)

And with such sacramentality as his ontological foundation, Scott's main enterprise is to describe the appropriate human relationship with this divine reality that surrounds and pervades us.

The proper human stance toward Being for Scott is what he calls, in a discussion of Walter Pater, "the ethic of *diaphanéité* (of openness, of transparency, of what Heidegger calls *Gelassenheit*)," which "is a kind of sacramentalism, a sense of a 'dearest freshness deep down things' that charges the world with a grandeur we ignore at very great cost to ourselves" (*Poetics of Belief* 67). Being, in its gracious generosity, "hails" us—the presence of the things of the earth "*is* the hail, the salutation, which Being addresses to us"—and "we respond to its primary hail by receiving and accepting the plenitude which it bestows upon us" (*Wild Prayer* 71). Our openness to the world, then, is "an affair of thanksgiving for the incalculable munificence with which Being lets things be" (*Wild Prayer* 71). It is a suspension of ego, a surrendering of "what Heidegger calls *the will to will*," for "it is only when we have consented to be *stupid* before the absolute presence of Being that it begins, translucently and radiantly, to disclose itself" (*Negative Capability* 66–67).

And this sacramental response to reality is, for Scott, exactly the source of good literature. A genuinely sacramental stance toward the world is an act of imaginative openness, not an act of cognition or will, so Scott agrees with Heidegger that "before the most ultimate realities which man faces, philosophy must at last give way to poetry. . . . For the poet (*der Dichter*) is, in Heidegger's view, far more than the thinker (*der Denker*) an adept in the art of 'paying heed' to the concrete actualities of earth" (*Wild Prayer* 73). Scott does not deny that poets also are adept at the "art of supervising language," but he maintains that "literary craftsmanship is wholly dedicated to the disclosure of the things and creatures of this world in their sheer specificity" (*Wild Prayer* 74). This is not to say that Scott is a naive mimeticist. Openness to Being for Scott is an act of meditative imagination, not a mere recording of objective facts; Scott considers mimetic theories of literature to be victims of what he calls "the Realistic Fallacy," which "conceives the world to be 'out there,' in its bare facticity, and that facticity is in no way felt to be itself a *figura* of any sort of radical significance. What man is understood to confront is a vast system of 'reified' fact which is something alien and detached from *la présence humaine* and which must therefore be approached impersonally, with the impassive precision of scientific objectivity" (*Wild Prayer* 19–20). But he is equally critical of extreme formalism or expressivism; these are founded, he says, on the "Angelic Fallacy," which "springs from a profound disenchantment about the possibility of ever realizing what Realism seeks in its effort at mastery

of the fact-world. Here . . . the artist elects, finally, to circumvent that solid flesh
and make do with his Cartesian vacuum. He opts for some version of the doctrine
that literary art should have nothing but itself in view" (*Wild Prayer* 20). Over
against both of these "fallacies," founded on a dialectical vision of the human subject standing apart from the real, Scott proposes that good literature is limited
neither to radical objectivity nor to radical subjectivity but is open to that shared
mystery which is Being: the analogical, reciprocal presence of the other to the
self, experienced neither as dead fact nor as impenetrable opacity but as overflowing with grandeur "like the ooze of oil / Crushed" (Hopkins, "God's Grandeur").
Imaginative literature, Scott says, is an especially effective vehicle for such a
vision of reciprocity between subject and world, and the poetic imagination expresses this reciprocity largely by its use of *metaphorical* language. Metaphors, by
their very nature, reveal connections, the "coalescence of the heterogeneities of
experience": "[I]n finding all the concrete realities of experience to point beyond
themselves, the poetic imagination is restlessly driven, from 'the visionary dreariness' of earth, towards 'unknown modes of being.' . . . [E]verything appears to
stand on the threshold of something else" *(Broken Center* 181). Metaphor, Scott
might say, is a linguistic equivalent of sacrament; with this emphasis on the connective rather than disjunctive aspects of metaphor, Scott's literary theory (whatever view of God it may emerge from) is decidedly *analogical.*

In practice, this devotion to a sacramental vision in literature has led Scott to
praise and criticize a wide variety of writers. In the late 1960s he tended to be critical of the great modernist fiction writers—Joyce, Woolf, Proust—because he felt
that in their creation of grand imaginative structures they are trying to flee the quotidian reality (the only reality there is, and hence the only place in which Being
hails us) and escape to some alternate created world. Joyce, Scott opined, attempts
to escape into mythic time (I tried to show in the previous chapter that he does no
such thing); Proust attempts to escape into memory; and Woolf attempts to escape
into pure, rarefied consciousness *(Broken Center* 43–100). Scott preferred such
postmodernists as Beckett, Robbe-Grillet, Grass, Burroughs, and Godard, because
they, he felt, rather than trying to escape the quotidian, radically open themselves
to all its ambiguity and even absurdity. They possess Keats's "Negative Capability": "they represent, generally, a firm disinclination to transfigure or to try
to subdue or resolve what is recalcitrantly indeterminate and ambiguous in the
human scene of our time" *(Negative Capability* xiv). It seems strange, perhaps, to
describe Beckett, Robbe-Grillet, and Burroughs as more sacramental—as having
more holistic, analogical imaginations—than Joyce or Woolf. But I think Scott's
preference here may have been more strategic than substantive; his avant-garde
writers do not possess sacramentality so much as *diaphanéité,* a radical openness
to *anything,* which must precede sacramentality. This was, I think, Scott's way of
critiquing the formalistic excesses of academic New Criticism. He was calling at-

tention to the limitations of texts that can be treated as pieces of self-enclosed architecture, and he noted, alternatively, the value of texts that are radically open to what is.

As postmodernism itself has spawned an entrenched, academic radicalism, however, Scott has largely turned away from the literary avant-garde and back to a British and American romantic and neo-romantic tradition. More recently his studies have focused on the likes of Coleridge, Arnold, Pater, and Santayana. And his 1993 book *Visions of Presence in Modern American Poetry* is a study of such modern and contemporary American poets as Wallace Stevens, Theodore Roethke, Elizabeth Bishop, Robert Penn Warren, and James Wright. Scott says that he is drawn to American poets because what has "chiefly distinguished the American imagination has consistently been an affair of wonder at the sheer 'presence' of all the remarkable things one finds outside oneself. . . . [T]he American poet more often than not has found the chief source of the sublime in the rich density of the quotidian and has felt there to be a sufficient affluence in the world at hand" (*Visions of Presence* 8–9). Scott praises in these poets the same quality that he earlier praised in Beckett, Robbe-Grillet, and their like: an openness to present reality. But of course Scott is aware of the beating that the word "presence" has recently been receiving from postmodern theories, which argue that presence is always deferred, that words are traces of an absence rather than signifiers mediating a presence. And Scott lately has been sounding downright scrappy in his criticism of the contemporary critical scene: "[O]ur native tradition," he says, after explaining why he is drawn to the American poets, "tends predominantly to yield a poetry of presence that pronounces a severe word of judgment on the received wisdom of our period" (*Visions of Presence* 9). Although Scott's critique of postmodernism is a bit one-sided (he does not, for example, take account of such nuanced, religious postmodernists as Kevin Hart, whose negative theology is actually quite close to Scott's own), it is emblematic of the passion with which Scott proclaims his own sacramental view. I end my analysis of Scott's literary/religious views with a short summary of this critique of currently prevailing literary theories.

In his 1985 book *The Poetics of Belief*, Scott's primary complaint about contemporary theory concerns its anthropology, its view of what human beings are and do. His main concern here is with presence *as experienced by the subject*, and he believes that a vigorous theory of the imagination is needed to show how humans are linked to the outside world.[2] For Scott, the imagination is something

---

2 William Lynch's own commitment to a substantive theory of the imagination is largely what Scott celebrates about Lynch in the essay I cited early in this chapter. Scott says that the term "imagination," for Lynch, "though never winning exact definition, always speaks of what is a part of our ordinary, habitual commerce with the things of this world: for him [Lynch], it speaks of our way of ordering experience" ("Theology, Poetics, Psychotherapy" 62).

like Bernard Lonergan's "transcendental exigence," conscious intentionality's orientation toward what is beyond itself and beyond what it already possesses. "Now
when we speak of the imagination," Scott says, "we mean, or ought to mean,
nothing other than this pushing of the mind beyond what is merely given, as it
reaches intentively after some fresh synthesis of experience" (*Poetics of Belief* 8).

In an essay on the philosopher George Santayana, Scott points out that this
is exactly the understanding that undergirds earlier theories of symbol—those
of "such people as Ernst Cassirer, Wilbur Marshall Urban, and Susanne Langer,"
who thought of "the great symbolic forms as structures wherewith human subjectivity constitutes and organizes its experience" (*Poetics of Belief* 104). But
contemporary theorists (Scott mentions Derrida, Foucault, Todorov, and Kristeva)
take it as their "*absolute* presupposition that the symbolic order so absolutely
precedes *le signifiant* that its work (*parole*), however elaborate it may be, must
be regarded as but a fragmentary expression of the *langue* from which it issues"
(*Poetics of Belief* 104–5). Scott's complaint, in other words, is that postmodernist
theories turn the human imagination into a mere epiphenomenon of the linguistic
system itself. It is not just the play of linguistic difference, always deferring a full
meaning, that renders presence unattainable within these current theories; it is
the lack of an active, imagining self to whom anything could ever be present in
the first place. Although Santayana, Scott says, is a careful post-Kantian who
acknowledges that humans have no direct access to the world but only to inner
mental images (which Santayana calls "essences"), he maintains an "animal faith"
that these images are at least analogous to an "environing world" that the human
imagination reaches toward "intentively" (*Poetics of Belief* 96): "Man does not
dwell, in other words, as Santayana wants to say, in his own brainpan but, rather,
in the presence of a world which, in respect to the human agent, is *wholly other;* he
is its witness, not its creator" (*Poetics of Belief* 94). But lacking the apparatus of a
vigorous, "intentive" imagination, Derrida and Foucault's human person, Scott
says, "does nothing with [the world] at all: he simply accedes to being puppetized
by antecedent linguistic codes whose constituent terms refer only to one another
and not at all to the circumambient world" (*Poetics of Belief* 109). For the Derridean and Foucaultian, "the distance between human subjectivity and the world of
'things' is so unbridgeable that, as a consequence, all our 'signifiers' are without
any 'signified' and . . . our gestures in the direction of *parole* are therefore fated to
figure forth nothing more than that system of norms and rules constituting the
langue off which they ricochet" (*Poetics of Belief* 112). Writing, in this poststruc-
turalist view, is mere "dancing about the Void" (*Poetics of Belief* 113).

More recently, Scott has criticized postmodernist theories from a somewhat different angle. In the 1993 book *Visions of Presence in Modern American Poetry*,
Scott's emphasis is less on the self that is imaginatively open to presence and more
on the sacramentally charged world itself: "[T]he poetic imagination," he says, "is

regularly captivated by things, by that which is *other than* the human mind" (*Visions of Presence* 5). Scott claims that such a world is precisely what does not exist for the Derridean postmodernist:

> Nowhere . . . is it possible within the terms of this scheme of thought to locate any kind of "presence," any kind of being or reality which is outside the play of signification and on which our thought and language might be taken to be grounded, for outside language there is only *le néant*—which, as Jacques Derrida would warn, is not itself to be taken as presenting any sort of alternative ontological principle, because nothing is, quite simply, nothing. (*Visions of Presence* 1)

Scott's argument, obviously, is with the extreme branch of postmodernism that Paul Lakeland calls the "radical historicist perspective," which decenters the subject, contextualizes and relativizes reason, and claims that any examination of reason "reveals its dependence on something else, perhaps on power relations or desire" (Lakeland 16); from such a perspective, not only can humans never quite attain a presence or center, but there is *no* presence or center to attain. Against such a position Scott offers the ideas of American philosopher Henry G. Bugbee, who notes that we do experience things as presences, and who argues that this experience seems to suggest an inherent relatedness of ourselves with these things, and even of all things with each other. Scott calls this reciprocal relatedness the "coalescence of the heterogeneities of experience," best expressed through poetic metaphor. Bugbee proposes that self and other are not polar opposites. Rather, they exist within a "closed circuit," and Scott asserts that "it is precisely 'the closed circuit' embracing both 'self and other' in which the poetic imagination finds its main ballast. . . . The intensity of its love for the quiddities and haecceities of experience conditions the poetic imagination . . . to view whatever it contemplates as ignited by the capacity for exchange, for reciprocity: it has the dimension of presence" (*Visions of Presence* 2–3). This description of a world that is outside the subject and yet at least partially and hypothetically present to it—and especially present to the open, diaphanous poet—complements Scott's earlier description of a vigorous human imagination. The two descriptions together add up to his analogical alternative to radical postmodernism's dialectical theory of absolutely deferred presence: for the latter theory, presence must forever be not-yet, but the metaphor of the closed circuit suggests that presence is always-already.

As I have already mentioned, Scott does not acknowledge other, less radical, versions of postmodernism (Kevin Hart's deconstruction, for instance), which claim to deal not with reality itself but merely with the limitations of human knowledge, limitations that Scott grants. But various forms of what Scott calls "Radical *chic*" ("Theology, Poetics, Psychotherapy" 69) do seem to have taken hold in the academy, and Scott holds up Santayana's vigorous theory of the imagination hoping to show, by contrast, "how drastic is the new hermeticism" (*Poetics of Belief* 113) and to invite us to decide which hypothesis about human symbol-making we prefer to adopt.

Nathan Scott is a remarkable critic in that over the years he has carefully and explicitly placed his literary theory and even practical analyses of literary texts within a coherent, intelligent, deeply felt and lived theological worldview. He is also remarkable for the way he unsettles the "analogical" and "dialectical" categories. As we have seen, his concept of God is in some ways quite dialectical, resistant as it is to any easy analogies between the divine and the worldly, the personal. And yet this dialectical concept serves, ironically, the very analogical function of infusing the world itself with a divine presence. Sacramentality is the key to Scott's vision of reality and of literature, so in our terms his imagination must be described as deeply analogical; Scott reminds us that a mature analogical imagination contains a strong (but not absolute) dose of the "no" as well as the "yes." Sallie McFague and David Tracy would perhaps argue that in resisting a personal image of God, Scott is losing a key Christian insight about humans' most intimate way of imagining themselves into relation with the whole, the limit-of. McFague, in overturning monarchical models of God, retains personal images of the divine because, she says, "One of the most distinctive aspects of the Judeo-Christian tradition is that in its kind of theism the deity is appropriately addressed as Thou, not It" (*Models of God* 18). She argues:

> To understand God as Thou, it seems to me, is basic for our relating to all reality in the mode of mutuality, respect, care, and responsibility. The qualities of personal relationship are needed in our time not only in the God-world relation but in the human-world relation as well. The problem, I believe, is not that personal metaphors and concepts have been used for God; it is not the personal aspect that has brought about the asymmetrical dualism. The problem lies, rather, in the particular metaphors and concepts chosen. (*Models of God* 19)

And Tracy similarly points out that the Christian, Jewish, and Islamic classics are all marked by their vision of a personal deity, "a faith that the whole is like a who, involved in a self-manifestation" (*Analogical Imagination* 255). Thus, McFague, Tracy, and others offer valuable analogical supplements to Scott's view. What they cannot better, though, is Scott's careful and passionate presentation of the sacramental vision itself.

William Lynch's Analogical Imagination

As Nathan Scott himself demonstrates in the essay I discussed at the beginning of this chapter, Scott's most obvious comrade in outlining an analogical literary/religious theory is William F. Lynch, S.J. Lynch is best known in literary circles as the author of *Christ and Apollo: The Dimensions of the Literary Imagination*, a

1960 book that defends a view of the imagination much like Scott's—as, at its best, incarnate, enfleshed, not ethereally detached from tangible reality. *Christ and Apollo* was an early effort, and Lynch went on to write cultural criticism (*The Image Makers* and *The Integrating Mind: An Exploration into Western Thought*) and psychology (*Images of Hope: Imagination as Healer of the Hopeless*). But almost as much as Scott has been, Lynch was committed, until his death in 1987, to integrating the literary and religious imaginations: he argues that image is a way of knowing, of truly entering reality, and that faith is a way of imagining. And, again like Scott, Lynch posits an *analogy of being*—"we are always in touch," he says, "no matter what the limitations, with the whole of being" (*Christ and Apollo* 53)—which organically connects the human subject and the other that the subject experiences. Lynch's theory, like the imagination he describes, is deeply analogical. In some ways, however, Lynch is a kind of reversal of Scott. If Scott founds his vision of analogical sacramentality on a dialectical, non-personal concept of God, Lynch uses a more orthodox, personal concept of God to found an analogical imagination that he says is explicitly *not* sacramental. So William Lynch complicates still further our picture of the dialectical and analogical imaginations, this time not by rejecting a personal concept of God but by rejecting sacramentality itself. Let us look, then, at Lynch's integration of the literary and the religious by examining first his personal, analogical concept of God, and then his analogical—but, it seems, not sacramental—picture of the world as imagined both by religion and by literature.

While Nathan Scott has rejected concepts of God as *a* being and *a* person, for William Lynch these ways of describing God are precisely what grounds the analogy of being. Imagining God is not for Lynch a matter of dialectical negation, of abstracting away such positive attributes as personality and substantiality, as it is for negative theology; rather, it is a vigorous way of imagining personhood, beinghood—human, earthly reality:

> We say we abstract from limitation and call it God. We have often abstracted from the actual existence of things and called it God. So we say that God is not heavy like iron. But suppose I say that he is even more actual than iron, meaning that if you think that iron is really there, that is the direction to take to imagine that God is there. (*Images of Faith* 63)

Lynch frequently asserts that "*[t]he task of the imagination is to imagine the real*" (*Images of Faith* 63), and this very substantive, very unghostly God is for Lynch the magnet drawing the imagination.

Lynch is critical of any theology that imagines that "man is terrible and God is distant" (*Christ and Apollo* 87)—a simple but not entirely inaccurate characterization of the picture often painted by the dialectical imagination. Lynch says that when the "search for man and the search for God remain totally disconnected," we have "a kind of theology, a kind of faith, a kind of leaping, which leaves the human situation untouched and in terms of which God is only being used as an escape" (*Christ and Apollo* 85). This, for Lynch, is a problematic form of imagination on which to base theology, because it is founded on a leap out of the human; Lynch, in many ways a reasonable Thomist, considers such an absurdist notion futile: "We cannot jump out of our skins, and if God cannot enter into the inmost part of us and our human reality, then all theology is a farce, a bit of magic which will never work or solve anything. All leaping is futile because leaping out of the human concrete is impossible" (*Christ and Apollo* 85). Far from being a leap out of the limited human, faith for Lynch is the initial context or paradigm within which humans originally experience anything at all. In the language of postmodern semiotics, faith is the *langue* within which all human meaning is formed. (For all his devotedness to concrete reality, Lynch is no naive empiricist; he sees faith as the necessary glue that turns a chaos of sensations into a meaningful world.) This initial, childhood faith is "a great primal and primitive force that precedes or even constructs knowledge itself," and its reigning god is "the ecstatic but unironic figure of Dionysus" (*Images of Faith* 35). For primal faith there are no differences, but only a sea of pure desire. Evolving faith founded on the imaging of the Hebrew-Christian God, then, is not for Lynch an ascent to some heavenly otherworld but rather a descent into the ambiguous, personal, limited human world.

God is not "out there," at an infinite transcendent distance from the human. Rather, God is in "the inmost part of us and our human reality." But that is just what Nathan Scott says about his Heideggerian Being. It is, in fact, to establish this very immanent view of God that Scott dispenses with images of a personal, all-sovereign Creator. Lynch, however, has no problem affirming the traditional definition of God as the Supreme Being, infinitely perfect, who made all things and keeps them in existence.[3] Although, as I will mention, the later Lynch moves to a somewhat more fluid—but no less personal—image of God, in the early work *Christ and Apollo* he talks confidently of God as providential artist maintaining "structural governance of supernatural history" (188). Indeed, God's personal

---

3 Hence it seems to me a bit disingenuous of Nathan Scott to suggest, in his essay on Lynch, that if Lynch had gone just a bit further in his thinking he would have arrived at Scott's own notion of God: "Ultimate reality," Scott says in this essay, ". . . or that which is symbolized by the term 'God' is not a specific thing or object, like a gazelle or an electron, which may be said to 'exist'" ("Theology, Poetics, Psychotherapy" 71). Scott suggests that "it is along this line of inquiry that Fr. William Lynch might well have felt himself propelled" if he had carried "the logic of his own theory of imagination" to its conclusions ("Theology, Poetics, Psychotherapy" 72). As I will discuss, Lynch does eventually move from strict Thomistic orthodoxy to an image of God similar to that of process theology, but he does this precisely to maintain a *personal* concept of God. I think it is unlikely that Lynch would ever have embraced Scott's abstract, negative, de-personalized concept of God.

concreteness—"God," Lynch says, "is infinite and endless in many ways, but He is also a completely determinate and personal being, full of identity and reality" (*Images of Hope* 72)—is the faithful imagination's protection against flying off into the gassy, non-human nothingness that Lynch joins Scott in finding distasteful and destructive. Lynch talks of God as the principle of all things' inner identity itself, in words that sometimes echo the non-personal tone of Nathan Scott's Heideggerian terms: "He is what He is, an absolute principle of identity, the God of complete inner life, and father of every other specificity in the universe" (*Christ and Prometheus* 131). But with both/and analogical logic, he also immediately asserts the likeness between divine and human *personhood*:

> But it is also as though He has put on the mind of man, engaging in a covenant with him, a God of promises, demander of fidelity, angry, jealous of his people, making specific decisions, committing himself to events, peoples, individuals, offering reconciliation. He is an action. (*Christ and Prometheus* 131)

As the principle of things' identity, and as a particular person and self, God is the very revelation of autonomy, specificity, self-identity:

> The religious imagination has fought a long struggle to separate God out from everything else in the world while keeping him altogether present to the world. The central history of the whole of the Old Testament is a separating out of God from all other gods and from all idols. The idea and location of the sacred as divine self-possession—to the point of adoration of that which reaches such a point of internality and selfhood—becomes absolutely clear. God tells the Jewish people who He is: "I am that I am." "Thus shalt thou say to the children of Israel, I AM hath sent me unto you." There are many other givings of an absolute name and an absolute identity to God. (*Christ and Prometheus* 130)

So autonomy and freedom are distinctive, positive attributes of God, and autonomy and freedom are what God communicates to creation and especially to humanity:

> If I were to add a study of natural theology (which I will not!), I would talk of a God who does not make things impotent, or annihilate their resources and their identity, by entering so deeply into them. The final test of his powers, as of all healthy human relations, is that he communicates autonomy: he does not destroy but creates by entering in. If, therefore, we really wish to imitate God, let us make men free. (*Images of Hope* 112)

Lynch's proposing of autonomy as *the* characteristic of God and humanity may seem naive in these days of intertextuality. But by "autonomy" Lynch does not mean post-Enlightenment atomism, something he is very critical of. He means, rather, fully incarnate, "sharp *haecceitas* or 'thisness'" (*Christ and Apollo* 130), which actually assumes a kind of intertextuality: an embeddedness in a concrete historical/cultural context. Only such an embedded subject, in reciprocal relationship with its context, has the thick actuality and inner depth that Lynch calls autonomy.

It should be clear that Lynch's God is as worldly and immanent as Scott's. Lynch's very concrete, personal portrayal of God, however, leads to a vision of the religious not as lyrical, epiphanic experiences of an oozing sacramental sacredness but rather as a dramatic experience of the unfolding of autonomous—specific, historically embedded—personhood. It is this dramatic element that pervades Lynch's writing about both religion and literature. It even leads him in his later work to begin describing God less in the traditional Aristotelian language of unchanging first cause and all-controlling providential manager and more in the language of postmodern process theology. Discussing modern science's increasing belief that the universe is open, surprising, not operating according to absolutely fixed mechanical laws, Lynch suggests in his 1973 book *Images of Faith* that God may be more fluid than orthodoxy has previously suspected: "Of course," he says, "there . . . is incredible order and harmony in the universe. But there is also incredible disorder, and the point I am . . . making is that perhaps God emerges incredibly greater for 'going ahead anyway with it all' on these and not other terms" (149). This means that perhaps God, too, changes:

> If God is only immutable (and not also mutable), if we are indeed really related to God but not he really to us, if the action of God in history produces no history in God, if all the sorrow of this world does not produce an affection within an all-perfect God, if nothing we do can add to the fullness of Being, then we are dealing with a God who satisfies the needs of a very distinctive rationality but cannot be said to satisfy the needs of biblical reality or human feeling. (150)

Lynch's implication here, of course, is that God *is* related to us, has a history, is affectionate, can be added to. Like any person or self, "autonomous" in the sense he uses the word, God has an unfolding, dramatic story.

For Christians, of course, the most fully dramatic, historically rooted and human revelation of God's personhood is Christ, and God-as-Christ is Lynch's key image of the worldliness of the sacred. Two of Lynch's books—*Christ and Apollo* and *Christ and Prometheus*—specifically set the imagination's engagement with Christ and Christ's specific, dramatic historicity over against forms of solipsistic thinking that, rather than engaging the real, fly off into ungrounded ("romantic") fantasy or pure, unimaginative cognition or willful absolutism. Imaging God as Christ roots faith in a God who, far from being dialectically separate from or hostile to human temporality, analogously and even incarnationally shares this temporality. God-as-Christ is a Man who, having "created" time, could not possibly be hostile to it; who had directed it from the beginning by way of His providence and His having substantially and inwardly shaped it (so that He is the master of both history and psychiatry), who finally entered it and grew into it with such subtlety and power that He is not the enemy of but the model for the imagination and the intelligence. He is the enemy only of the romantic imagination and the pure intelligence as ways of life. (*Christ and Apollo* 50)

If *Christ crucified* for Karl Barth reveals the impotence of the human and temporal, and the radical need for grace, *Christ resurrected* for Lynch reveals that the temporal and human is blessed—and always has been: "It is completely false to say that Christ redeemed time. For time has never needed redeeming; it only needed someone to explore its inner resources fully, as He did. And so powerful and new is the exploration, in His case, that it is crowned not only with insight but with the Resurrection" (*Christ and Apollo* 51).

The dramatic story of Christ, in all its narrow specificity ("the time structure, the event structure, the mysteries, of the life of a Nazarene carpenter" [*Christ and Apollo* 52]), reveals that "time, even on the natural level, *is* a kind of ontological prayer. There is no other form of union with God" (*Christ and Apollo* 50). It is hard to conceive of a more analogical way of imagining the relation between the divine and the human. And this analogical theistic framework, with its emphasis on unfolding dramatic action rather than on discrete moments of sacramental radiance, is the metaphysic and governing metaphor grounding both Lynch's general vision of humans' relationship with reality and his more particular theory of the purpose and value of literature.

For Nathan Scott, as we saw, the analogy of being permits and even mandates humans' diaphanous openness to concrete reality, to "the quiddities and haecceities of experience" (*Visions of Presence* 2). William Lynch, similarly, says that "the heart, substance, and center of the human imagination, as of human life, must lie in the particular and limited image or thing" (*Christ and Apollo* 4) and that "[w]e waste our time if we try to go around or above or under the definite; we must literally go through it" (*Christ and Apollo* 7). But this *going through* the definite is, for Lynch, a dramatic process, as dramatic as the life of Christ or the story of Oedipus. One alternative, he fears, is what he calls the "univocal mentality," a drive to reduce all reality to one clear abstract idea, obliterating the differences that are the very texture of thingness. Such a mentality is, for Lynch, a form of Manichaeanism, a refusal to accept the human and limited: "[T]he univocal man aspires to the condition of an angel and he is a rebel" (*Christ and Apollo* 129). In the terms of this study, such an attitude would reflect an extreme dialectical imagination's divorce of the messily worldly from the transcendently pure—as would Lynch's other alternative to the dramatic imagination, the "equivocal mentality." As Nathan Scott explains it, Lynch's equivocal mentality "recognizes the infinite variousness of the world, though never discovering any intrinsic unity" ("Theology, Poetics, Psychotherapy" 67). Equivocality defends the autonomy of concrete reality, but not out of "a love of the clarity and light that comes from" the autonomous thing, and not from "the joy that comes out of the sharp *haecceitas* or 'thisness,'" but from "the love of the darkness and pain that is present to some minds in the fact that no one thing seems to be truly connected with anything else" (*Christ and Apollo* 130).

If the univocal mentality rejects dramatic imagining because the dramatic is swamped in concrete details rather than fixed on the pure and single, the equivocal mentality rejects dramatic imagining because the dramatic form implies that concrete details have some organic meaning and order. The univocal believes only in unity, the equivocal only in difference. The dramatic imagination, however, is for Lynch precisely analogical: it believes that unity only unfolds within difference—flexibly, tentatively, always open to supplementation:

> [W]ith an analogical idea . . . [t]he work, the thinking of it, is never done. The process of adaptation is eternal. We can never come up with one logical core and say it will satisfy the requirements of all the subjects. Only the proportion is the same; but the two parts of the proportion are always changing. (*Christ and Apollo* 150)

Analogy, therefore, possesses *obscurity* ("for it is impossible to abstract the same from the different so that they become two clearly demarcated univocal ideas") but also *glory*: "[I]t is through this obscure but actual interpenetration that by living in the world of men, with all its weaknesses, we can live with knowledge in the world of God" (*Christ and Apollo* 152). To know God, we do not need to "change our ways and thoughts," Lynch says; "we need not utterly jump out of our skins to get to Him" (*Christ and Apollo* 152).

Nathan Scott claims that his own sacramental vision is "radically secular": in seeing that the most ordinary human things (bread, wine) can radiate the sacred, the sacramental imagination is "not concerned with any special world of sacred things that is conceived to stand over against the commonplace and the everyday; on the contrary, it has a lively vision of the sacredness of the commonplace" (*Wild Prayer* 51). It is in his celebration of the secular—his refusal to separate the secular from the sacred—that William Lynch sounds most analogical, most undialectical, most like Nathan Scott. And yet it is the issue of secularity that leads Lynch specifically to distance himself from the sacramental imagination. Lynch's 1970 book *Christ and Prometheus* is subtitled *A New Image of the Secular*, and Lynch argues here that the secular has an inner depth, what Hopkins would call "inscape," entirely on its own terms. The secular—"the march of mankind, in the autonomous light of its own resources, toward the mastery and humanization of the world" (*Christ and Prometheus* 7)—only *seems* to need to be infused from outside with radiance by some totally other "Being" because a demythologizing, mechanistic form of the univocal mentality has stripped secular images of all their vitality. Worse yet, Lynch says, theology has tried to demythologize *itself* in order to stay in step with modernity, but this demythologizing merely leaves theology eviscerated and marginalized. What Lynch calls for is a dramatic journey of the religious imagination toward a reenvisioning of the secular and the secular project, toward a respect for secularity's autonomous, unconditioned inner life—its always-already possession of the very qualities that, as we have seen, are the mark of the sacred.

Lynch specifically says that this renewed analogical imaging of the secular is not the same thing as sacramentality. The secular, he believes, is intrinsically endowed with inner depth and goodness; it is *unconditional*, not dependent on anything outside: "There is an inner all-rightness of things as they are and as I see them, in their own identity, without going out of themselves" (*Christ and Prometheus* 49). But the Catholic imagination, he says, "has not been happy in this state of unconditionality and tends much more to seek the final sacramental view" (*Christ and Prometheus* 49). Protestantism, he says, has been more willing to accept the unconditionality of the secular—but the "fervent defense of secularity by some Protestant images is rooted in a dialectical theology which comes to a nonsacramental view of the world because of the absolute and radical abyss between God and the world" (*Christ and Prometheus* 50). What Lynch is calling for is a nonsacramental *Catholic* (for him this means, I think, analogical) imagination.

I am not sure, however, if there finally is an essential difference between Lynch's analogical imagination and Scott's sacramentality. Sacramentality, for Scott, does not condition the world of things; it is not extrinsically imposed. It is, rather, the radiance of Being itself, Gerard Manley Hopkins' "dearest freshness *deep down things*." And if Lynch were to counter that Scott's Heideggerian Being is immanent but also "wholly other," Scott could point out that the same ambiguity exists in Lynch's model. Lynch himself says that the inwardness of secular reality, analogous to the inwardness of God, comes *from God*:

> I want to talk about the interplay, within the religious imagination, of the great contrariety of *inside* and *outside*. This imagination has begun to tackle the difficult, painful problem of secularity and to grant it autonomy and inwardness. It is at this point that the dialectical action must occur. What seems a contradiction (because we incline to think, as logical atomism did, in absolute units of thought) comes to life. This inwardness of secularity comes from the outside and is all the more inward and autonomous for doing so. It is a creation of the outside and stands in continuous relation to an outside. This means that the inwardness of secularity is a creation of God and the sacred. (*Christ and Prometheus* 137–38)

Depth and value for Lynch, like sacred radiance for Scott, infuse the secular both from within and from without; as is often the case with the analogical imagination, the dialectic is resolved not by an either/or but by a both/and. But whether or not Lynch's model of the relation between the sacred and the secular is essentially different from Nathan Scott's sacramental model, its dramatic/active expression of the analogical imagination forms a useful supplement to Nathan Scott's more lyrical portrait of this imagination—and to David Tracy's more overtly mystical "manifestation" model as well.[4]

The question remains, however, considering his thoroughgoing rehabilitation of the secular, what a specifically *religious* imagination would be for Lynch. And it turns out that this topic serves as an excellent introduction to Lynch's more specific literary theory. The religious imagination for Lynch is faith itself—or, rather, faith is that form of imagination which, in David Tracy's terms, imagines the whole of reality. And the shaping of this imagination is a lifelong task. Everyone has faith—everyone begins life with that wild, primal experience of the whole—but this faith must undergo a process of connection to the real, a connection that is always tentative, incomplete, in need of supplement, and hence marked by irony. This maturing faith learns to deal with the expected and the unexpected both: "It is only by keeping the expected and the unexpected together in an irony of a definite character that faith is able to compose and recompose evidence according to its own epistemology. To learn to recompose is the heart of its education" (*Images of Faith* 126). Faith learns to build a present moment; it moves through infinite possibility, through "the curse" (Lynch's word for the Fall as it is experienced by the imagination), through the tragic, through death and nothingness (*Images of Faith* 133–75). Faith, the religious imagination, is in short the paradigm within which humans experience their own life stories.

And this explains why Lynch so thoroughly links the religious to the literary. "The first and basic image of the literary imagination," Lynch says, "is the definite or the finite, and not the infinite, the endless, the dream" (*Christ and Apollo* 3); entering into such richly imagined definiteness develops and maintains in people the "taste of existence" ("Life of Faith and Imagination" 8), a grounding of the imagination (and hence of faith) in real human action. This ability to "taste" present reality is the only way of analogically joining inside and outside, of seeing

---

4 For Tracy, as I discussed in chapter 1, "manifestation" and "proclamation" are the two classical forms of religious expression: "When the dialectic of intensification of particularity releasing itself to a radical sense of participation predominates, the religious expression will be named 'manifestation'; when the dialectic of intensification of particularity releasing itself to a sense of radical nonparticipation dominates, the religious expression will be named 'proclamation.' . . . In Christian theology, the alternatives are ordinarily formulated under the rubrics 'sacrament' and 'word': the emphasis upon sacrament distinctive of Catholic and Orthodox Christianity and the emphasis upon word distinctive of Protestant Christianity" (*Analogical Imagination* 203).

inscape within the actual rather than drifting into either univocal or equivocal thinking, neither of which imagines the real. So Lynch's theory of literature is pragmatic; this is not an art-for-art's-sake or formalist theory. But his theory is not naively mimetic. Literature, for Lynch, does not just imitate the real; it also trains the audience to vigorously shape the real with their own imaginations. Nor does the theory reduce literature to rhetoric. Literature is not just a dressing-up of previously formulated theological concepts, and Lynch makes fun of theologians who treat it that way ("Life of Faith and Imagination" 12–14). Literature, maintaining the "taste of existence" in and underneath ideas, is a *"permanent* feeder of human beings with the taste of the actual world and the taste of the actual self" ("Life of Faith and Imagination" 8). Because faith-imagination is the context or paradigm within which humans form and experience a synthetic meaning, images (unless demythologized by a mechanistic worldview) have a rich cultural/cognitive density that, Lynch believes, must not be ignored by any who wish to contemplate religious questions. And, although he does not directly say this, Lynch's claims also suggest that its vigorous engagement with images inherently leads literature, analogically, to engagement with the limit, the whole—that is, the religious.

This is only the sketchiest of glances at William Lynch's theories. What I have not conveyed is the way he himself integrates the literary and the religious: the way, for instance, he builds his discussions around (or within) literary texts— especially, in *Christ and Prometheus*, the *Oresteia*. But I think it is more important, in the current critical climate, to play Lynch against contemporary theory—to see what he has to add to the postmodernist conversation about what meaning, if any, can reside in a literary (or any other) text.

In an obvious way, of course, Lynch is as adamant as Scott that literature, like theology, is about presence, about a real encounter with the real; "the very deepest need the people have," he says, "is the need for closeness to, union with, things and persons and God" (*Integrating Mind* 134). With his robust theory of the imagination as a capacity that *imagines the real*, Lynch seems to think that we do have access to presence of some kind, that presence is not indefinitely deferred. He asserts, in fact, that making presence present is precisely the "passionate vocation" of religion and art:

> It is the passionate vocation of theology, or religion and art, real art, to satisfy, each in its own way, this tremendous need by putting men in touch with things and people and God. Theology and art are always searching for reality and are always using different techniques to *uncover* it so that we may be in touch with it. (*Integrating Mind* 135)

Lynch sets true art—which uncovers or unveils the real—against "the commercial instinct," which uses things only for profit and hence ignores or even suppresses, *covers up*, the unconditioned inner reality of the real. He would perhaps, then, see the postmodern proclamation of the veiledness of reality, the indefinite deferral of presence, to reflect not so much the way things are as the way they appear within a commercialized, demythologized imaginative paradigm—which makes radical postmodern theories not rejections of bourgeois culture but rather representatives of that very culture.

And yet at times there is a downright postmodern resonance in Lynch's work. His argument that real things and selves and even God exist in contextual fabrics—indeed, as I mentioned above, this is part of Lynch's rather paradoxical notion of "autonomy," the key attribute of all actual existents—ties him to post-modern theories and leads him to defend them against post-Enlightenment positivism and atomism, which he finds much more distasteful. Indeed, in his 1970 book on secularity, Lynch explicitly defends modern attempts to "de-pack or de-symbolize our images of the world" (surely if he were writing today he would use the word "deconstruct"), because he sees these as strategies to retrieve autonomous thingness:

> The aspiration toward an unconditional image in things may be the largest factor behind the increasing hostility to metaphysics in our time. What is really at stake is hostility to a long history of finding the meaning of the literal things in front of us *outside*, in the form of double and external images of themselves. There is a general effort to de-pack or desymbolize our images of the world—an effort to start with their unconditionality. (*Christ and Prometheus* 47)

Kevin Hart, as we saw, in his postmodernist work *The Trespass of the Sign* endorses a negative theology that dismantles metaphysical "onto-theology" in order to show that the word "God" always has a supplement that overflows any human definitions. And although William Lynch, who so adamantly describes God as a definite person, is hardly a negative theologian, his claim that the definite—with its thick, contextualized concreteness—always overflows the absolutizing ambitions of the "univocal mentality" is a call to recognize images' incompleteness, their need for ironizing supplementation. Hence it is not surprising to find that he is an admirer of Samuel Beckett, who supplements images of the human by uncovering the suppressed dimension of *failure* (*Christ and Prometheus* 67–68). Nor is it surprising to see him endorse Jacob Bronowski's rather Derridean description of the proper attitude scientists should take toward what is now seen as an open universe: "The step by which a new axiom is added cannot itself be mechanized. It is *a free play of the mind*, an invention outside the logical processes" (*Christ and Prometheus* 96, emphasis added). Most important, perhaps, Lynch's claim that faith is a paradigm through which we view reality from the very beginning means that he believes humans never get "behind" a signifier to reach a signified: "There is not even such a thing as pure appearances (the first look of things before we think or imagine or believe). We have already given a structure, from the very first, to appearances" (*Images of Faith* 16). These, I think, are the reasons that Lynch, in a 1982 article, says that he is not particularly threatened by postmodern denials "that prior to thought there is an altogether separate, basic, direct, immediate image before the invasion of intelligence" ("Life of Faith and Imagination" 16). For Lynch, a release of images to free, ungrounded play is preferable to the univocal mentality's attempt to freeze images into absolute intellectual meanings. With the postmodern "philosophy of perception," he says, "we would go with more ease and less fear to the marvelous images of our true artists, without the 'theological' fear that we will be lost if we do so" ("Life of Faith and Imagination" 16).

But I will not try to transform this orthodox, neo-Thomist Jesuit into a radical postmodernist; he shares with Nathan Scott a devotion to the presentness of presence and to a robust theory of the human imagination. Indeed, although his way of describing our experience of the world is relativized and intertextual, the background against and within which we experience "reality" is not, for Lynch, "text" or "*différance*" (which would be merely an "equivocal" background, in his terms). It is *faith*:

> Faith . . . provides a structure or context. It is a way of experiencing and imagining the world; or it is a world within which we experience or imagine. It composes it or, if you will, it recomposes the world according to its terms. For example, the beatitudes totally recompose ordinary experience. To believe that the poor are *blessed* puts an entirely different light on things. (*Images of Faith* 17).

William Lynch's contribution to literary theory, and especially to my discussion of the analogical and dialectical imaginations, lies in his suggestion that such a contextualizing can actually add thickness to an image rather than denuding it, and I join Nathan Scott in considering Lynch "an 'original' whom we ought to try to recover from the obscurity into which his career has been allowed to descend" ("Theology, Poetics, Psychotherapy" 75–76). If Scott points to the thickness of human images by seeing them as sacramental reservoirs of sacredness, Lynch does so by calling attention to their temporality and hence dramatic extension and energy; this, I think, is why he must describe even God as a person who has a story. And by virtue of an intuition of the analogy of being that seems to link subject, other, and Other, Lynch can talk of this "thick" image as at least a hypothetical and partial (always waiting for supplementation) entrance into the real— a glimpse into reality's inscape, the "dearest freshness deep down things."

Cesáreo Bandera's Dialectical Imagination

Cesáreo Bandera begins his book *The Sacred Game: The Role of the Sacred in the Genesis of Modern Literary Fiction* with a discussion of the "sacred allergy"— the allergic reaction many literary critics feel to the "mixing of the sacred and the profane" (2) in literary analyses. Bandera dates the modern outbreak of this allergic reaction to the Renaissance, when the confident Dantesque integration of the religious and the secular broke down. And although it would seem that "this 'allergic' reaction to the mixing of 'the human and the divine' must have something to do with the generally acknowledged process of desacralization that took place in the transition from the Middle Ages to the modern era" (3), Bandera has written his book in order to argue that these phenomena "are not only *not* the same thing, but are in principle opposites" (3). For Bandera, an allergy between the secular (or profane) and the sacred is not an indication of desacralization but is part of the very nature of the sacred itself. The emergence of the sacred allergy in the Renaissance is, Bandera thinks, a sign that sacralization still lingered in the desacralized modern era.

Bandera, following René Girard's anthropological literary model, builds his theory of the emergence of a truly desacralized modern literature—a literature that, spurred by Christianity and the central event of the Cross, has truly superseded the literature of the "old sacred"—on this notion of the radically dialectical relationship between the sacred and the secular. Bandera's Cross-centered rather than Incarnation-centered or sacrament-centered view of Christianity bears comparison with Barth's or Altizer's. And Bandera's book provides a valuable counterpoint to the works of Nathan Scott and William Lynch, founded as they are on analogical ways of imagining the religious: *The Sacred Game* is a richly nuanced example of contemporary literary criticism, with postmodern elements, emerging from a *dialectical* religious imagination.

Bandera's religious theory is built not on a concept or image of God—a gracious limit-of or ground of being—but rather on a theory of the "sacred." And even with regard to the sacred, Bandera eschews the "manifestation" language that generally marks David Tracy's analogical imagination. Bandera does not talk about the sacred in terms of Rudolf Otto's "Holy"—the numinous, the self-disclosive ground of Being on which Nathan Scott grounds his "sacramental principle": "that certain objects or actions or words or places belonging to the ordinary spheres of life may convey to us a unique illumination of the whole mystery of our existence, because in these actions and realities (to use Rudolf Otto's famous term) something 'numinous' is resident, something holy and gracious" (*Wild Prayer* 49). Rather, Bandera's sacred is always dialectically opposed to, rather then analogically present in, the secular.

This is not to say that the sacred is, for Bandera, a Barthian transcendent reality separated by a great gulf from the fallen human world. Bandera's sacred, despite its dialectical relationship with the profane, is immanent, part of the fallen human world; in a sense, the sacred is the trace of the Fall itself. The human-created sacred is "transcendent" only in that its reality grows from human interrelationality and so it is not controllable by any single individual. Bandera needs no "manifestation" principle on which to found the sacred because the basis of his sacred is not a transhuman numinosity but a wholly human experience: the experience of violence. The sacred, Bandera says, emerges as an attempt to mask or project out interrelational human violence.

Bandera begins his explication of his theory of the sacred with Emile Durkheim, who emphatically affirmed the dialectical separation of the sacred and the profane: "In all the history of human thought," Durkheim wrote, "there exists no other example of two categories of things so profoundly differentiated or so radically opposed to one another" (Bandera 17). The sacred, Durkheim claimed, is the untouchable; it needs to be kept at a distance from everything else. It is this fearsomeness that gives the sacred its holy quality. And Bandera asserts that "this is just another way of saying that the power of the sacred is the power of undifferentiation itself" (18): the notion of the sacred "is inseparable from the notion of chaotic undifferentiation" (18). So if a member of a "primitive," sacralized society can "keep the sacred away from everything else, . . . everything is differentiated" (18). The sacred, then, is different from the profane in that the profane exhibits difference while the sacred is the *source* of differentiation. The sacred is chaotic undifferentiation, which must be expelled in order to usher in order; the sacred is, in its very makeup, dialectical. The dialectic of the sacred and the profane is the necessary basis for the birth of order from chaos.

Since the undifferentiated sacred must be expelled in order to make possible the differentiated profane, Bandera, following Girard, declares that a prototypically dialectical act is the very essence of the sacred: "[T]he sacred-making institution par excellence," he says, is "ritual sacrifice" (19)—the sacrifice of a sacred victim, which purges a primitive society of chaos.

Declaring the centrality of blood sacrifice to the emergence of and the very essence of the sacred allows Bandera, again following Girard, to found an anthropology of the sacred on the human propensity to violence itself.[5] The evolution of human beings, Bandera says, introduced a serious danger to the species' very ability to survive: an increased capacity for violence. All animals are violent, of course, but "[b]y comparison with animals human beings are extremely mimetic creatures. The human capacity for imitative behavior is enormous. On the one hand, this capacity signifies a vast learning capability; on the other, it amplifies human rivalries and conflicts well beyond the threshold where they can be contained by instinctual animal mechanisms of survival" (21). So humans have an unprecedentedly "contagious and open-ended" (21) capacity for vio-

---

5 Bandera asserts that he is not claiming "the ontological priority of violence, or turning violence into some sort of metaphysical absolute" (25). But this is, I think, because his Altizer-esque dialectical immersion in secularity, his disinterest in any notions of a transhuman numinosity, obviates ontological or metaphysical discussions altogether.

lence against members of their own species, and a new mechanism is necessary for controlling this violence. That mechanism is the "sacrificial mechanism" or "sacred ruse."

Bandera compares the emergence of this mechanism to the moment, in the physical theory of Lucretius, when *something* emerges from chaos. For Lucretius, in the beginning the universe was the great "inane," and matter was a chaos of atoms falling downward: "This dynamic equilibrium is described by Lucretius as an endless fall of the atoms through the void, each one carried by its own weight, but all traveling at exactly the same speed because the void offers no resistance at all to their fall" (160). This chaotic state is analogous to the sea of random, imitative violence that marked the beginning of the human species. But then, says Lucretius, one atom, by accident, swerved: "A deviation from symmetry must occur, a break in the equilibrium, a minimum of disorder, before anything can be born. This is, of course, Lucretius's famous *clinamen* (swerve)" (160). That tiny deviation from symmetry is the origin of difference, of things rather than chaos. It is notable that the deviation is utterly haphazard, not guided by any gracious, self-disclosive Being at the heart of being, and that matter is always on the verge of returning to the great inane, the symmetrical plunge of atoms.

In anthropological history, Bandera says, the sacred victim is the *clinamen*, the swerve emerging from the undifferentiated inane—in this case, the sea of mimetic human violence—by sheer accident:

> Everything emerges from the victim. Before the victim there is nothing but silence, the perfect symmetry of the atoms cascading into bottomless inanity. The "indignant moan" of the victim breaks the primeval silence. From then on there is language and meaning, and everything becomes possible. But everything will also bear the mark of the original random victimization. (162)

The way this works in human society is that prior to the emergence of the victim, the human habitat is a formless chaos, ravaged by undifferentiated violence; it is ripe for a *clinamen*: "[T]he very mimetic character of human violence, which increases in direct proportion to its intensity, makes it, statistically speaking, highly probable that all the violent participants in a collective crisis will eventually end up agglutinated against one" (21–22). The sacred, in other words, for Bandera as much as for Tracy, emerges at the *limit*, "in extremis"—the crisis point of intense violence that will jeopardize species survival itself. This is Bandera's state of original sin, "a human condition of helplessness and despair" (165). And at this limit the victim emerges, the *one* who will receive the violence in place of the group. The victim has the aura of the sacred, precisely because he or she must be expelled. This is the ambiguity of the sacred *pharmakos*: the victim is profoundly good (the source of healing for the community) but also evil (the victim must be destroyed). The sacred, then, for Girard and Bandera emerges when the realization that violence can destroy all society causes that society to establish ritual sacrifice to drain off this undifferentiated violence. So the sacred, the undifferentiated, simultaneously emerges and is driven out. The victim "is made sacred in the very act of being sacrificed" (19). This is the "sacred ruse" (27), which drives out the sacred—the undifferentiated, which is violence itself. The dialectic of the sacred and profane is, therefore, *the* establishment of difference; prior to the sacrifice, there is undifferentiation, Lucretius's symmetrical fall of atoms through inane space. The expelling of the victim establishes the essential gap, the primal difference: "The 'absolute' difference between the sacred and the profane is but the gap created in the midst of internally uncontrollable, undifferentiating violence by the elimination of the victim" (23). Creating this gap makes a crucial difference—"the difference, literally, between life and death" (23).

But this mechanism is a "ruse," Bandera points out, because although it pretends to drive out violence, the sacrificial mechanism is of course itself drenched in violence; it *is* the very violence that it affects to expel. So the foundation of "the sacred game," for Bandera, is a kind of despair, an exit from human depravity that is no exit. The sacred mechanism pretends to stand apart from the violence by claiming that in *this* particular victim "it has found the one and only cause of its trouble" (22). But this conviction hides the true depravity beneath the sacred game; because of the "liminal character" of the sacred, the fact that the sacred emerges *at the limit*, the victim appears "either prior to any system of meaningful differences or at the moment when all such differences have lost their meaning; that is, when nothing makes any difference any longer" (136). Violence has so destroyed meaning that normal difference—one person rather than another—no longer means anything. Hence, the choice of the victim is necessarily arbitrary, not divinely determined at all; it is the sacred mechanism, not some inherent holiness, that endows the victim with sacredness:

> The "one for the many" remedy is indeed very violent; it only works, literally, in extremis. The violence that kills the saving victim must have leveled everything; it must have turned the cultural landscape into a flat wasteland. . . . All that is required is that the victim be one of those many who are to be saved through her demise, for the formula promises that all will be saved minus one. (136)

So in "rational, differentiated, terms, the 'choice' of the saving victim can only be described as utterly arbitrary and random" (137). The liminality of the sacred, in other words, guarantees that its victimizing mechanism is merely arbitrary, drenched in the very violence it affects to purge. This means, of course, that Bandera's idea of liminality is based on something like David Tracy's notion of a dialectical *limit-to*, without any analogical *limit-of*: the sacred emerges at the extremity at which human society dissolves into undifferentiated violence, but Bandera never suggests that there is a gracious limit-of beyond this extremity.

The idea that the victim is arbitrary—is really no different from anyone else in the community—is the deep secret of the sacred mechanism, which depends on the expulsion of the victim and hence on the dialectical differentiation between the sacred (the victim) and the profane (everyone else). This is why, for Bandera, an allergy between the sacred and the profane is a sign not of desacralization but rather of the continuing power of the sacred itself.

Bandera ultimately demonstrates a great respect for Christianity, which he feels undermines and even dismantles the sacred by revealing the terrible secret about the sacred victimization: that it is not a moral, divinely validated act at all, but is merely a bit of cruel human bloodletting. For Bandera the value of Christianity is that it breaks the grip of the sacred by revealing "the true human source of the fictitious idol's power, the intersubjective breeding ground from which idols emerge, public idols whose sacred character hides their purely human etiology" (231). Nonetheless, Bandera believes that the sacred mechanism served an important function in the evolution of human culture. The recurring dialectic of the sacred was crucial for human survival in more primitive times, because it channeled violence that is human but also "transcendent"; that is, because the violence is "trans-individual," arising from the system of human relations rather than from single human persons, it could not be curbed by any individual's will but only by the systemic, dialectical ritual of sacrifice. If such a mechanism had not evolved in early human culture, humans would likely have combined their intelligence with their violence and wiped themselves out. Within the sacred system, the sacred victim—viewed with both awe and hatred—receives and purges the violence. And yet the sacrifice itself embodies the violence that it supposedly purges; far from overturning systemic, interrelational violence, the sacred game remains very much within the system. Hence, the sacred remains even as it is expelled, and the ritual needs to be repeated again and again. Although Bandera claims that he is not asserting "the 'ontological' priority of violence, or turning violence into some sort of metaphysical absolute" (26), it is clear that he is not basing the sacred on anything other than human violence. There is no experiential presence or Being or limit-of (or "God") grounding his theory; the "etiology" of the sacred is "purely human." Bandera's fundamental theological position, then, is dialectical in two ways: it is predicated on a radical gap between the sacred and the profane, and it is radically immersed in the immanent human world. And from this radically immanent standpoint emerges Bandera's Christianity, focused—as dialectical Christianity tends to be— not on the Incarnation but on the Cross.

Most explanations, Bandera asserts, of the birth of modern Europe claim that modernity is based on humanity's "heroic" experience of independence from the gods or God. But Bandera reverses this, claiming that the modern era is founded on a rejection of heroism and a Christian admission of human fallenness: "[T]he human spirit only crosses the threshold of the modern era as it drops all claims to heroic status and is forced to confront itself through an unavoidable sense of individualized guilt and responsibility" (233).[6] This realization is founded, for Bandera, on a radical desacralization effected by "the Christian text," an event or story that destroys the authority of the sacred game.

The essence of the Christian story, Bandera says, is that "in the course of an immemorial sacrificial history, at a given moment, the sacrificers come upon a victim who refuses to play the sacrificial game. This victim does not refuse to be killed, but he reveals to the sacrificers in no uncertain terms the truth of what they are doing. He tells them they are hypocrites; they claim innocence but their hands are bloody with the killing of all their victims 'since the foundation of the world'" (24). Christ is the first sacred victim who commands not awe and hate but pity, and in doing so he reveals that the sacrificial mechanism is not a divinely justified act but is a merely human act of cruel violence. What Christ reveals is that the victim is not inherently sacred at all—neither evil nor heroic—but is merely human, and that to kill the victim is not a holy act but an atrocity. This "nonsacrificial, Christian revelation" (28) is a hard truth to swallow, Bandera says, and so for many centuries the Christian tradition buried it beneath various theories of Christ's death as "atonement"; the European Renaissance, however, assimilated the true, underlying Christian revelation "at an unprecedented rate" (28). And Bandera connects this assimilation of Christianity's desacralizing truth with the late Middle Ages' sudden "increased awareness of Christ's Passion" (29) and with the period's discovery of "the spirituality of the Cross" (246). The modern era was made possible, Bandera asserts, "with the advent of Christianity, insofar as the sacrificial killing of Christ—the historical event to which Christianity became the witness—shatters the sacred cover-up of the collective victimizing mechanism and forces each and every one of the persecutors to discover him or herself as such, as a violent persecutor. This is precisely what transfers the responsibility for the historical here and now from the hands of God to the hands of man, not as crushing burden . . . but as a foundation for hope and relief" (234).

Traditional religion and even philosophy, Bandera says, are tinged with the sacred. Both try to maintain order by expelling a sacred victim; Platonic philosophy's expulsion of the poets in favor of pure reason is, Bandera asserts, just another example of the sacred mechanism. But Christianity permits no such expulsion, descending instead into the ambiguous, flawed human world, finding no awesomely heroic, damnably evil sacred victim on whom to project human violence. If this is a dialectical vision of Christianity, at first glance it looks quite

---

6 In my discussion of literary modernism's response to and reaction against modernity at the beginning of chapter 2, I described both of these dimensions of the modern situation: the triumphalist celebration of the subject's independence from transcendent truth and the corresponding sense of disquiet and uncertainty.

similar to the Christian attitudes of both William Lynch and Nathan Scott, whom I have been describing as primarily analogical. For Lynch, as we saw, Christianity is a descent into the ambiguous human world, and for Scott it is a radical, transparent openness to haecceity, thingness, the secular here and now rather than a gassy transcendent realm. The difference, I think, is that both Lynch and Scott claim that the Christian descent into the secular is actually an encounter with the sacred, while for Bandera it is an exposure of the sacred sham. The human autonomy celebrated by Christianity is, for Lynch, analogous to God's: "The final test of [God's] powers, as of all healthy human relations, is that he communicates autonomy: he does not destroy but creates by entering in. If, therefore, we really wish to imitate God, let us make men free" (*Images of Hope* 112). And that reflective, inward-looking, autonomous secular self is, Lynch asserts, not freed from the sacred but precisely created by it: "[T]he inwardness of secularity is a creation of God *and the sacred*" (*Christ and Prometheus* 138, emphasis added). That Bandera would perhaps say that Lynch here is misusing the word "sacred" and is actually talking about a *de*sacralization is not, I think, just an issue of semantics. The point is that Lynch and Scott do not make such distinctions between the secular and the sacred, while for Bandera the sacred by its very nature is in radical contradistinction from the secular (or, for him, the "profane"). And this difference is neatly encapsulated in the different images at the center of these respective views of Christianity: at the center of Lynch's and Scott's Christianity is the Incarnation, the bridging of the divine and the human, while Bandera builds his theories of Christianity, of modernity, and of modern literary fiction on a theology—or, to be more precise, an anthropology—of the Cross.

In a discussion of the philosopher Hans Blumenberg, Bandera writes that Blumenberg places at the threshold of modernity Giordano Bruno, who even as he was about to be burned at the stake expressed his autonomy by averting his face from a crucifix held out to him. This gesture, for Blumenberg, shows that Bruno had the "self-assertion" of the modern age; the power of the Cross had failed, and autonomous humanity had been born. Bandera claims, however, that "the failure Blumenberg describes is not the failure of the Cross, it is the failure of philosophy to deal with the Cross" (242–43). Blumenberg, Bandera says, does not really talk of the Cross but of the Incarnation—as an "idea" that "cannot be integrated into a fully coherent philosophical system . . . and should be discarded as irrelevant" (243). But, says Bandera, "[t]he anthropological and historical context from which the Cross derives its meaning and upon which it impacts with devastating and liberating force is prior to and far more universal than philosophy" (243). Philosophy itself, Bandera has argued earlier, arose as a way to tame and hide the violent truth underlying the sacred. Blumenberg, therefore, is trapped within the philosophical system, which is just another form of the sacrificial system; he "has no credible explanation for the ancient fears that drove the Greeks to the philosophical construction of their reassuring cosmos, because he does not understand the terrifying 'rumblings of hungry Acheron'" (243)—that is, he does not know Girard's theory of the human violence, always seeking purgation through a sacrificial victim, that underlies religion and philosophy both.

Bandera sees the Cross as an anthropological event that little by little desacralized human culture, which had previously depended on the sacrificial game to displace human violence: "The desacralizing potential of Christianity . . . rests specifically on the historical account of the life of Christ leading to the Crucifixion and the Resurrection" (245). This story or "text" is the "clear and explicit unmasking of the sacrificial mechanism" (245). Because it radically undermines culture's central (if deceptive and corrupt) survival mechanism, the Christian text could be digested only a bit at a time, and Bandera traces the way explanations of what happened on the Cross—theories of the atonement—increasingly evolved toward a concentration on "the suffering humanity of Christ" (246).

The earliest view of the atonement stresses neither Christ's human suffering nor humanity's guilt for Christ's murder; in this view, a lordly Christ liberated humanity from objective demonic forces, from bondage to "Sin, Death, and the Devil" (252). But even this view, Bandera says, contains a trace of the full Christian revelation. The "demonic" forces that Christ fought on the Cross are representative of the systemic force of human violence—an interrelational system not controllable by any individual. These are entirely immanent, this-worldly forces.[7] The point for Bandera is that evil is initially experienced by humans as "something that transcends the power of any single individual" and involves, rather, the whole network of human interrelationships; this notion of possession by demonic forces "expresses . . . a powerful intuition into the *systemic* character of the transindividual reality of evil" (253). The demonic, in other words, is a primitive symbol of a key aspect of Bandera's dialectical theory: human fallenness. So even in its earliest form, Bandera says, the doctrine of the atonement contained an insight: "to say that the sacrifice of Christ breaks the power of the devil amounts to saying that it breaks the power of the system of death, the power that systematizes death, that derives its strength from the systematic use of death—or, to put it in the context of our theory of the sacred, the power of the victimizing or sacralizing system" (253).

The next version of the atonement was Anselm's: the legalistic view that God is "the *pantokrator*, the universal ruler" (247), who demands a blood sacrifice in

---

7 Tellingly, Bandera quotes religious historian Colin E. Gunton's definition of the "demonic"— an expression of "the helplessness of human agents in the face of psychological, social, and cosmic forces in various combinations" (253) —and remarks, "I do not know what Gunton means by 'cosmic forces'" (253). The religious, for Bandera, emerges entirely from intrahuman, not extrahuman (or "cosmic"), forces.

reparation for human sin. No merely finite human could satisfactorily provide reparation to such a transcendent God, however, so God had to send a son to be the sacrificial victim. Obviously the sacrificial mechanism has returned in a powerful way in this theory of the atonement, but at least there is a growing notion that what is at issue is *human* sinfulness.

Just as Nathan Scott thinks that humanity has outgrown an image of God as *pantokrator*, so does Bandera. For the analogical Scott, however, the evolution is away from an image of God as ruler and toward an image of God as immanent, numinous, sacramental presence; the dialectical Bandera's immersion in the secular has no such sacramental component (the word "sacrament" itself would for him be yet another attempt to smuggle the sacred game back into desacralized Christianity). The late Middle Ages and Renaissance dislodged the divine *pantokrator* from their view of the atonement to install not a sacramental vision of an immanent God but rather a vision of humanity's compassionate potential. In the new view, Bandera says, Christ's death is not a payback to a God who condones blood sacrifice but is "instead an extraordinary act of sheer generosity out of pure love for an undeserving humanity: an act of love that begs to be imitated, that invites and challenges the individual to do the same, to bear his cross willingly, even joyfully" (248). After quoting the popular Spanish Renaissance sonnet "To Christ Crucified," Bandera says: "This radical interiorization of the human drama of the Crucifixion also frees the outside world of its sacred attachments" (250). A deep understanding of the "sacrifice" of the Cross reveals the terrible secret of the sacred mechanism: that it is not something *out there*—not God, not the Law— which demands blood, but it is the human individual. "The problem," Bandera says, "lies inside; the sacrificial guilt is 'my' guilt" (250). When the human individual acknowledges, through attention to the Cross, that the world's evil is internal not external, then that individual can truly turn toward the external world with pure, dispassionate, scientific interest. For Bandera, then, nothing less than the birth of the modern scientific spirit is attributable to the Cross.

So within Bandera's anthropological history, Christianity and especially the Cross are instruments of a positive human enlightenment. Bandera describes this "historical progression" as moving "from the breakup of the sacrificial idolatrous system toward a deepening sense of individual responsibility and, therefore, freedom, in the face of the crucified" (254). He does not, however, endorse the emergence of a new Christian system to replace the old sacrificial one; human systems, he maintains, are always versions of the old sacrificial system. So Christianity introduces into the system "a nonsystemic element, an element that cannot be assimilated by the system qua system. This is the element that keeps the system from ever closing itself completely. This is the expulsion that cannot be expelled, that is to say, justified, glossed over, hidden. It is also the element that opens the system to an authentic future, a future that is unpredictable from within the system itself"

(254). The Christian Cross, in other words, is Bandera's version of the deconstructive supplement—that which inherently subverts any system. Let us end this discussion of Bandera's contemporary contribution to the dialectical religious/literary imagination by examining how this "nonsystemic" Christian element is, for him, the literally *crucial* catalyst for the development of modern fiction.

"Modern literary fiction" is, for Bandera, primarily represented by the novel, which emerged in the early Renaissance in Spain and spread to England and elsewhere shortly thereafter. And Bandera's theory of the novel is that it blossomed in European soil that had been newly desacralized by a genuine embrace of Christianity and especially of the Cross. Novelistic narrative about ordinary, nonheroic characters is, Bandera asserts, founded on a truly, thoroughly immanent world in which the sacred is not continually being ritualistically expelled (that mechanism, as we have seen, keeps the dialectical power of the sacred at its peak); rather, the sacred has simply imploded on itself, the sacred sham having been exposed on the Cross.

Bandera asserts nothing less than that "there would have been no such thing as modern poetic fiction without Christianity" (29). What he means is that traditional literary fiction—classical tragedy, say—is a direct child of the sacred spirit. The naming of the sacrificial victim is the prototypical fictive act, but its fictiveness—the secret fact that the "sacred" victim is actually no different from anyone else in the community—must be hidden. The naming and telling of the grand (implicitly if not explicitly sacred) literary hero repeats this fictive act, but again the fictiveness of the hero and of the hero's awesomeness must in traditional literary stories be suppressed. Christianity, however, exposes the sacrificial game, and hence the grand narrative of the hero, as *fiction, not truth;* in doing so, Christianity sets fiction free from the pretense of being either true or heroic. Christianity, in other words, destabilizes the heroic/sacred system and in doing so ushers in a new, nonheroic narrative form. Literary fiction's crucial event, its Cross event, is for Bandera Cervantes's *Don Quixote*, a comic exposure of a character who mistakes fiction for truth—"a most un-Christian thing to do in Cervantes's eyes" (30).

Bandera maintains that even the radically desacralizing worldview of Christianity has had trouble shaking literature loose from the sacrificial mechanism precisely because literature itself has such a fierce affinity for the sacred. Again and again, even in the modern era, literature has been resacralized, re-endowed with sacred status. Even if European culture no longer believes in gods or spiritual reality, the Matthew Arnolds and Edgar Allan Poes continue to baptize poetry itself as a sacred space. (It is precisely, according to Bandera, this disguised *re-*sacralization of literature, not desacralization at all, that has revitalized literature's "allergy" to the sacred. Bandera's sacred is, as I have repeatedly noted, profoundly dialectical.) A truly modern literature, therefore, needed more than just the original Christian revelation. A further historical development was necessary to usher in a fully desacralized modern fiction: the revelation of the individual "human being as alone responsible for his own violence against a foundational victim who, amazingly, instead of pointing an accusing finger, offered the possibility of a nonviolent rescue from violence" (37). Modern individualism, then, is for Bandera an intensification of the revelation of the Cross. So it is once again the Cross that founds what Bandera considers truly modern literary fiction.

This emphasis on the Cross obviously places Bandera at odds with the analogical followers of Gerard Manley Hopkins, say, who see literature as a repeated affirmation not of the Cross but of the Incarnation—of the "dearest freshness deep down things" ("God's Grandeur") that Nathan Scott so enthusiastically celebrates. Bandera's emphasis on the Cross does lead him to claim that modern literary fiction is wholly immanent, concerned with individual human reality rather than with the ideal and heroic, and in this sense he bears some resemblance to both William Lynch and Nathan Scott. Lynch's analogical imagination, remember, is called to imagine the real, to enter into specific historical contexts, thick actualities, autonomous human depths; literature, for Lynch, is imagination's encounter with "the particular and limited image or thing" (*Christ and Apollo* 4). Scott's diaphanous imagination, similarly, is intensely open to the immanent, the here-and-now; for Scott, "the poet . . . is . . . far more than the thinker . . . an adept in the art of 'paying heed' to the concrete actualities of earth" (*Wild Prayer* 73). But Bandera's Cross-centered tone is quite different from either Lynch's incarnationalism or Scott's sacramentality. Unlike the classical literary protagonist— a hero/victim drawn from "the typical sacrificial scenario"—Bandera's modern protagonist is one among many, a member of the crowd yet seen individually, "who, revealed as a persecutor in his heart, will no longer be able to hide among the faceless many" (38). Bandera's is a "world of pure immanence" not because the gracious is immanently manifested but because the individual is guilty and responsible: "[I]n radical contrast to the sacrificial vision, what this new vision reveals is that it is totally arbitrary and unjustified for anybody to throw the first sacrificial stone, a terrifying thing to discover in the midst of a sacrificial world that had always survived by sacrificing someone" (38).

So while Scott and Lynch maintain the sacred within the immanent, Bandera uses the Cross to dismantle the sacred altogether; what Bandera sacrifices on the Cross is ultimately the sacred mechanism itself. After the Cross, there is no analogical, incarnational presence of the sacred, but merely an exposure of the hollowness of the sacred. The resultant guilt, which represents individual humans' acknowledgment of their own responsibility for the violence that creates the sacred, frees humans to confront the world out there, outside them; the birth of modern, desacralized literature is simultaneous with the birth of the scientific spirit. The much more romantic Scott sees self and world as being joined by the shared mystery of which they are both a part, and literary metaphors for Scott represent the connections, the "coalescence of the heterogeneities of experience": "[I]n finding all the concrete realities of experience to point beyond themselves, the poetic imagination is restlessly driven, from 'the visionary dreariness' of earth, towards 'unknown modes of being.' . . . [E]verything appears to stand on the threshold of something else" *(Broken Center* 181). But such a threshold would be, for Bandera, an untenable state—it would be that violent moment of undifferentiation awaiting the *clinamen*, charged with a sense of mystery precisely because the victim is about to emerge. Scott's "threshold," in other words, exists for Bandera precisely within that sacred mechanism that is obliterated by the Cross. Bandera wants to step outside this sacred dialectic altogether, and he claims that Christians are called to do just that. Both Scott with his lyrical sacramentalism and Lynch with his interest in drama and story see an analogy of being: the poetic and the dramatic are a window into a gracious limit-of. Bandera will not follow analogical imaginers to the limit-of. With the prophetic fervor of a dialectical theologian, Bandera warns that such seemingly hopeful religious metaphors have a dark, idolatrous side. For him, the introduction of the sacred is always a mask of the mere limit-to—the guilty human encounter with interrelational violence. Bandera's immanence, then, must remain radically desacralized.

Acknowledging this desacralization, Bandera is led to ask what really is left for literary fiction—born of the hero-naming sacrificial mechanism—to do. The fruit of desacralization, according to Bandera, is the birth of modern science; freed from the sacred game, modern desacralized humans have themselves taken responsibility for the world's violence and thus are able to look at the outer world not as a projection of good and evil but just as itself. But if the new desacralized society favors scientific truth above all else, that places literary fiction at the bottom of the knowledge hierarchy—and romantic or Arnoldian attempts to invert the hierarchy and claim for literature a higher truth are, says Bandera, a return to the sacred game, a covering up of the scientific truth with a "sacred veil" (127).

If we want to avoid resacralizing, Bandera says that we are faced with the need "of having to accept poetry's status at the bottom of the hierarchy of knowledge; in other words, with having to accept what, to sacrificial eyes, is the marginal place of the outcast" (127). Humans resist outcasts, wanting either to expel them (as Plato wanted to expel the poets) or to place them on a pedestal (as Arnold venerated poets). But for Bandera the Christian revelation is that outcasts truly are neither heroic nor demonic; they are just like those who want to elevate or expel them. Hence poetic fiction, while at the bottom of the knowledge hierarchy, is still *part of* that hierarchy, just as an outcast is simply another member of the community. And since literature contains "error and confusion," it reveals that error and confusion are themselves inside, not outside, the system of knowledge: "what the fiction of poetry enacts or represents is nothing short of the collapse and dissolution of the hierarchical structure" (128). Literary fiction, in other words, is important to Bandera as an inherent destabilizer of the sacrificial system, the too-easy solution to human violence that is always attempting to reconstitute itself. The sacrificial mechanism—a seething interrelational stew finally reaches a crisis of undifferentiated chaos, which is purged by the arbitrary naming of the sacrificial victim—was exposed as a sham by Christ on the Cross, and it is continually exposed by modern literary fiction: "To accept poetry as the bottom of the shared hierarchy of knowledge is to look the crisis in the face: . . . the crisis of difference itself, the undifferentiating spread of violence that is the totalizing crisis of the sacred; the very crisis that is at the root of the sacred" (128).

So by keeping literary fiction at the bottom of the knowledge hierarchy, neither elevating nor expelling it, we resist resacralization, Bandera asserts. Elevating and expelling are two sides of the same resacralizing coin: "Our Arnoldian worshipers of poetry are the predictable heirs to many generations of angry antipoetic moralists" (128). Poetic literature is the *undifferentiated* form of discourse which all other discourses evolved from and are hierarchically superior to (because they are more objectively true); literature is, then, the primitive, undifferentiated sacred from which everything else emerges and maintains its distance. "In nonsacrificial hands," says Bandera, "this old sacrificial tool is capable of revealing, through a sustained act of self-examination, the deepest secrets of mankind" (130). Modern literary fiction, then, is the Cross, that which constantly subverts the old sacrificial system, the basis of all hierarchy, by exposing its sham: the victim is *not* separate from the human community; fiction is *not* separate from the hierarchy of knowledge. In practice, this means that with the help of the Christian nonsacrificial vision, the modern poet does not present super-human heroes having epic adventures; the Christian "'fallen man,' understood in the sense in which the Judeo-Christian text means it, cannot be a hero. It is certainly not for a hero that the Christian promise of redemption is meant" (183). Christian narrative "is inspired by a logos or spirit that undermines the setting up of a human being on a pedestal, because it has discovered that such a pedestal is the altar on which the sacrificial victim is immolated" (186).

So the new literary subject is not epic or tragic heroes but ordinary human people in relationship with each other. For sacrificial eyes, the chaos of violence reaches a crisis that is resolved by a manifestation of the sacred; for the Christian, however, at the crisis nothing is there except other humans themselves:

[A]t the crucial moment when all eyes turn in search of the one culprit, the ultimate source of all the trouble, they are seen to be searching in vain, and yet the situation does not become hopeless, it does not lead to utter despair. The great modern poet now has the possibility of letting the spectacle stand of those human eyes looking into each other. He now has the possibility of exploring at length and in detail the infinite ways in which human beings relate to one another for good and for bad, even beyond the point where his predecessors would become scandalized and the victimizing mechanism would be triggered. (300)

In the Renaissance, Bandera says, the best modern literary writers "were discovering in amazement all the intricate ways in which human beings get themselves into troubles of their own making" (196).

Bandera rejects those literary theories—whether Arnoldian or Nietzschean—that see modern literature as the great replacement for a lost religious vision, having sprouted "spontaneously on the soil of a world 'abandoned by the gods'" (300). In such a world in crisis, in which people wearily long for a retreating "Sea of Faith" or try heroically to create a new, triumphant, super-human spirituality, a culture is really looking for a victim to reconstitute the sacred. But for Bandera the hope for maintaining a truly desacralized "open society" comes, rather, from turning the sacrificial mentality "upside down": "renouncing the search for the victim altogether" (301). Like Christianity, modern literature cannot generate a new system, for any system for Bandera is at root the sacrificial game all over again. Rather, the literary artist must stand in quicksand, a hopeful destabilizer of all systematizing: "The purely immanent interacting of violently undifferentiated human beings was something like a quicksand on which he [the modern literary artist] stood, not only as a human being, but also, specifically, as a poet, for such a quicksand is precisely the soil on which poetry prospers, the stuff it is made of" (301).

For Cesáreo Bandera, the sacred is not a numinous presence experienced through the analogy of being: it is not Nathan Scott's Being or even Kevin Hart's negative, deconstructed not-Being. While Scott's and William Lynch's sacred is analogical, the proportional intersection of the divine and the human, Bandera's sacred is thoroughly immanent (wholly human) and radically dialectical (inherently set against the profane). In a sense, Bandera does end up with the same modern literature that Scott and Lynch endorse: domestic, immanent, human rather than mythic and transcendent. But it is fascinating to see the way a different religious imagination—one that emphasizes the Cross, violence, human guilt, as opposed to sacrament and Incarnation—gives Bandera's description of this modern literature a different, more prophetic, more doggedly secular tone. And all three of these critics demonstrate the continuing centrality of a religious imagination, a way of imagining humans' relationship with the whole of reality, to the creation and understanding of literary fiction.

4

Realism/Postmodernism:
Contemporary Religious Imaginations

Joseph Conrad and James Joyce, as we saw earlier, were pioneers of English-language modernist fiction, fiction that eschewed objective, empirical reality, the domain of what is too loosely called "realism." The modernists had become disenchanted with the Arnoldian attempt to found objective, Enlightenment certainties on human experience rather than on otherworldly authority and instead had rejected those certainties altogether and had fully turned toward the subject; the modernists became, in David Lodge's words, "concerned with consciousness, and also with the subconscious and unconscious workings of the human mind" (*Modes* 45). But despite their skepticism about dogmatic religion, the modernists' subjectivism—founded on an encounter with epistemological *limit*—has an inherently religious dimension, which Virginia Woolf calls a concern for "the spirit" (209), and I have argued that modernists' encounters with this religious dimension can be described in terms of David Tracy's two theological imaginations, the dialectical and the analogical.

The period after modernism has slammed into an even more fundamental limit, the limit of human language itself and its ability to mediate anything at all—any reality transcending the self or even any integral self. This is the *postmodern* context, which I described in my first chapter: a context marked by the "linguistic turn," which sees human societies and even human selves as constituted by language rather than having a substantial reality independent of the historical, linguistic situations in which they are embedded. As Paul Lakeland says in his book *Postmodernity*, from which I have previously quoted: "It is not Being or God or *nous* or reason that is the foundation of thinking, and hence of the subject, but language. What can be said lays down the boundaries of what can be thought, and this insight has profound historicizing and contextualizing implications" (19).

At the end of *The Modes of Modern Writing*, throughout which he has been discussing such modernists as Joyce and Woolf as well as later "antimodernists" who returned to more empirical, "realistic" fictional techniques, David Lodge describes the fiction that has emerged in this skeptical context, "a certain kind of contemporary avant-garde art which is said to be neither modernist nor antimodernist, but postmodernist" (220). This is the art of the radical literary experimenters—Beckett, Vonnegut, Pynchon—who truly push the limits of humans' ability to *say* and the world's ability to *mean*. Postmodernist fiction, Lodge says, subverts the meaningfulness of both conventional narrative fiction and unconventional modernist fiction by exemplifying "endemic" *uncertainty*: labyrinthine plots that cannot be unraveled and that have, in place of a clear ending, "the multiple ending, the false ending, the mock ending or parody ending" (226). These works employ *contradiction*, text that "cancels itself out as it goes along" (229); *permutation*, a presentation not of one unfolding plot but of "alternative narrative lines in the same text" (230); *discontinuity*, a jarring disruption of unified discourse "by unpredictable swerves of tone, metafictional asides to the reader, blank spaces in the text, contradiction and permutation" (231); *randomness* (235); *excess*, an exposure of the inadequacy of narrative by a relentless and parodic overuse of traditional literary devices and details (235); and *short circuit*, an exaggeration of the "gap between the text and the world, between art and life" (239) in order to expose language's inassimilability to any reality transcending it.

Postmodernist fiction, according to Lodge, exemplifies a deep skepticism, an encounter with the existential absurd: "[T]he general idea of the world resisting the compulsive attempts of the human consciousness to interpret it, of the human predicament being in some sense 'absurd,' does underlie a good deal of postmodernist writing" (*Modes* 225–26). This sense of absurdity drives postmodernist fiction to seek "formal alternatives to modernism as well as to antimodernism" (*Modes* 226). The modernists, like the postmodernists, were interested in exposing the "falsity of the patterns imposed upon experience in the traditional realistic novel," but to the postmodernists "it seems that the modernists, too, for all their experimentation, obliquity and complexity, oversimplified the world and held out a false hope of somehow making it at home in the human mind" (*Modes* 226). Joyce's *Finnegans Wake,* for instance, "the most extreme product of the modernist literary imagination," certainly resists reading and interpretation because of "the formidable difficulty of its verbal style and narrative method"; nonetheless, says Lodge, we try to read even this supremely difficult modernist novel "in the faith that it is ultimately susceptible of being understood—that we shall, eventually, be able to unpack all the meanings that Joyce put into it, and that these meanings will cohere into a unity." But, Lodge asserts, "[p]ostmodernism subverts that faith" (*Modes* 226).

It is arguable that this contemporary subversion of faith is the death knell of the religious altogether. Carl A. Raschke, remember, calls postmodern deconstructionist theory "*the death of God put into writing*" (3). But, as we have seen, postmodernism need not be fundamentally at odds with a religious understanding of reality. Paul Lakeland describes conservative and moderate versions of postmodernism (17), which he considers quite open to the religious. And although Lakeland suggests that the most radical branch of postmodernism—the "radical historicist perspective" (16) of Foucault, Derrida, Rorty, etc.—is intrinsically atheistic, we have seen that according to Kevin Hart, David Tracy, and others, even this need not be the case. In *The Trespass of the Sign*, as I have noted, Kevin Hart claims that even "radical historicist" postmodernism deals with epistemology, not reality itself; to say that truth claims are radically suspect does not imply that nothing exists but only that human access to reality is always deferred, mediated through language, and hence limited. And such a profound awareness of *limit* reintroduces one of David Tracy's key modes of experiencing the religious. In his very postmodernist work *Plurality and Ambiguity*, Tracy continues to affirm the validity of "religious or limit questions," suggesting that postmodernism's very "resistance" to earlier, more naive theories of meaning and selfhood reveals an underlying "strange and unnameable hope, however inchoate" (*Plurality and Ambiguity* 87). Tracy suggests that "secular postmodernity" and the great religions actually have a common goal: to retrieve a sense of mystery by resisting "earlier modern, liberal, or neoconservative contentment with the ordinary discourse on rationality and the self" (*Plurality and Ambiguity* 84). Far from rendering religious forms of imagining outmoded, postmodernity—like modernism before it—has a decidedly religious bent, a concern with limit and ultimacy.

In my final chapter, then, I will examine a few contemporary works of English-language fiction to see how David Tracy's categories of religious imagination play out in the contemporary postmodernist climate. I am choosing works that exemplify David Lodge's specifically "postmodernist" characteristics to a varying degree: two works, Anne Tyler's *Saint Maybe* and Muriel Spark's *Symposium*, are somewhat conventional narratives, while two others, Thomas Pynchon's *The Crying of Lot 49* and D. M. Thomas's *The White Hotel*, significantly subvert traditional narrative forms. All, however, are very much a part of the highly compromised narrative scene that has followed literary modernism and can hence be broadly called *post*-modern. And the two religious imaginations, it turns out, leap across the gulf between the traditional and the experimental. It would seem that traditional narrative would favor an analogical assimilation of the transcendent to human language, while the radically postmodern would always stress the gaps between the transcendent and the human; in fact, however, Muriel Spark—a kind of traditional realist, and a Catholic to boot—ends up with a primarily dialectical vision, while D. M. Thomas, whose mixture of fantasy, fictionalized psychological case study, poetry, letter-writing, straight storytelling, and other genres explodes traditional realism, is deeply analogical.[1]

---

1 Of the two contemporary representatives of the dialectical imagination that I will discuss here, one, Thomas Pynchon, was raised Roman Catholic and the other, Muriel Spark, is a Roman Catholic convert. Spark and Pynchon demonstrate what we have already seen several times: that Andrew Greeley's linkage of the analogical imagination with Catholicism and the dialectical with Protestantism is—as he himself admits—at best an overgeneralization.

An Analogical Imagination in a Realistic Narrative

As compared with a Thomas Pynchon or a Don DeLillo, Anne Tyler is surely a traditional realist. But she is not quite one of David Lodge's "antimodernists." Her novels, for all their narrative conventionality, frequently play with point of view in a modernist way: her typical device is to build a unified narrative whole from seemingly disconnected parts, chapters that are each narrated from a different character's point of view. The gaps between these viewpoints are, in my terms, dialectical—indications of the limits of one system of discourse to systematize the world. But the unified architecture of Tyler's novels is an implicit act of analogical faith: a faith in the common "analogy of being" uniting each seemingly self-enclosed narrative unit.

In *Art and the Accidental in Anne Tyler*, Joseph Voelker has contrasted Tyler with John Updike, whom he calls "two of our most masterful fictional realists" (2), and he suggests that Tyler's and Updike's differences are based on their dissimilar religious backgrounds: Updike's Lutheran and Puritan influences and Tyler's Quaker upbringing. Updike, Voelker says, was "[b]orn and raised a Lutheran" in Pennsylvania; then he moved to New England, where, "haunted by Hawthorne," he "gave free rein to the Protestant aspect of his imagination and provided the steepled backdrop for his lyricism and his abiding obsessions, sex and the demonic" (2). Tyler, on the other hand, "grew up in an experimental Quaker community outside Raleigh, North Carolina, a circumstance she considers formative" (2), and Voelker calls her sensibilities "essentially Quaker": "the distrust of glamour, the quiet resistance toward moral authority, the conviction of human goodness, and the calm insouciance toward sexuality" (3).

Although Voelker does not use the terms "dialectical" and "analogical" to differentiate Updike's and Tyler's works, the contrast he draws between the imaginations underlying their fictions is very much along these lines. Updike's novels, Voelker suggests, are infused with a sense of sinfulness and a vision of God as *absent* but *proclaimed*; Tyler's novels are grounded in a sense of human decency and a vision of the Good as *present*, immanently *manifested*. "The Updikean narrative voice," Voelker says, "is rooted—however remotely—in a culture founded upon the conviction of sin" (4), and we have seen that Roger Lambert's voice in *Roger's Version* is very directly, not remotely, rooted in such a conviction. Furthermore, Voelker says, an "Updike novel naturally gravitates toward hellfire sermon" (3). Tyler's "conviction of human goodness," on the other hand, allows her to favor manifestation over proclamation, the Quaker sense that the Good is so immanently available that everyone, not just a "hellfire" preacher, has access to it: "Invariably, Tyler hands over spontaneous inspiration to one of her characters, none of whom is denied at least the potential to see and speak the gently surprising truth, each of whom is permitted captainship of his or her destiny within the confines of a random and ungovernable external world" (3).

Although Voelker completed his study before the publication of *Saint Maybe*, it is perhaps in this novel that Tyler most self-consciously reveals the religious imagination that Voelker attributes to her Quaker roots. If all Tyler's novels have a religious subtext, a groping for a vision of the whole in the face of the limits of finite viewpoints (the separate narrative points of view from which her fictions generally emanate) and of human folly and mortality (Voelker's "confines of a random and ungovernable external world"), *Saint Maybe* brings this subtext into the open. In *Saint Maybe* the central character, Ian Bedloe, explicitly places the issue of life's meaningfulness in a religious context, not specifically Quaker but nonetheless marked by a Quaker sense of immanent, analogical spirit. And the religious movement of the entire narrative is, as I see it, a movement from a naive analogical imagination, through a harsh dialectical disruption, to a reaffirmed analogical vision that is a great deal more mature, nuanced, and hypothetical; the book ends with a vision of immanent sanctity . . . *maybe*.

The book seems to start not with the dialectical specificity of a single narrative viewpoint but with the analogical confidence of an omniscient narrator. "On Waverly Street," we are told, "everybody knew everybody else" (1). Apparently this is a world without dialectical gaps or painful, alienating limits, troubling mysteries; it is perhaps a naive, suburban version of a placid Quaker community. The truth about this neighborhood is clear, out in the open: "The squat clapboard houses seemed mostly front porch" (1).

And the epitome of this out-in-the-openness is the family who will dominate Tyler's novel: "Number Eight was the Bedloe family. They were never just the Bedloes, but the Bedloe *family,* Waverly Street's version of the ideal, apple-pie household: two amiable parents, three good-looking children, a dog, a cat, a scattering of goldfish" (1). The Bedloes are nearly a caricature of the blandest and most optimistic version of David Tracy's analogical imagination, an imagination that sees goodness as so thoroughly immanent that it takes not the slightest leap of faith for it to see the Good as always already present: "There was this about the Bedloes: They believed that every part of their lives was absolutely wonderful. It wasn't just an act, either. They really did believe it. Or at least Ian's mother did, and she was the one who set the tone" (6). This is a simplistic analogical imagination, lacking what Tracy calls "that sense for the negative, that dialectical sense within analogy itself" (*Analogical Imagination* 413).[2] Certainly problems have occurred for this family, but the Bedloes—especially the mother, Bee (one, perhaps,

---

2 David Tracy, as we have seen, criticizes an analogical imagination that has lost a sense for the negative: "Where analogical theologies," Tracy says, "lose that sense for the negative, that dialectical sense within analogy itself, they produce not a believable harmony among various likenesses in all reality but the theological equivalent of 'cheap grace': boredom, sterility and an atheological vision of a deadening univocity" (*Analogical Imagination* 413).

for whom *Be*ing *is*, always-already, never not-yet?)[3]—can accommodate any of
these problems. They incorporate everything into their happy family story, a story
in which all is analogically related, all is part of the same "lighthearted," but at
bottom sterile, "ongoing saga":

> When bad things happened—the usual accidents, illnesses, jogs in the established
> pattern—Bee treated them with eye-rolling good humor, as if they were the stuff of
> situation comedy. They would form new chapters in the lighthearted ongoing saga
> she entertained the neighbors with: How Claudia Totaled the Car. How Ian Got Sus-
> pended from First Grade. (6)

Little by little, however, it becomes clear that this first chapter is settling into
the point of view of one character, that of Ian Bedloe. And he is the family's—as
well as the novel's—"sense for the negative," an initial hint of a dialectical "limit
to" the Bedloes' easy tapestry of analogical order. The above passage, the last bit
of narrative omniscience, is followed by a small trace of Hamletian doubt. The rest
of the Bedloes, we have just been told, truly believe that "every part of their lives"
is "absolutely wonderful." And then there is Ian, the character who bumps into a
tiny limit to this faith, a "hitch" that will be the source of disaster (the limit-to) but
also ultimately of grace (the limit-of): "As for Ian, he believed it too but only after
a kind of hitch, a moment of hesitation" (6). For example, ideas pop into Ian's
head that his father, a teacher at Ian's high school, "was something of a joke at Poe
High" (6); that his sister Claudia, "the family's one scholar," has gone off track by
marrying, dropping out of college, and having babies "so thick and fast that they
had to be named alphabetically" (6); and that older brother Danny, merely working
at the post office, is something of a loser (7).

For now, Bee's good cheer is able to smooth over Ian's glimpses of these limits:
"Then Ian readjusted; he shifted gears or something and *whir!* he was rolling along
with the others" (7). This works, at least, until the arrival of Lucy Dean, who permanently disrupts the Bedloes' easy analogical ability to imagine that everything
can be assimilated to their happy, integrated family saga. What Lucy does is tear
open the "hitch" that Ian has always experienced but suppressed.

Lucy is the limit, the inassimilable reality that the novel, the Bedloes, and especially Ian run up against. When oldest son Danny introduces Lucy as his fiancée,
it at first seems that she will be easily—even physically—assimilated into the

---

3 Voelker claims that Tyler's protagonists tend to have a Quaker ability to let life roll off them, an
ability just *to be:* "All of Tyler's protagonists share aspects of this style of consciousness, as it settles
toward the passivity that enables them to become perceptive witnesses. . . . The dynamic of their
thought is a slow jettisoning of the thingliness that attaches to an Updike protagonist" (7). By these
terms, Bee would represent a rather negative, immature version of such passivity, which in her case
allows her to be a witness, but not a perceptive one.

family: "His mother, skipping several stages of acquaintanceship, swept Lucy into a hug. (Clearly more was called for than a handshake)" (3–4). But then Lucy casually mentions her ex-husband, and the whole family experiences a "little jolt" analogous to Ian's frequent "hitch":

> "I was mailing some odds and ends to my ex-husband and I wanted to be shed of them as fast as possible," Lucy said.
> A little jolt passed through the room.
> Bee said, "Ex-husband?" (5)

The divorced Lucy is the unconventional that the Bedloes cannot assimilate. This, in fact, is what has drawn Danny to her in the first place; he met her in the post office when, in her attempt to "shed" those "odds and ends," she airmailed a bowling ball to her ex-husband. "If she had said parcel post I might have let her go," Danny says. "But airmail! I admired that. I asked if she'd like to have dinner" (5). Bee does manage, after the jolt, seemingly to assimilate Lucy after all; after Danny and Lucy leave, Bee jokes that if Lucy has lots of children, "we can mix them in with Claudia's and form our own baseball team," and Ian reflects that "[a]lready she had passed smoothly over to unquestioning delight" (9). But the jolt has occurred.

Lucy is the biggest and most permanent "hitch" Ian has ever experienced. He tries to picture her bowling, but his image is inadequate ("Illogically, he pictured her in the shoes she had worn to the house—little red pumps with red cloth roses at the toes" [9–10]). At Lucy and Danny's wedding, all Ian sees is the seams on Lucy's stockings ("He had never seen seams on stockings before, if you didn't count old black-and-white movies. He wondered how she got them so straight" [11]). After Lucy and Danny have been married for a while, Ian almost manages to "take her for granted"—but "still when she turned her silvery gaze upon him he had an arrested feeling, a sense of a skipped beat in the atmosphere of the room" (21). Clearly Ian is erotically attracted to Lucy, and yet neither he nor the book will ever acknowledge this fact. Hence, a reductive reading of the novel might suggest that Ian's subsequent quest for God—sparked, as we will see, by his violently ambiguous feelings about and actions in relation to Lucy—is nothing more than a displaced quest for the erotic. But I think that the book, by making Lucy's eroticism so distinctly a *limit*-experience, equally indicates that Ian's quest for the erotic is nothing less than a quest for God.

The stakes rise when the limit encountered by the Bedloes is death itself. Seven months after the wedding, Lucy gives birth to a baby girl whom Ian, with another "hitch," realizes *"is not a premature baby"* (25); Lucy, Ian concludes, had another lover right before marrying Ian. Then, when Lucy shows Ian a new dress that supposedly cost her only $19.59, Ian—after an electrically erotic moment when he touches "the fabric at her waist . . . so fine-spun it made his fingers feel as rough as rope" (30)—concludes that the dress is a gift from a lover, someone she meets during her frequent excursions. Ian feels "malicious satisfaction" (32) at having solved this mystery about Lucy, but it is worth noting that the book never validates Ian's solution. In fact, Ian will later—with miserable guilt, considering the tragedy that he incites by voicing his suspicions—come to a very different hypothesis about Lucy: that she was a shoplifter, not an adulterer (107). The point, I think, is that the book, limited in viewpoint, never reveals the "truth" about Lucy, just as it never acknowledges Ian's infatuation with her; she remains the inassimilable limit. And Ian figuratively and Danny literally crash into this limit. Infuriated that Lucy has left him stranded baby-sitting her children when he has a date with his girl-friend, Ian blurts out his suspicions to Danny: that Daphne is not his daughter, that Lucy goes out with lovers who buy her expensive gifts. This spurs the book's dis-astrous pivot, the moment at the end of the first chapter that forever cancels the easy analogical optimism of the Bedloe family. Indeed, it marks their disintegra-tion as clear-cut referent for the word "family" at all. Ian listens to Danny crashing his car into "the stone wall at the end of the block" while he himself stares at his face in the mirror, watching his identity transform from easy, regular Bedloe boy to someone guilty of his own brother's death:

> [T]here was a gigantic, explosive, complicated crash and then a delicate tinkle and then silence. Ian went on staring into his own eyes. He couldn't seem to look away. He couldn't even blink, couldn't move, because once he moved then time would start rolling forward again, and he already knew that nothing in his life would ever be the same. (49)

This event and its meaning are the dialectical "limit-to" that Ian cannot assimi-late. Assimilation of meaning for Ian becomes not a clear, conclusive project but an endless and futile repetition; its only analogy is deeply, absurdly reductive:

> In his ninth-grade biology class, Ian had watched through a microscope while an amoeba shaped like a splash approached a dot of food and gradually surrounded it. Then it had moved on, wider now and blunter, distorted to accommodate the dot of food within.
>   As Ian accommodated, over and over, absorbing the fact of Danny's death. (88)

This grotesque analogy suggests Ian's way of accommodating, but it also re-veals the limit to his ability to do so. Yes, he can—painfully—deal with Danny's death ("It felt like swallowing" [88]); he can *swallow* most of a series of horrible thoughts about this event: "*Danny is dead. He died. Died. . . . He died on purpose. He killed himself*" (88). But the final thought—"*Because of what I told him*" (88)— is the limit that he cannot accommodate:

> And then finally the last thought.
> No, never the last thought. (89)

In the face of this limit, Ian is even less than the amoeba under his microscope. He cannot think "the last thought," nor can he talk to others about it; it is that which cannot be mediated. Ian tries to imagine confessing this to his mother, but the imagined dialogue merely reveals the ludicrous inadequacy, the limit, of his mother' usual attempts to accommodate:

> Maybe if he went and confessed to his mother she would say, "Why, sweetheart! Is that all that's bothering you? Listen, every last one of us has caused *somebody's* suicide."
> Well, no. (89)

In any case, such an act of confession would be hopelessly paradoxical. Though it would be a confession of the truth, and hence seemingly good, it would be hurtful, and hence seemingly bad; if he confesses, then his mother will know that her son's death was suicide rather than an accident: "That was the trouble with confessing: it would make him feel better, all right, but it would make the others feel worse" (89). So Ian has confronted that which is, in every way, unspeakable, inassimilable to human language. And this reveals, by extension, the ultimate fraudulence of *all* his mother's assimilations of events to her neat, conventional meanings; the dialectical has exploded the analogical.

This is the new situation that Ian finds himself locked into. He desperately wants to back away from the dialectical limit, but instead he is thrust against it again and again. Soon it is Lucy who has died, after taking an overdose of sleeping pills, and Ian, horrified at the price he is paying *"for just a handful of tossed-off words"* (96), wants to return to the simpler past: *"Can't we just back up and start over? Couldn't I have one more chance?"* (97). Return he does, but only back to the prototypical limit-experience itself. Waking or dreaming, Ian keeps reliving the night he baby-sat Danny's children and then listened to Danny kill himself: "He felt he was traveling a treadmill, stuck with these querulous children night after night after night" (104).

Ian's Bedloe-like trust in the inherent graciousness of the world—which is a naive form , I am arguing, of the analogical imagination that the novel will ultimately endorse—has been crushed, and so far nothing but profound skepticism has replaced it. When the clergyman Dr. Prescott visits the Bedloe house to make arrangements for Lucy's funeral, he asks Lucy's children if they would like to ask him any questions; the children are indifferent, but Ian thinks, *"I would! I would!"* Sadly, however, "it wasn't Ian Dr. Prescott had been addressing" (105).

Clearly there is no return to past naïveté. In any case, with that "hitch" he always experienced Ian has never had the easy ability to accommodate all troubles that marked the other Bedloes; Ian's imagination has always been somewhat dialectical, compared with that of the rest of the family. The question is whether there can be a hitch beyond the hitch—something that can jolt Ian out of this entrapment in absurdity. In other words, ironically Ian now needs a jolt or "hitch" to work in the opposite way from his earlier hitches, not to undermine his mother Bee's too-easy ability to assimilate all to her analogy of *Bee*-ing, but rather to undo his own dialectical dissociation of self—*I*-an—from world: Ian wonders "if there was any event, any at all, so tragic that it could jolt him out of this odious habit of observing his own reaction to it" (99). But can a jolt undo a jolt? Can the analogical be retrieved by an encounter with the dialectical limit to the dialectical itself? Can Tracy's limit-of be a dialectical canceling of the limit-to? This is the problem the novel will proceed to address, and the answer it gives is a resounding "maybe."

The resolution of Ian's despair comes in what seems to be a terribly conventional and potentially simplistic way: Ian joins a church, appropriately called "the Church of the Second Chance." But we are warned ahead of time that this is a playful, decentered resolution. At Lucy's funeral service at Dober Street Presbyterian, Ian has a foreshadowing of his own religious renewal; as he listens to Dr. Prescott pray for God's mercy to "pour like a healing balm upon our hearts" (109), Ian feels "limp and pure and pliant as an infant. He was, in fact, born again" (110). But *this* kind of second chance, a conventional "born-again" experience (founded on a dialectical vision of religious purity that is radically separate from the messy secular world), is exactly what will not be available to Ian, and it is quickly negated. The born-again glow lasts only until Ian returns to the imperfect ordinary world that is home; he picks up baby Daphne, who is "far too heavy," and notes that the "air in the room seemed dull and brownish" (112). Ian then has a dream that signals another kind of "chance": "At night, Danny stood at the blackboard in front of Ian's English class. 'This is a dream,' he announced. 'The word "dream" comes from the Latin word *dorimus*, meaning "game of chance"'" (112). A second *chance*, then, might be playful and fluid and slippery, more like the unpredictable, metaphorical gift of a comforting dream—or like the rough-and-tumble, unpredictable world of flawed, middling humans—than like the clear dialectic of Calvinist born-again salvation.

The church Ian stumbles upon, the Church of the Second Chance, at first glance seems like the church of any small evangelical sect, founded on a straightforward, dialectical theology of the Cross and of grace. But Tyler's comic tone—or, rather, Ian's ironic point of view—undercuts the apparent evangelical fervor of this church. When the minister, for instance, announces that it is time for people to share their petitions to God, he states that "No request is too great, no request too trivial in the eyes of God our Father," provoking Ian to weave a humorously homey analogy: "Ian thought of the plasterer who'd repaired his parents' bathroom ceiling. NO JOB TOO LARGE OR TOO SMALL, his panel truck had read" (126). And then, when a woman in the congregation tells of a terrible limit-experience— her son was killed in Vietnam because he forgot his parachute—Ian mentally leaps from the tragic to the ridiculous:

Maybe it had slipped his mind he *couldn't* fly, so in the first startled instant of his descent he supposed he had simply forgotten how. He may have felt insulted, betrayed by all he'd taken for granted. *What's the big idea here?* he must have asked.

Ian pictured one of those animated films where a character strolls off a cliff without noticing and continues strolling in midair, perfectly safe until he happens to look down and then his legs start wheeling madly and he plummets.

He gave a short bark of laughter. (128)

Ian feels horribly guilty for laughing, but in a sense his laughter is precisely the kind of hitch-beyond-the-hitch that he has needed. For Ian the limit, this time, is itself limited by comedy. And then Ian learns that in this church grace, though certainly amazing, is not dialectically separate from the human world. Rather, it needs to be earned by real people living in real situations; if the church's pastor, Reverend Emmett, is a Calvinist (as at least his evangelical fervor would suggest), he is a Calvinist whom Calvin would regard suspiciously. Ian tells Reverend Emmett after the service that he needs God's forgiveness for causing his brother's death, and Reverend Emmett informs Ian that he needs to do specific human work to win the grace of forgiveness:

"... Don't you think I'm forgiven?"

"Goodness, no," Reverend Emmett said briskly. ...

"But ... I thought that was kind of the point," Ian said. "I thought God forgives everything."

"He does," Reverend Emmett said. "But you can't just say, 'I'm sorry, God.' Why, anyone can do that much! You have to offer reparation—concrete, practical reparation, according to the rules of our church." (133)

According to "the rules" of the Church of the Second Chance, grace may be radically transcendent and unearned (if the sin is "something nothing will fix," then "that's where Jesus comes in, of course" [133]), but it is also something that needs to be worked for in the gritty and imperfect world in which Ian lives. If so far Ian has been bumping up against the *limit to* his human decency, the absolutely and terribly transcendent, Reverend Emmett now offers him a glimpse of what David Tracy calls the gracious *limit of* the human world—Gerard Manley Hopkins's "dearest freshness deep down things," the immanent spirit of Tyler's Quaker tradition. Ironically, more than purely transcendent grace would, this immanent grace demands work and sacrifice; Reverend Emmett tells Ian he must drop out of college and raise Lucy's children.

When Ian tells his family about his new religious involvement, and especially about the fact that he now feels that he must give up his education and raise the children, the other Bedloes of course think that Ian is breaking from what I am calling their analogical vision of things; for his family, Ian has taken a radically dialectical turn. Their traditional Presbyterian church, his mother argues, "never asked us to abandon our entire way of life," but Ian answers: "Well, maybe it should have" (138). But I suggest that Ian is actually returning to the native Bedloe analogical imagination, though this time in a sophisticated rather than naive way. Ian's

rejection of the easy Bedloe prescription for living a good life is simply the dialectical movement that for Tracy must be enfolded within any analogical imagination that is not bland and simplistic (as, I have suggested, the Bedloe imagination
has been).

Tracy, remember, criticizes analogical imaginations without "that sense for the
negative, that dialectical sense within analogy itself" as "the theological equivalent of 'cheap grace': boredom, sterility and an atheological vision of a deadening
univocity" (*Analogical Imagination* 413). Ian's newfound analogical imagination,
with its profound sense for the negative, is a full dialectical step ahead of that of
his family. For Ian, the Bedloe world has already been negated, prospectively by
those little "hitches" and then definitively by Danny's death. His new change
of direction (his "second chance") is a second "hitch," a second negation, which
at first rips through the family like a divorce. At Reverend Emmett's insistence,
Ian confesses to his parents that he caused Danny's death—a suicide, not an
accident—and this effects the sharpest and most shattering of "hitches":

> His mother moved her lips, which seemed unusually wrinkled. No sound
> emerged. . . .
> For the first time it occurred to him that there was something steely and inhuman
> to this religion business. Had Reverend Emmett taken fully into account the lonely
> thud of his sneakers on the steps, the shattered, splintered air he left behind? (139)

What I am suggesting, however, is that this shattering is really a shattering of the
prior shattering—an attempt to negate the negation, to tentatively and playfully
reapproximate faith by negating radical doubt.

This new negation is not some sort of clear-cut "salvation by faith"; Tyler is
too playful for such dogmatic propositions. When Ian becomes a carpenter, for
instance, the text reverses the conventional analogy; Ian has not become "like
Christ" so much as Christ is revealed, comically and humanly, as being *like Ian*:

> ". . . Sometimes when I look at paintings of Him I try to see what kind of muscles He
> had—whether they're the kind that come from hammering and sawing. I like to
> think He really did put a few bits of wood together; He didn't just stand around dis-
> cussing theology with His friends while Joseph built the furniture." (283)

Ian has come not to a definite salvation but rather just a *dream* of peace. The final
dream he has about Danny reflects this peace in a playful, metaphorical way. In the
dream, Danny helps Ian carry a heavy carton for the moving company Ian works
for: "'Here,' Danny said, 'let me help you,' and he took one end and started back-
ing down the steps with it. And all the while he and Ian smiled into each other's
eyes" (140). Ian wakes from the dream "clenched and anxious" (140). But then he
thinks of his church's hymn about "leaning on the everlasting arms," and he lets
go, allowing his imagination to weave analogies between Danny and God, healing
his sense of both of them: "Gradually he drifted loose, giving himself over to God.

He rested all his weight on God, trustfully, serenely, the way his roommate used to rest in his chair that resembled the palm of a hand" (141). This way of imagining ultimate reality is at least partly dialectical—the Ultimate is something Ian gives himself over to, transcending the burdensome human world. And yet this dialectic is enfolded within a nest of homey analogies; God is like his roommate's chair, like the palm of a hand, like Danny. God is the limit-to that surprises Ian by revealing itself as a gracious limit-of, holding him up like a chair or a hand or a brother. In a sense, the remainder of the novel simply elaborates on this final dream.

The indefinite nature of Ian's sanctity (he is "Saint Maybe" and also "a saint . . . maybe") remains Ian's hallmark throughout the rest of the novel. He finds himself, for example, teetering between two conflicting notions of sin. Would-be girlfriend Jeannie tells him that he is "sinning not to walk away" from Lucy's children: "I think," she says, "we're allowed one single life to live on this planet. . . . And if you let it go to waste—now, *that* is sinning" (231). But Reverend Emmett tells him to accept the burden of raising the children, to "[l]ean into it . . . View your burden as a gift. . . . Accept that and lean into it. This is the only life you'll have" (235). When the children are more or less grown up, Ian—at Reverend Emmett's urging—considers entering the ministry, but again he wavers; he goes into a Methodist church and prays for a sign: "*Nothing fancy. Just something more definite than Reverend Emmett offering a suggestion*" (278). But all he gets is the sight of Gideon, the boyfriend of Lucy's now-high-school-age daughter Daphne, with his arm around another girl. "What if that was the sign he had prayed for inside the church?" Ian wonders. "But if it was, he had no idea what it meant" (288). Worrying that her boyfriend will hurt her, Ian tentatively warns Daphne that "some *people* aren't what they seem" (290); Daphne, however, tells him not to interfere in her relationship with Gideon: "You think I'm some ninny who wants to do right but keeps goofing. But what you don't see is, I goof on purpose. I'm not like you: King Careful. Mr. Look-Both-Ways. Saint Maybe. . . . Mess up, I say! . . . Make every mistake you can think of! Use all the life you've got!" (291). And then Ian realizes the meaning of the "sign" he received: he remembers "Lucy rushing home out of breath, laughing and excited, and his own arrogant certitude that he had an obligation to inform his brother" (292), and he knows that this time, toward Daphne, he must not act so rashly. He must remain uncertain.

So being Saint Maybe, being uncertain, is precisely Ian's virtue. Even as a boy, with his "hitches," Ian lacked Bedloe certitude, and this lack turns out to be the source of his generous spirit. It also means that he will not become a minister; he would not be able to give people the definitive answers a minister needs to give, and, more important, he would not want to (292). His lack of certitude forces Ian to do without clear dialectical concepts about "right" and "wrong" or about "transcendent" and "worldly" but rather to contextualize these things within the real human stories he is involved in. And it forces him to pray not definitively but analogically: "not forming actual words but picturing instead this spinning green planet safe in the hands of God, with the children and his parents and Ian himself small trusting dots among all the other dots" (293). This is a good image of the whole of reality as interconnected rather than divided—or, in the words of Catholic feminist theologian Elizabeth Johnson, an image of "the nature of divine relatedness to the world as a whole: not a distant, dominating transcendence but otherness that freely draws near, bringing new life, sustaining all lives" (169). Ian has come back to that analogical Bedloe belief in neighborhood, in community— primary values of Tyler's Quaker heritage. But Ian's new version of this belief is softer, more uncertain, more humble than the clear but sterile belief previously held by the Bedloes.

Ian's return, in this new way, to the analogical vision of his family ushers in the other gracious returns or repetitions that mark the final section of the novel. The most important of these repetitions is Rita, a "clutter counselor," who comes to the Bedloe house in order to help them clean out the mess that has collected, and who then ends up Ian's mate. Rita is a kind of repetition of Lucy; Ian describes her, with a surprising sensuous accuracy, as "tall and slim and beautiful," a woman who "could easily be an Indian. She has beautiful black hair and she moves in this loose, swinging way, like a dancer" (339). While playing Scrabble with Rita, Ian wanders over and looks at a picture of Lucy. Rita is trying to get him to trade two of her vowels for one consonant; Lucy in the picture is leggy and spunky— like Rita. At this late date, Ian is still trying to get some perspective on Lucy, "to understand what Lucy's meaning had been in his life" (355). Meanwhile Rita yells in the background, "Okay, *three* of my vowels. For one lousy consonant. You drive a hard bargain, you devil" (355). Ian puts down the picture of Lucy, "no wiser" about what he has felt for her, though the answer is under his nose: Lucy was someone to whom he was very erotically attracted, and Rita is her gracious repetition, her echo, the erotic returned and now earned as good.

And at the end of the novel, when Rita gives birth to Ian and Rita's son, Joshua, Ian has a final vision of the way things have echoed, analogically, through his life. People are visiting him and Rita to see Joshua, and Ian feels an "echo effect" (372)—he vividly recalls Danny presenting his own "firstborn" (Daphne). But the moment skips, like a phonograph needle, to Danny presenting Lucy to the Bedloe family: "I'd like you to meet the woman who's changed my life" (372). Lucy, Ian remembers, just "tipped her head and smiled. After all, she might have said, this was an ordinary occurrence. People changed other people's lives every day of the year. There was no call to make such a fuss about it" (372–73). Those are the novel's final words.

This has been a novel about people who have changed Ian's life. That, finally, is the significance of Lucy. She was the unexpected grace, the limit-experience or "hitch" that broke the too-easy Bedloe trust in the analogical connectedness of everything. By itself, of course, such an encounter with limit was a dialectical experience; the Bedloes encountered the *limit to* their suburban ease. But by virtue of his gentle openness to experience, Ian achieves a renewed analogical imagination, one that is able again and again to experience the grace that Lucy brought, and increasingly to find this grace not as shockingly external to the everyday but as part of the warp and woof of family life. Lucy is part of a chain that eventually includes such further revelations of grace as Daphne and Rita and ultimately Joshua. These are people who in various ways give Ian limit-experiences; they reveal the "limit to" the Bedloe routine and the gracious, grounding "limit of" the larger world. Ian, merely a Saint Maybe, is by virtue of his very uncertainty—his tendency to experience that "hitch" of doubt—open to such grace. So he is able to experience the gracious repetition of Daphne, Rita, and Joshua, after his sin has made him lose his original treasures, Danny and Lucy.

Anne Tyler's novel is itself very Ian-like. The book, as I suggested earlier, is not daringly postmodernist, and yet it is not coolly certain about its own narrative either. Like many of Tyler's novels, *Saint Maybe* is a collection of chapters that bounce from viewpoint to viewpoint; although Ian's point of view dominates, chapters are also narrated from the points of view of Lucy, Agatha (Lucy's older daughter), Doug Bedloe, and others. What Tyler accomplishes with this modernist technique is similar to what Ian himself achieves over the course of the book: Tyler presents a collection of narratives between which there are gaps but nonetheless analogical linkages, a kind of gentle Quaker community of separate but connected voices that are all capable of expressing small, immanent experiences of grace. Anne Tyler's *Saint Maybe* is a good example of a contemporary novel that uses fairly conventional storytelling to convey an analogical vision of the relation between the ordinary and the Ultimate, and the book's overt religious content suggests that this is explicitly what Tyler was up to.

A Dialectical Imagination in a Realistic Narrative

If in *Saint Maybe* Anne Tyler complicates a traditional story by playing with points of view, building shifts into her narrative that initially establish dialectical gaps or "hitches" that are ultimately healed by imperfect but real analogical links, in *Symposium* Muriel Spark complicates her rather simple story of a murder by playing not with viewpoints but with time. Spark's novel shifts between present and past tense, and at the end even leaps into a future tense, in a fragmented manner that is in some ways postmodernist. Indeed, David Lodge himself calls Spark's time shifts postmodernist. In *The Modes of Modern Writing*, Lodge treats Spark briefly in his "Postmodernist Fiction" chapter (226–27); in *The Art of Fiction*, furthermore, Lodge states that "Muriel Spark's combination of frequent time-shift with authorial third-person narrative is a typical postmodernist strategy"

(77), and he then goes on to compare Spark to Kurt Vonnegut. And Spark herself has sharply distinguished her own fiction from traditional twentieth-century social realism. "We have in this century," she writes, "a marvelous tradition of socially-conscious art. And especially now in the arts of drama and the novel we see and hear everywhere the representation of the victim against the oppressor" ("Desegregation of Art" 34). Time has run out on such social realism, Spark says; "it isn't achieving its end or illuminating our lives any more," and the time has come to cultivate "a more effective technique" ("Desegregation of Art" 34). The valid literary form for the present absurd world, she says, is one with a sharply dialectical edge, satire: "[T]he only effective art of our particular time is the satirical, the harsh and witty, the ironic and derisive. Because we have come to a moment in history when we are surrounded on all sides and oppressed by the absurd" (36). If Lodge is correct in considering postmodernism a response to the existential absurd, then Spark's work shares common ground with the postmodern.

Yet there is, finally, something deeply traditional about *Symposium*, the Spark novel I wish to consider. Behind the fragmentations is a crisp British comedy of manners, with wittily drawn and generally realistic characters and incidents. More important, even the temporal leaps are confidently controlled by a very omniscient narrator, one who sees and authoritatively describes past, present, and future events; far from undermining narrative authority, the seemingly postmodernist leaps actually *affirm* such authority. This is not a fragmented, centerless novel in which truth is radically relativized. And it is primarily this authoritative narrator that establishes the novel's dialectical vision: the narrator is a portrait of a transcendent, omniscient Other, which towers over the petty world of human desire and action. According to *Village Voice* reviewer Jane Mendelsohn, Spark's "favorite theme" is "omniscience, authorial and divine. . . . She's always hinting at the parallels between fictional and physical creation, torturing her characters and readers with the unpredictable attention of an Old Testament deity" (25). The characters in *Symposium* encounter that transcendent otherness most vividly when, at the end of the novel, they crash against the murder, the evolution of which we have been watching throughout the narrative. The murder gives the characters an experience of the *limit to* their own ability to act, an ultimacy that frames their world but that remains impenetrable. Hence, although *Symposium* is a realistic comedy of manners, its religious imagination, like its satirical tone, is distinctly dialectical.

As Mendelsohn points out, a temporally omniscient narrator is something of a Muriel Spark hallmark. Spark gives her narrator the same uncanny control over past, present, and future in her most famous novel, *The Prime of Miss Jean Brodie*, and this novel, too, presents a dialectical vision of limited humans over against utter transcendence. In that earlier novel, however, Spark—a Roman Catholic convert—also planted an alternative analogical, sacramental vision. The awe-inspiring teacher Miss Brodie acts as a kind of analogue of the omniscient narrator; she teaches the protagonist, Sandy Stranger, about divine transcendence—but in a somewhat mediated and at least potentially sacramental way.

On the one hand, Miss Brodie towers dialectically over the girls in her charge, standing as a type of the transcendent, Barthian Other. Even to the extent that she ultimately fails to control the girls' destinies (Sandy finds that she is able to "betray" Miss Brodie and end her domination over young students), Miss Brodie reveals the dialectical Other: her very failure reveals the inadequacy of any human analogue to mediate divine omnipotence.

But on the other hand, Miss Brodie is more than a negative analogue of the divine; her power really does teach Sandy about the way amazing—and, surely, sometimes terrible—grace can come down to earth. The narrator suggests that what is missing from the Calvinist, predestining Brodie is a sacramental imagination:

> Her disapproval of the Church of Rome was based on her assertions that it was a church of superstition, and that only people who did not think for themselves were Roman Catholics. In some ways, her attitude was a strange one, because she was by temperament suited only to the Roman Catholic Church; possibly it could have embraced, even while it disciplined, her soaring and diving spirit, it might even have normalized her. (125)

It is Sandy who supplies the sacramentality that Brodie needs, and by doing so she separates the good of Brodie (her sense of wonder) from her evil (her Hitlerian desire to be all-powerful). The title of the book Sandy, as a psychologist nun, later writes is *The Transfiguration of the Commonplace*, which suggests that its contents unfold something like David Tracy's theory of the analogical imagination.

Nonetheless, even this Spark novel has no easy analogical vision. Although Sandy writes her psychological treatise and explicitly attributes its inspiration to "a Miss Jean Brodie in her prime" (187), she also remains dissatisfied, struggling, clutching "the bars of her grille more desperately than ever" (186). Sandy has become a Catholic, but not an uncritical one. We sense that her relationship with Catholicism in general, as with the convent in particular, is a dialectical tug of attraction and distaste: Sandy "had entered the Catholic Church," Spark states late in the novel, "in whose ranks she had found quite a number of Fascists much less agreeable than Miss Brodie" (183). Similarly, Spark herself has described her own relationship with the religious tradition she has adopted in rather dialectical terms. On the one hand, she describes her conversion as natural, a recognition of the analogy between the Roman Catholic Church and her own way of thinking. The "simple answer" to the question why she became a Catholic is, Spark says, "that I felt the Roman Catholic faith corresponded to what I had always felt and known and believed; there was no blinding revelation in my case" (*Curriculum Vitae* 202). And yet her reasons for converting are also unspeakable, untranslatable into the terms of the day-to-day world: "The more difficult explanation would involve the step by step building up of a conviction; as Newman himself pointed out, when asked about his conversion, it was not a thing one could propound 'between the soup and the fish' at a dinner party. . . . Indeed, the existential quality of a religious experience cannot be simply summed up in general terms" (*Curriculum Vitae* 202). And Spark's relationship with fellow Catholics is as dialectical as that of her creation, Sandy Stranger: "I was put off a long time by individual Catholics," Spark writes, "living ones, I mean. Good God, I used to think, if I become a Catholic, will I grow like them?" ("My Conversion" 24). In fiction and in life, Spark's Catholic religious imagination appears to be more dialectical than analogical.

As I have stated, Spark typically presents her dialectical religious vision by employing a satirical and omniscient narrator who looms over the text and its limited characters much as Miss Brodie looms over her students. In *Symposium*, such a narrator intrudes quickly and abruptly, informing us on the novel's first page that she towers over the characters and events with a definitive authority. After tossing us into her story *in medias res*—presenting, in a brief first paragraph, an unnamed character who shouts, "This is rape! . . . This is violation!" (7)—the narrator stops and interjects a sudden, even shorter second paragraph: "It was not rape, it was a robbery" (7). This is a narrator who *knows*, and knows more than her characters; she exists above the characters' limited individual viewpoints. She refuses to respect the narrative convention of learning of events along with the characters, allowing the reader to travel to the end of a story step by step. Rather, she relates the story's end nearly at the beginning. The novel's plot spins around a dinner party at the end of which the characters learn that a murder has been committed, but the narrator leaps to that ending, subverting any sense of surprise, already in the fourth of her fourteen chapters. When the hostess, Chris Donovan, tells one of the guests, Margaret Damien, that her mother-in-law, Hilda, will "look in after dinner," the narrator interrupts: "But Hilda Damien will not come in after dinner. She is dying, now, as they speak" (45).

The narrator's absolute knowledge cuts across the limited knowledge of the characters, dialectically jarring us with a sense of the *limit to* the characters' experience. The foreknowledge also creates a sense of fate, a view of the Big Picture in which each person or event or thing is not a sacramentally grace-filled analogy of the whole, but rather each is a meager, limited piece in a predestined design. The entire novel becomes a kind of jigsaw puzzle, and all the pieces fit together to depict Hilda's inevitable death. And this overall design is mirrored in all sorts of mini-narratives that the narrator enfolds in the text. For example, in the midst of the more important task of filling in the story of Margaret Murchie Damien, whom I will discuss at length, the narrator interjects a few sentences about Margaret's sister Jean, who is shipped off to a convent in Liège after her and Margaret's grandmother is murdered. The narrator reduces Jean to the merest pebble in the inexorable unfolding of the predestined events of the novel. Jean's long, loving relationship with a man named Paul is of no intrinsic value but is only an offshoot of the main story's unfolding "destiny": Jane's relationship with Paul "is another story, or would be but for the mere fact that her destiny was contingent upon the murder of her grandmother" (74–75), an event that *is* important to the novel's main narrative. Similarly, the lives of six nuns are equally dismissable, from the narrator's imperial viewpoint. While telling the story of the time Margaret spent in an Anglican convent some years prior to her new marriage to William Damien, the narrator coolly notes that only three of the nine nuns of the convent are "of vital interest"; the other six are "dreary as hell" (103). Such examples neatly sum up the dialectical gap between the transcendent narrator and her utterly dependent characters, who are only as important as she wants them to be. This is a narrative world in which the characters are radically limited, and ultimate reality (the reality of the narrator) is at a radical distance from the characters.

Another way that Spark—both in her own narration and in comments made by her characters—diminishes the importance of people and events is by inserting witty, satirical, distinctively Sparkian non sequiturs. Issues and events normally considered important are juxtaposed with statements of the trivial in a way that ironically undermines any sense that the merely human is ever anything but trivial. For example, after describing a champagne grower who was killed by his wife with a champagne bottle, Hurley Reed (Chris Donovan's lover and the host of the party) remarks, "The French make their bottles very heavy. Especially champagne" (88). Helen Suzy, whose house has been ransacked by the same burglars who will soon kill Hilda Damien, describes the event this way: "I was truly sorry our stuff was stolen, and that they urinated all over. We had to get the walls done anyway. I never liked those chair covers" (97). And after the murder of a nun in the convent where Margaret Damien lived for a time, another nun inadvertently mixes the sacred and the profane with this funny non sequitur: "We can't help feeling the hand of the supernatural in this tragic event. The house is to be taken over by a firm of lawyers" (121). In a sense, the entire novel is one huge non sequitur: the story of the evil Margaret and her desire to kill Hilda ends with the murder of Hilda—by burglars who have nothing whatsoever to do with Margaret:

> Destiny, my destiny, thought Hilda. Is she [Margaret] going to poison me? What is she plotting? She is plotting something. This is a nightmare.
>   Hilda was right. Except that in the destiny of the event Margaret could have saved herself the trouble, the plotting. It was the random gang, . . . of which Margaret knew nothing, who were to kill Hilda Damien. (176)

These non sequiturs, large and small, are embodiments of a dialectical imagination: a vision of the disjunctions between occurrences and human responses to them, or between human intentionality (presumed causes) and ultimate effects.

"Chronology is not causality" (122), says the oracular Magnus, Margaret's mad uncle, and this might well be the novel's—and especially the narrator's—motto.

This statement makes explicit the novel's most important dialectic, the one that for David Lodge pushes the book toward postmodernism: that of *time*. The narrator, as I have illustrated, exists in an eternal now for which there is no chronology, for which human past and future are always present. In case Spark has not sufficiently suggested this throughout the rest of the novel, the narrator's transcendence of time is nailed home in the book's final pages when the narrator— who throughout has freely alternated between a present-tense description of the dinner party and past-tense descriptions of earlier events—leaps to the future tense. She briefly describes what *will* happen the next day to Andrew J. Barnet, a man who recently met Hilda and intended to take her to dinner, but whose potential relationship with her has been truncated by the murder. Hence, the characters are all trapped in their limited chronologies, and only the time-transcending narrator has any real control, any ability to cause events. Chronology, indeed, is not causality.

By establishing two incompatible time frames—the narrator's all-knowing "causal" time and the characters' limited "chronological" time—Spark suggests a vision of ultimate reality as outside the flow and flux of worldly temporality. The mathematical physicist and theologian John Polkinghorne talks about this "classical" view of God's relation to time, and he compares it with an alternate view:

> Among the most puzzling, and the most pressing, of general questions about God are those concerned with how he is to be understood to relate to time. . . . The classical answer . . . is to say that God relates to the whole of cosmic history "at once." The quark soup and sinful humanity are equally present to the One who, in Aquinas's phrase, does not foreknow the future but, from the perspective of his eternity, simply knows it.
>
> . . . The trouble with the timeless view of God's relationship with his creation is that it is in danger of denying the reality of becoming. . . . It seems to me that it is not sufficient for God just to know that events are temporal, he must know them as temporal in their due succession. . . .
>
> Thus, I am persuaded that in addition to God's eternal nature we shall have to take seriously that he has a relation to time which makes him immanent within it, as well as eternally transcendent of it. (59, 61)

The analogical imagination, I would argue, imagines the divine in the temporally immanent way that Polkinghorne endorses; this is a God infused in the flow and flux of "chronology." The transcendent, eternal dimension of the divine— Polkinghorne's "classical" picture of a timeless God who "relates to the whole of cosmic history 'at once'"—is what the dialectical imagination points toward. As I have noted repeatedly, this notion of the radical transcendence of God can be grasped only indirectly. There are no analogies for such a God; there is only the experience of the finitude of the human, the *limit-to*. Although Spark seems to break this rule, using her temporally omniscient narrator to suggest analogously the transcendent dimension of God, the narrator is not quite an analogue in the full sense of the word. The narrator remains little more than a cool, witty abstraction enfolding the story, a limit-to but not a gracious limit-of, in David Tracy's terms. To the extent that the narrator may operate as an analogue of God, it is an analogue that stays at the novel's envelope, its limit; this "God" cannot enter inside the novel, so to speak—it cannot be incarnated within the story, or within any character. And the other seeming analogue of the divine omnipotence—the novel's main character, Margaret Damien—is, even more than Miss Jean Brodie (who, as I noted, does manage with her underlying, pitiable humanity partly to reveal to Sandy Stranger the Transfiguration of the Commonplace), ultimately a non-analogue. The character of Margaret depicts the way presumed human potency ultimately runs smack against its limits, its impotence.

At the center of the novel, woven into the narrative about the dinner party and its preparations, is the story of the perversely evil Margaret Murchie Damien. Although this story is enfolded in, and hence framed by, the chronologically jumpy overall narrative, and although it has uncanny and even latently supernatural elements, the tale of Margaret is told in a realistic, straightforward way.[4] Margaret's story is about human and even, perhaps, metaphysical evil, and yet at the end her story slams, impotently, against a limit: abstract, incomprehensible Fate.

Margaret is introduced into the novel as a pretty, "romantic-looking" young woman, though the narrator adds an ironic twist to her description—Margaret's "long dark-red hair" is "a striking colour, *probably* natural" (12, emphasis added)—which hints at something artificial and unseemly. Margaret also reveals in these earliest pages her dialectical divorce from the material world; as people at the party sympathize with Lord and Lady Suzy, who have recently been robbed, Margaret notes placidly that "[a]ccording to some mystics . . . the supreme good is to divest yourself of all your best-loved belongings" (15). Margaret's theme, it seems, is a kind of romantic transcendence, with a hint of possible fraudulence. (Hilda Damien, we are later told, has judged her to be "that goody-goody type of girl, how could she be real?" [55].) The saintly Margaret, whom her new husband, William Damien, likes for her "moralistic tendency, and especially her refusal to speak ill of anybody" (30), is being linked with the dialectical morality of the saint whom Hurley Reed, the host, speaks of during the party: "St Uncumber . . . to whom people, especially women, used to pray to relieve them of their spouses" (13). If marriage is a human image or analogy of the divine linkage with the world, divorce

---

4 This is another reason that I am treating *Symposium* as a "realistic," not "postmodern," novel: apart from Spark's play with time, the central story of Margaret, like the narrative that frames it, exemplifies traditional formal realism.

suggests the dialectical wrenching we have been discussing in these pages. Although a newlywed, the placidly detached—Un(en)cumber(ed)—Margaret is quickly introduced as a patron saint of divorce.

By the seventh chapter, after swinging back and forth between the party and its preparations, the narrator is ready to back up several years and tell in earnest the story of Margaret. Murder, it turns out, has tended to happen around her rather regularly.

Margaret's family, the Murchies, are a decidedly drab Scottish family, though they have one "imaginative factor": Margaret's father Dan's brother Magnus, whom Dan and his wife, Greta, treat as a kind of oracle—"but unfortunately he was mad" (65). Magnus, in Margaret's presence, suggests that Dan get their elderly mother to change her will, cutting out Magnus and three sisters and leaving all her considerable money to Dan. Margaret quietly gets the family lawyer to arrange this, and then old Mrs. Murchie is immediately murdered by a female inmate of Magnus's asylum. Apparently this is just a random act by an insane woman, occurring at a coincidentally convenient time, and Margaret practices the dialectical renunciation that is her hallmark, refusing to accept any of her grandmother's fortune: "If there is one thing I could not bear to do . . . it is to profit by darling Granny's death" (79). Dan and Greta fear that Margaret somehow orchestrated the murder, and Dan nervously asks Magnus if he thinks Margaret is sane. Magnus expresses his indifference with a typical Sparkian non sequitur: "Probably not. Perhaps she inherited something wild from me. Is it time for a drink?" (81).

Soon Margaret, further accentuating her dialectical renunciation of the world, enters an Anglican convent, a comical place in which the other nuns seem more attached to secular Marxism and to foul-mouthed talk than to religious renunciation. But Margaret remains pure, detached: "I believe I have a vocation," she writes to her father. "It is all a question of thinking of *les autres*" (104). "*Les autres*" becomes Margaret's code phrase for renunciation of personal desires. In a sense her use of the phrase is ironic, since she ultimately reveals herself to be supremely, demonically self-centered; yet her desires do not tend toward ordinary worldly things or people but toward a kind of transcendent power, the power of *the Other*, so "*les autres*" really are what she has set her mind on.

Once again Margaret finds herself adjacent to a murder. Sister Rose, assistant to the amusingly proletarian plumber Sister Rooke, is murdered at the convent, and the ailing Mother Superior, with whom Margaret has been sharing a room, confesses to the murder and then dies. Margaret, of course, is technically innocent; she was away at the time of the murder. And yet the incident provokes Uncle Magnus to make his cryptic Schopenhauerian comment about the design of Spark's universe: "Chronology is not causality" (122).

Eventually we learn that, as Jane Mendelsohn puts it in her review, Margaret "seems to have been, since childhood, a magnet for catastrophe" (26): as a child Margaret watched a school friend drown, and later she was at a tearoom with a teacher who then permanently disappeared (Margaret, at the time, calmly drank tea and "ate two biscuits" [138]). But for all her coolness and cruel intent, Margaret has not actively caused any of these deaths. Rather, her "capacity for being near the scene of tragedy was truly inexplicable in any reasonable terms. . . . [T]here was absolutely no link of any rational, physical or psychological nature between Margaret's personal activities and what went on around her" (142). Like her Sparkian predecessor Miss Brodie, and like the omniscient Sparkian narrator of whom she seems to be an image, Margaret is not content with such passivity: "I'm tired of being the passive carrier of disaster," she says to Uncle Magnus. "I feel frustrated. I almost think it's time for me to take my life and destiny in my own hands, and actively make disasters come about" (143–44). And Magnus, ever the oracle, precisely locates evil in the Spark universe: in malicious human *desire*, not in actual accomplishment. "The wish alone is evil," Magnus tells Margaret, at which she answers, "Glad to hear it" (144).

What Margaret is about to discover, however, is that this desire is all she has. She is not an analogue of the omniscient narrator; no such analogues—not even the passionately willful Margaret—exist in the human world. All that exists is Margaret's malicious will—and her impotent fury when she crashes against the limit to her will, an external Design that ironically matches her will but that she has had no hand in engineering.

Yes, she engineers her marriage to William Damien. They meet in a grocery store, and the story of their meeting, as Mendelsohn says, "is repeated hypnotically throughout the book . . . until it takes on a magical quality like the dinner party itself" (26); this repetition gives the event a bizarrely predestined quality. And it turns out that this encounter has been carefully arranged by Margaret, who decides to meet and marry William after she learns he is the son of the extremely wealthy Hilda. Up to a point, then, Margaret *is* a prototype of the Sparkian predestining power. But only up to a point.

Tired of merely being nearby when violent deaths occur, Margaret vows to Magnus that she will not be satisfied to wait for something to "happen" to Hilda: "I want to actively liquidate the woman. Compared with the evil eye, what I have in mind is just healthy criminality" (159). But when Margaret states that she will arrange an accident for Hilda, Magnus oracularly declares: "Like it or not . . . destiny might do it for you" (160). And destiny does. In the very event of fulfilling Margaret's desires, destiny defers the fulfillment. The narrator, in writing the completion of Margaret's wish—*Hilda is murdered*—*un*writes Margaret's wish: the murder is committed not by Margaret nor by anyone connected with her, but by the burglars whose operation has been indicated little by little over the course of the novel.

The sheer, inexorable mechanism of this murder becomes retrospectively clear, as it has *always* been clear to the narrator in her eternal, transcendent now. The American student Luke, it turns out, has taken a job helping butler Charterhouse with the dinner party. Charterhouse conveys the time of the party and the guest list to Luke, who then tells one of the band of robbers that William Damien and his very rich mother, Hilda, will be at the party, leaving a Monet painting in William and Margaret's flat:

> "Damien."
> "Damien?"
> "Yes, Damien. Mother and son he seemed to think are expected. She's doing up a flat in Hampstead. A picture on the wall by that artist named Monet, that French—"
> "You said Monet?"
> "Just bought it, just the other day." (125)

The last, slight chance that the scheme may be foiled is itself foiled by the merest accident (or, which is the same thing, by the narrator, who has precisely the control that Margaret craves but falls short of): on the day of the party, host Hurley Reed is warned that his chef is suspicious of Charterhouse, but Hurley has no time to look into the matter because his mother suddenly and unexpectedly needs him to help her move furniture. So the terrible machine clicks into gear. Hilda arrives at the flat just when the robbers, who have been informed that she will be at the party, are there to steal the Monet. The robbers "are unmasked, recognizable." Hilda's arrival "is something they have not expected and this is the tragic fact for which Hilda dies" (190).

Obviously the narrator is using the word "tragic" ironically. This random accident has no tragic grandeur; its effect, rather, is to reduce the human actors to mere pawns, dialectically wrenched from any sort of ultimate meaning. And Margaret, of course, realizes this all too painfully. When the news of Hilda's murder reaches the party, Margaret shrieks hopelessly, "It shouldn't have been till Sunday!" (191). All the characters have encountered the *limit to* their freedom and power. But the diabolically clear-sighted Margaret is the only one who knows this.

Muriel Spark, it seems to me, is as traditional a storyteller as Anne Tyler. Tyler embeds a vision of analogical grace within a straightforward, comic-realistic saga of an ordinary Baltimore family; she uses her trademark modernist device—an alternation from chapter to chapter between various characters' third-person-limited points of view—but there is no full-scale postmodernist shattering of the very narrative enterprise itself. Spark uses an even more conventional genre, the suspense-mystery, complicating it with her own trademark modernist device, an omniscient narrator who can leap back and forth in time. But if Tyler is a rather traditional storyteller who, in *Saint Maybe*, uses her craft to explore the ultimate graciousness that is woven analogically throughout the ordinary, Spark—a Catholic who is more generally known than Tyler as an overtly religious writer—suggests ultimate reality only indirectly, as a dialectical limit to the ordinary upper-class social milieu she depicts. In this novel, as Jane Mendelsohn says, "the sherry glass is drained while bagpipes moan ominously in the background, and Spark's only glimpse into the numinous is through the wreckage of the moment" (26). The numinous inferred through wreckage: that is as good a definition as any of the dialectical imagination.

A Dialectical Imagination in a Postmodern Narrative

Biographical information about the notoriously reclusive Thomas Pynchon is hard to come by, but a memoir by Jules Siegel, Pynchon's next-door neighbor in a Cornell University dormitory in the 1950s, contains some provocative details about the religious traditions that surrounded Pynchon as he grew up. Siegel remembers Pynchon as a practicing Catholic and a rather conservative young man:

> Tom Pynchon was quiet and neat and did his homework faithfully. He went to Mass and confessed, though to what would be a mystery. He got $25 a week spending money and managed it perfectly, did not cut class and always got grades in the high 90s. He was disappointed not to have been pledged to a fraternity, but he lacked the crude sociability required for that. (84–85)

Pynchon's mother "had a lot of Irish in her and was a Catholic." Pynchon's father "was a Protestant," a member of "an old American family" in Massachusetts; one Pynchon was a prominent moderate during the witch trials, and another "appears in a not very attractive characterization" in Hawthorne's *The House of the Seven Gables* (Siegel 86–87). It does not seem far-fetched, therefore, to suggest that Pynchon combines his mother's Catholic tradition's attraction to symbols with his father's Calvinist tradition's tendency to expose those symbols' inadequacy and hollowness. In any case, I wish to argue that in his 1966 novel *The Crying of Lot 49*, Pynchon's imagination is distinctly religious and decidedly dialectical.

But if it is somewhat unusual to claim that Pynchon's imagination is religious and dialectical, it is hardly even necessary to argue that Pynchon is a postmodernist. Indeed, the massive *Gravity's Rainbow* has become such a classic English-language example of postmodernist ambiguity that for some English and American critics "postmodern" and "Pynchon-esque" are probably more or less synonymous. *The Crying of Lot 49*, like Pynchon's other works, seems to me obviously to exemplify the "endemic" uncertainty that for David Lodge constitutes postmodernist literature: its plot—about the search for what it seems cannot, by its very nature, be found—is a kind of metafictional presentation of the ambiguous activity of postmodern fiction-making and fiction-reading. Furthermore, although actually very carefully constructed (as most postmodernist literature is), the novel creates a sense of discontinuity and randomness rather than smooth connectedness, and with its parodic, ridiculously named characters and bizarre incidents, it demolishes the conventions of formal realism.

I should note, however, that some critics have resisted categorizing the novel as strictly postmodernist. Edward Mendelson, for instance, in a discussion of the book's dialectic between the sacred and the profane (to which I am indebted for my own analysis), differentiates "subjunctive" from "indicative" fiction and claims that *The Crying of Lot 49* is ultimately "indicative." "Subjunctive" fiction is Mendelson's term for postmodernist works "concerned with events that can occur only in language, with few or no analogues in the phenomenal world," while "indicative" fiction is his term for more traditional narrative works "that transmit, through . . . no matter how wide or narrow a focus, information about the emotional and physical world of nonliterary experience" (214). The works of Nabokov and Borges, Mendelson says, are truly subjunctive, works that radically resist affirming anything about any "real" world outside the texts, but Pynchon's *Lot 49* is comparatively quite empirical, concerned with telling a story about actual reality. Pynchon's novel, Mendelson says, "insists on its indicative relation to the world of experience" (214). Since for Mendelson "subjunctive" fiction is that "with few or no *analogues* to the phenomenal world" (emphasis added) while "indicative" fiction affirms such analogues, Mendelson seems to be doubly refuting my thesis about this novel; he seems to be suggesting that the book is empirical and analogical, while my position is that it is postmodern and dialectical. But Mendelson's analysis—which, in its entirety, is insightful and compelling—simply illustrates that such categories, including those that govern my own argument throughout this work, are an unscientific shorthand rather than an absolute. The novel's emphasis on the dichotomy of the sacred and the profane, which Mendelson wisely analyzes, reveals a deeply *dialectical* religious imagination. And Mendelson's assertion that the book is "indicative" rather than "subjunctive" does not fundamentally contradict my claim that it is postmodern but rather reminds us that postmodernist ambiguity is usually not just play for its own sake but is a profound reflection on contemporary existential experience.

Similarly, although in her discussion of the novel's metaphoricity N. Katherine Hayles seemingly rejects strict postmodernist readings of this novel, she does not, in the end, negate my own claim that *The Crying of Lot 49* exemplifies David Lodge's postmodernist "endemic" uncertainty. Hayles uses something like Mendelson's differentiation between subjunctive and indicative fiction (though she does not use those terms), suggesting that metaphors can be employed from a "strict constructivist position," which maintains that "whatever we can speak or know is always already a representation, not reality as such," or from an epistemologically realistic position that affirms "the possibility of literal speech, since metaphor is a concept constructed through its difference from literal signification" (97). Hayles asserts that *The Crying of Lot 49* is not strictly postmodernist, which she associates with the fully constructivist position, but rather that it exists in an uncertain tension between these poles: "The text cannot quite make up its mind whether its 'verbally graceful' metaphors can reach a reality beyond language, and more fundamentally, cannot resolve whether the endeavor to do so is insane or inspired, divine or demonic. . . . [I]t is never able to resolve whether its language play is a postmodern excursion into consensual constructions or a thrust through the theater curtain to a higher order of reality" (121–22).

But this radical uncertainty is precisely what, for me, firmly establishes the novel as a postmodernist text. The book's protagonist, Oedipa Maas, can never find what she is looking for, the elusive "Tristero" mail system. She is never even sure that there is a "what" out there to find. And the reader, as Lance Olsen points out in an essay relating modern science's Uncertainty Principle to this novel, is equally frustrated:

> Nor is Oedipa the only one reduced to such continual uncertainty. Because of the intrinsic positionlessness of the text, the reader too finds himself stumbling among the matrices of a great digital computer. . . . As the textual centers begin shifting, Truth dissolves, and as an opaque haze settles on the words, frustration mounts.
>
> The true effect of the last page is not to glide the reader out of the text with a sense of completion as in a myth, a romance, a high mimetic or many low mimetic works, but to cast him back into the book's intricacies. (161–62)

The Crying of Lot 49 is also a latently—and eventually even explicitly—religious text. Oedipa's groping for the truth about the Tristero becomes emblematic of a groping for Truth, for ultimate reality, itself. And Pynchon uses his postmodernist literary form to express not the analogical, sacramental immanence of ultimate reality but rather its distance, even its absence; human access to Truth, or even to truth, in this novel is always subverted, deferred. Indeed, the entire novel builds to the moment before a revelation—the moment before the seemingly pentecostal "crying of lot 49." The epiphany of the Ultimate is always not-yet, and the book embodies what Sallie McFague describes as "the iconoclastic tendency in Protestantism, what Paul Tillich calls the 'Protestant Principle,' the fear of idolatry, the concern lest the finite ever be imagined to be capable of the infinite" (*Metaphorical Theology* 13). Thomas Pynchon's *The Crying of Lot 49* is postmodernist fiction as an expression of the *dialectical* religious imagination.

The novel begins with the main character, Oedipa Maas, learning that she has become the executor of the estate of a recently deceased lover, Pierce Inverarity. The novel immediately indicates that this is a comic/sacred jarring loose of Oedipa from mundane ordinariness; she has just come from a Tupperware party in her very middle-class hometown, Kinneret, in Northern California. But now "Oedipa stood in the living room, stared at by the greenish dead eye of the TV tube, spoke the name of God, tried to feel as drunk as possible" (9–10). Martin Green argues that *The Crying of Lot 49* is Pynchon's *Heart of Darkness*—that Oedipa, like Marlow, is being drawn into a limit-dimension, that her journey through California "traverses a landscape filled with intimations and shadows of the darkness which is the underside of the bright and plastic landscape of America" (30), and that Pierce Inverarity is a kind of Kurtz:

> In a way, all the strands of imagery in *The Crying of Lot 49* lead to Pierce, just as all the strands of imagery in *Heart of Darkness* lead to Kurtz. Like Kurtz, Pierce seems to have been a devouring ego, trying to incorporate into himself "all the air, all the earth, all the men before him," as Marlow says of Kurtz. (35)

So Oedipa, in seeking the truth about Pierce and his estate, is, like Marlow, going to the limit. And, as in Marlow's hazy heart of darkness, Oedipa's revelations will always be not-quite—an experience of the religious as a dialectical awareness of the *absence*, within this world, of any divine, providential reality. In David Tracy's terms, Oedipa has intimations of the whole or the Ultimate not as *participating in* but as *distanced from* the secular California landscape through which she travels.

When, after leaving Kinneret, she approaches Pierce's Southern California home base (called "San Narciso," the patron saint, presumably, of self-enclosedness), she has an almost-epiphany that sets the tone for the dialectical not-quiteness that will mark all the revelations of ultimacy throughout the book. The houses and streets of San Narciso, seen from the road above, have the "unexpected, astonishing clarity" of a circuit card in a transistor radio. Yet she knows nothing about either Southern California or printed circuits, so this supposed "clarity" has no clear referent:

> [T]here were to both outward patterns a hieroglyphic sense of concealed meaning. . . . [I]n her first minute of San Narciso, a revelation . . . trembled just past the threshold of her understanding. Smog hung all round the horizon . . . ; she and the Chevy seemed parked at the centre of an odd, religious instant. As if, on some other frequency, or out of the eye of some whirlwind rotating too slow for her heated skin even to feel the centrifugal coolness of, words were being spoken. (24–25)

The veils and *not*-language in this passage could hardly be more insistent: meaning is "concealed," a revelation is "just past the threshold of her understanding," smog hangs all around, words are spoken on another frequency, and wind blows that she cannot feel. A few pages later, Oedipa again feels "some promise of hierophany" (31). Thus, her first visit to San Narciso sounds the theme of the novel—Oedipa is awaiting hierophany, revelation of the religious (which Tracy, as we have seen, defines as "what is sensed as the whole of reality" [*Analogical Imagination* 157–58]).

Edward Mendelson asserts that the movement of the novel is toward the fulfillment of this waiting: "This 'promise of hierophany,' of a manifestation of the sacred, is eventually fulfilled, and her 'sense of concealed meaning' yields to her recognition of patterns that had potentially been accessible to her all along, but which only now had revealed themselves" (190). With his strong sense of the gap between the sacred and the profane in this novel, Mendelson's reading is already rather dialectical. Yet I would go an additional dialectical step and state that Pynchon's imagination here is fully dialectical in that the "promise of hierophany" is never fulfilled in the novel; just as the postmodernist form defers narrative resolution, so Oedipa's awaited manifestation of the sacred, of the whole or the Ultimate, remains deferred, not-yet.

At first, of course, her expectation that this visit to San Narciso, merely a mundane trip to execute a dead man's will, will yield such a manifestation seems madly unfounded, which in itself casts doubt on the legitimacy of Oedipa's expectations of transcendent revelation. But quite soon hints begin to emerge that the Kurtz-like Pierce has drawn her into something bigger than just handling the legal details of an estate.

The vehicle for Pierce's not-quite-revelation to Oedipa is as mundane as it could be, a collection of stamps: "Much of the revelation was to come through the stamp collection Pierce had left, his substitute often for her—thousands of little colored windows into deep vistas of space and time" (44–45). In San Narciso, Oedipa is "sensitized" to experience this revelation (or almost, though not quite, to experience it) by a dialectical immersion in narcissistic secularity: she undergoes a "peculiar seduction" by the lawyer Metzger—who, according to Edward Mendelson, "seems to serve in the novel as the representative of the entirely profane" (196)—and then by "other, almost offhand things" (45). It is these "offhand" things that now begin to proliferate. Oedipa, in seedy and utterly secular, profane places, hears rumors of the overwhelmingly Other—"what she was to label the Tristero System or often only The Tristero (as if it might be something's secret title)" (44).

Newly "sensitized," Oedipa picks up slight traces of something that resists secular American culture. In a bar called the Scope, she learns of an alternate mail system used by a group of ultra-right-wingers as a way to resist the mainstream federal postal monopoly. And in the bar's rest room she encounters for the first time the symbol of the other alternate mail system that will become her obsession throughout the rest of the book: she sees a muted post horn, which is drawn beneath a notice that refers to a message-carrying system called "WASTE" (52). It will be many pages before she learns that "WASTE" stands for the apocalyptic-sounding "We Await Silent Tristero's Empire" (169), but already she thinks, "God, hieroglyphics" (52); both words, of course, link the Tristero, whether directly or parodically, with the religious themes of *God* and *revelation* ("hierophany"). As Mendelson says:

> The manifestations of the Trystero (an alternate spelling), and all that accompanies it, are always associated in the book with the language of the sacred and with patterns of religious experience. . . .

> To enter the Trystero, to become aware of it, is to cross the threshold between the profane and sacred worlds. (188, 205)

So Oedipa enters the Tristero, which begins to reveal itself, the narrator says, as a stripper slowly reveals her body:

> So began, for Oedipa, the languid, sinister blooming of The Tristero. Or, rather, her attendance at some unique performance, prolonged as if it were the last of the night, something a little extra for whoever'd stayed this late. As if the breakaway gowns, net bras, jeweled garters and G-strings of historical figuration that would fall away were layered dense. . . . (54)

But what is going to be behind these dense, veiling layers? The narrator is ambiguous. Perhaps it will only be a tease ("Would its smile, then, be coy, and would it flirt away harmlessly backstage . . . ?"), or perhaps it will cut through the mundane, secular world with prophetic "words she [Oedipa] never wanted to hear" (54). So far, at least, the Tristero remains at a radical dialectical distance from the human world, and Oedipa's access to it is problematic at best. Oedipa's search for the Tristero already seems likely to be doomed, and Oedipa seems likely to remain trapped in the San Narciso of self, just as, for dialectical theologian Karl Barth, human beings even when sincerely praying cannot escape self and experience a revelation of God:

> because even the most sincere, most heroic, most powerful prayers . . . do but serve to make clear how little the man of prayer is able to escape from what he himself has thought and experienced, how utterly he—yes, precisely he—is a man and no more, how completely the bravest leaps and the boldest bridge-building activities of so-called "piety" occur within the sphere of this world and have in themselves nothing whatever to do with the incomprehensible and unexperienced but living God. (316)

If *The Crying of Lot 49* exemplifies the dialectical imagination, as I think it does, it is highly unlikely that Oedipa will ever truly, in Edward Mendelson's terms, "enter the Trystero" by crossing "the threshold between the profane and sacred worlds" (205).

It is not surprising, then, that Oedipa hears the word "Trystero" itself only indirectly, during the performance of a play, rather than in any actual, literal context. She has been provoked to attend the play because she has heard that its plot echoes details of her own escalating quest. And although at the play she finally actually hears the secret word, "Trystero," this stripping is more tease than full unveiling. The revelation still remains deferred, not-yet, as Kurtz's revelation in *Heart of Darkness* is veiled and deferred by Marlow's circuitous way of telling a story—or, perhaps more accurately, only such a circuitous form of storytelling can mediate what Conrad and Pynchon seem to agree is the deferred nature of truth.

The play Oedipa attends is called *The Courier's Tragedy* (another reference to mail carrying), a rather conventionally melodramatic seventeenth-century drama about battles for power between heroes and villains of the Holy Roman Empire. But in act 4 a new, quite unconventional element enters the play, a suggestion of something unspeakable, something that cannot be dramatized but can only be pointed toward dialectically, by indirection, by saying what this something is *not* rather than what it is:

> It is at about this point in the play . . . that things really get peculiar, and a gentle chill, an ambiguity, begins to creep in among the words. Heretofore the naming of names has gone on either literally or as metaphor. But now . . . a new mode of expression takes over. It can only be called a kind of ritual reluctance. Certain things, it is made clear, will not be spoken aloud; certain events will not be shown onstage. (71)

This is a good description of the dialectical imagination: incapable of speaking literally and distrustful of metaphor, ritually reluctant to speak or to show. Such reluctance enters the play, for example, when the hero is attacked by figures in black and he cannot name his assassins but, as he dies, merely stutters "the shortest line ever written in blank verse: 'T-t-t-t-t . . .'" (73). And then, only once, the word "Trystero" is spoken, as the name not of a concrete entity but only of that which silences, renders "Tacit" the "gold once-knotted horn" (the post horn of the imperial Thurn and Taxis postal service—Trystero is that which *mutes* the *post horn*), yet is so powerful that no positive fate can save one from it: *"No hallowed skein of stars can ward, I trow, / Who's once been set his tryst with Trystero"* (75).

Ambiguous as this not-quite-revelation of Trystero is, however, it is then even further deferred, pushed back into the kind of foggy, subjective context of a story told by Conrad's Marlow. Oedipa goes backstage at the theater and visits the play's director, Randolph Driblette, and he demolishes any notion that the words of the play—especially, no doubt, that barely spoken word "Trystero"—have a referentiality outside his own mind: "You guys," he says, "you're like Puritans are about the Bible. So hung up with words, words. . . . The words, who cares? They're rote noises. . . . But the reality is in *this* head. Mine. I'm the projector at the planetarium, all the closed little universe visible in the circle of that stage is coming out of my mouth, eyes, sometimes other orifices also" (79). Without Driblette, the play's only truth would be the flattest historical facts that the author based his work on, and this past facticity is trivial and in any case unreachable: "Dead, mineral, without value or potential," says Driblette (80). But Trystero, although apparently far from trivial, is not even one of these historical fossils, now unreachable but once factual; it is precisely nothing.

Still, this nothing from nowhere continues to tantalize Oedipa. A visit to a senior-citizen home erected by Pierce Inverarity, for example, leads Oedipa to a chance meeting with an old former Pony Express rider named Mr Thoth. He shows

Oedipa a ring he cut many years ago from the finger of a marauder who attacked mail deliverers (muting postal communication, so to speak), and on the ring is engraved the Tristero symbol, the muted post horn. "My God," Oedipa says, and Mr Thoth answers, "I feel him [God], certain days. . . . I feel him close to me" (92–93). Maybe Mr Thoth feels God close, but this God—or Tristero or Trystero or whatever—remains for Oedipa as mysterious and transcendent as ever. It is true that details such as Mr Thoth's ring keep circling around this empty center, keep repeating, pointing Oedipa toward some heart of darkness. But these little traces or grace notes are repetitions for which the original is beyond access, as an actual, ecstatic seizure is beyond the access of an epileptic's memory, with the epileptic consciously remembering only the unecstatic "secular announcement" (what David Tracy might call the "limit to" the seizure): "She could, at this stage of things, recognize signals like that, as the epileptic is said to—an odor, color, pure piercing grace note announcing his seizure. Afterward it is only this signal, really dross, this secular announcement, and never what is revealed during the attack, that he remembers" (95). This is exactly how the sacred is experienced by fallen human nature, according to Luther, Barth, and other dialectical theologians: it is that which is *not* the secular depravity in which the human person is immersed. Like the Catholic tradition in which he grew up, Pynchon is using items from the mundane world as symbols that point toward the transcendent; so far, however, rather than sacramentally manifesting the presence of an ultimate reality, Pynchon's "grace notes" underline its absence.

But the trail of these secular grace notes eventually brings Oedipa to Berkeley, California, where she encounters what may be the central image or symbol or metaphor (or grace note) in the novel: the Nefastis machine. The crazy inventor John Nefastis—who, Oedipa discovers later, communicates via the Tristero system (131)—has developed a machine that he believes can drive a piston without any expenditure of energy. And at first it appears that Oedipa has finally found an object that truly is sacramental and analogical: the machine brings into the material world a principle that seems spiritual, a principle of life and energy and resurrection not as other and unreachable but as present and available.

Specifically, Nefastis's machine is concerned with entropy, which in lay terms is *disorder*; a good image of entropy is the shuffling of an initially sorted deck of cards. As N. Katherine Hayles explains: "Thermodynamic entropy is a measure of the amount of heat lost for useful purposes in a heat exchange. The second law of thermodynamics states that in a closed system, entropy always tends to increase. This means, in effect, that the universe is constantly running down (assuming it is a closed system)" (110). In other words, the material process is a continual shuffling of the physical universe's cards, which thermodynamically means that the world is inexorably dying: "Thermodynamic entropy, then, is akin to the dissipating processes in *The Crying of Lot 49*, pointing toward an attenuation whose end point is the cessation of life" (Hayles 110). But using a thought experiment of the actual nineteenth-century physicist John Maxwell, Nefastis tries to reverse this process—to bring heat from cold, life from death. "Communication is the key," says Nefastis (105). Nefastis's machine is a box in which, he claims, there is a Demon that collects data on all the gas molecules in the box and conveys this huge amount of information to a psychically gifted observer (a "sensitive"), who feeds the information back to the Demon. This flow of information between Demon and sensitive allows the Demon to reverse thermodynamic entropy—to unshuffle hot (fast-moving) and cold (slow-moving) molecules, and then to direct hot molecules into a separate compartment in the machine until enough are there to push the piston.

This is, of course, a ridiculous invention, but it is a marvelous metaphor for the intersection of the sacred (life, resurrection, psychic communion) and the secular (molecules and a piston). "On the secular level," Nefastis says, "all we can see is one piston, hopefully moving" (105–6). But at "some deep psychic level"—the level of the sacred—the Demon (a transcendent power) has managed to "get through" to a human person (105).

What Pynchon is doing here is playing the theories of thermodynamic and informational entropy off each other. Citing Claude Shannon, "the father of modern information theory" (111), Hayles summarizes the relevance of entropy to information theory:

> In Shannon's view, systems rich in entropy are not simply poor in order; rather, they are rich in information. The key is to think of disorder as maximum information. So influential has this view become that in contemporary irreversible thermodynamics, entropy is seen as an engine driving systems toward increasing complexity rather than dissolution. In cosmology, it has recently been used to construct a model of the universe that does not end in heat death, because entropy bestows upon it the capacity to renew itself. (111–12)

Entropy is a good metaphor for the postmodernist vision itself—literature in which the cards, so to speak, are increasingly shuffled, endemically uncertain. And Nefastis's machine seems to be Pynchon's way of meditating on the possibility that this chaos is more richly alive than any neoclassically ordered structure could ever be. A sorted deck of cards is clear and easy to memorize, but it is not very interesting. Shuffled decks, however, have innumerable, uncertain, imaginatively fascinating webs of interconnections from card to card and from individual card to the whole. So Nefastis's machine reverses thermodynamic entropy (heat loss) by actually *increasing* informational entropy—generating a huge, complex information flow between "Demon" and "sensitive."

Such a vision of chaos as something rich in vital complexity allies Pynchon with science's own postmodern "chaos theory," which Hayles is alluding to in her description of a new cosmology that sees entropy as a principle not of dissolution but of renewal. Physicist/theologian John Polkinghorne describes chaos theory as "a 'third revolution' in physics, comparable to the discoveries of Newtonian mechanics and quantum theory" (196). According to this theory, says Polkinghorne, "[p]hysical systems . . . often display such an exquisite sensitivity to their detailed circumstance that their behaviour becomes intrinsically unpredictable" (196). The universe envisioned by chaos theory, Polkinghorne argues, is a leap away from positivistic science's soulless machine; rather, chaos theory suggests that "actual physical reality is subtle and supple in its character; that physical process is open to the future. We live in a world of true becoming" (25). For Polkinghorne—and, I suggest, for Pynchon—chaos lives and breathes; Oedipa Maas, having left the predictable American suburbs and stumbled into postmodern, unpredictable, chaotic Pynchonland, has entered a sacred (or almost-sacred) space.[5]

This is, in fact, Edward Mendelson's argument: Oedipa, he claims, leaves the secular and enters the sacred. Mendelson correctly notes the deep religious undercurrents of Pynchon's fiction, but I think he makes the space of Pynchon's novel sound more fully sacramental than it is, and he makes the revelation sought by Oedipa sound sacramentally and analogically available within the images and metaphors that surround her. The fact is, as Hayles points out about Nefastis's invention, "of course the machine doesn't work" (113). The Nefastis machine, like the other "grace notes," is more *un*-sacrament than sacrament. Nor, I think, do the other revelations come. Rather than being given an analogical manifestation of— of what? (the fact that I am unable to say what is to be manifested shows how dialectical this vision is)—Oedipa is left just with a number of alternatives for which there is no basis to adjudicate in this fallen, benighted world:

> Now here was Oedipa, faced with a metaphor of God knew how many parts; more than two, anyway. With coincidences blossoming these days wherever she looked, she had nothing but a sound, a word, Trystero, to hold them together. . . .
> Either Trystero did exist, in its own right, or it was being presumed, perhaps fantasied by Oedipa, so hung up on and interpenetrated with the dead man's estate. (109)

Later in the novel Oedipa more thoroughly thinks through the dialectically incompatible, but all equally possible, alternatives. Perhaps the Tristero is a truly sacred, mystical alternative to the "spiritual poverty" that people experience in their secular lives (represented by the world of conventional communication, the U.S. postal system), but perhaps it is not:

---

5 It seems appropriate that Pynchon has become a darling of cyberspace. The Tristero—a vast, unregulated communication network, a chaos teeming with information—is a kind of foreshadowing of the Internet (which of course did not exist in 1966, when *The Crying of Lot 49* was published).

Either you have stumbled indeed . . . onto a secret richness and concealed density of dream; onto a network by which X number of Americans are truly communicating whilst reserving their lies, recitations of routine, arid betrayals of spiritual poverty, for the official government delivery system; maybe even onto a real alternative to the exitlessness, to the absence of surprise to life, that harrows the head of everybody American you know, and you too, sweetie. Or you are hallucinating it. Or a plot has been mounted against you, so expensive and elaborate, involving items like the forging of stamps and ancient books, constant surveillance of your movements, planting of post horn images all over San Francisco. . . . Or you are fantasying some such plot, in which case you are a nut, Oedipa, out of your skull. (170–71)

Faced with these alternatives, Oedipa becomes painfully conscious of the dialectical limit to her human ability to know. Far from receiving a revelation, a sacramental experience that breaks into the here and now, she encounters only the human limit itself: "For this, oh God, was the void. There was nobody who could help her. Nobody in the world" (171).

This is not to say that Oedipa receives no glimpses at all of a graciousness beyond the void; the sacred revelations that John Mendelson traces throughout the novel are there—almost. There is a sacramental as well as dialectical thread in this novel—almost. For example, with great postmodern playfulness Pynchon has Oedipa, wandering through San Francisco, run into a man named, of all things, Jesús Arrabal, who apparently uses the Tristero system of communication. Arrabal is an anarchist, hence a friend of *chaos*, and he seems to indicate that chaos can indeed usher in not death but life. Oedipa remembers that years ago, when she met him in Mazatlán, Arrabal talked about the miraculous (sacramental?) manifestation of the transcendent within the immanent: "You know what a miracle is? . . . another world's intrusion into this one" (120). And now, meeting him again, she sees he carries a newspaper (stamped with the Tristero muted post horn) with the Easter-like title "*Regeneración*" (121).

An even more striking manifestation of present graciousness occurs in Oedipa's encounter shortly afterward with a drunken sailor, tattooed with the muted post horn, who wants to find a Tristero mailbox in which to post a letter to his wife. When Oedipa tells the sailor she does not know where to find such a mailbox, he makes the very hopeful claim, "Always one. You'll see it" (125). And then, in the novel's most genuinely tender moment—all the more tender for appearing in this otherwise tough, funny, sharply satirical novel—Oedipa embraces the poor sailor: "Exhausted, hardly knowing what she was doing, she came the last three steps and sat, took the man in her arms, actually held him, gazing out of her smudged eyes down the stairs, back into the morning. She felt wetness against her breast and saw that he was crying again" (126).

Realizing that the sailor suffers from DTs, Oedipa thinks about the fact of his inevitable death, and about all the unique and amazing information stored in his brain that will be forever lost—no longer accessible even to Nefastis's

Demon. This leads Oedipa to spin a metaphor based on her memory of freshman calculus—"DTs" are also "dt": "'dt,' God help this old tattooed man, meant also a time differential, a vanishingly small instant in which change had to be confronted at last for what it was, where it could no longer disguise itself as something in-nocuous like an average rate; . . . where death dwelled in the cell though the cell be looked in on at its most quick" (129). Her playful metaphor, therefore, has given Oedipa access to a deep truth, and she comes to an understanding of metaphor that is deeply relevant to the two kinds of literary imagination I have been discussing throughout these pages:

> Behind the initials [DT] was a metaphor, a delirium tremens, a trembling unfurrow-ing of the mind's plowshare. . . . [A]ll act in the same special relevance to the word, or whatever it is the word is there, buffering, to protect us from. The act of metaphor then was a thrust at truth and a lie, depending where you were: inside, safe, or out-side, lost. (128–29)

Oedipa has inferred the two attitudes toward metaphorical images that, as I suggested in my first chapter, distinguish the analogical from the dialectical imagi-nation. The analogical imagination—while honestly acknowledging metapho-ricity—feels itself sufficiently *inside* truth to affirm the proportionate, analogical relationship between things, the carrying-between (*meta-pherein*) of meaning, that constitutes a metaphor. The dialectical imagination, hyper-aware that humans are *outside* ultimate reality, stares sternly at the limitations of metaphorical language and image, and it drives wedges between human images and truth or limit. This imagination immerses itself in the secular/profane, spinning connective metaphors in order to expose their falsity.

Surrounded by the potentially enlivening chaos of the Tristero, encountering the possibly miraculous Nefastis machine, embracing a drunken sailor, and spin-ning a wise and compassionate metaphor, Oedipa seems to be making an ana-logical "thrust at truth"; this is what to a different degree both Edward Mendelson and N. Katherine Hayles assert. But Pynchon's novel as a whole works much more emphatically to undermine that "thrust," to stress the "lie" of the metaphor and to leave Oedipa "outside, lost." I hope I have demonstrated that negative, skepti-cal emphasis throughout my analysis of Pynchon's novel, and I suggest that the book's unresolved, endemically uncertain postmodernist ending strongly reaffirms this dialectical orientation.

As the novel approaches its conclusion, Oedipa learns from Genghis Cohen, the philatelist who has been going over Pierce Inverarity's stamp collection, that this collection is about to be auctioned off and that the "Tristero 'forgeries'" (those stamps containing subtle symbols of the Tristero system) are to be sold "as lot 49" (175). Oedipa reflects yet again on the dialectical alternatives that her journey to Inverarity's heart of darkness has led her to see. If Tristero is Inverarity's hoax to make Oedipa paranoid, so Inverarity can possess Oedipa's mind even after his death, then the only reality is deeply profane: Inverarity's acquisitive possessiveness ("his need to possess, to alter the land, to bring new skylines, personal antagonisms, growth rates into being" [178]). But if Tristero is real, then there is an actual, sacred underground of American exiles in communication, community, with each other: "Suppose, God, there really was a Tristero then and that she *had* come on it by accident. . . . Were the squatters there [by old Pullman cars] in touch with others, through Tristero: were they helping carry forward that 300 years of the house's disinheritance?" (179–80). Thus, either the Tristero sign has a signified or it does not:

> Behind the hieroglyphic streets there would either be a transcendent meaning, or only the earth. . . . Another mode of meaning behind the obvious, or none. Either Oedipa in the orbiting ecstasy of a true paranoia, or a real Tristero. For there either was some Tristero beyond the appearance of the legacy America, or there was just America. (181–82)

Either way, the only way Oedipa can now be an American is as an alien—alone, set apart, thrown back into her own powerless humanity by a profound experience of limit. Yes, there is hope: when "lot 49" is auctioned, when the auctioneer calls out ("cries") lot 49, perhaps the bidder will be an unequivocal representative of the Tristero, a fully present manifestation of this mystical otherness. In David Tracy's terms, the dialectical not-yet will transform into the sacramental always-already.

But of course, the postmodern and dialectical Pynchon will not satisfy such a desire for presence. The book ends, quite precisely, with a not-yet: "Passerine [the auctioneer] spread his arms in a gesture that seemed to belong to the priesthood of some remote culture; perhaps to a descending angel. The auctioneer cleared his throat. Oedipa settled back, to await the crying of lot 49" (183). Mendelson explains that the moment following the crying of lot 49 may be epiphanic, pentecostal, a manifestation of the Ultimate, but he acknowledges that this Pentecost is deferred, that Pynchon withholds the epiphany. Mendelson's analysis here— which, I think, contradicts his earlier claim that the "'promise of hierophany,' of a manifestation of the sacred, is eventually fulfilled" (189)—seems to me very insightful and accurate:

> [T]he word Pentecost derives from the Greek for "fiftieth." The crying—the auctioneer's calling—of the forty-ninth lot is the moment before a Pentecostal revelation, the end of the period in which the miracle is in a state of potential, not yet manifest. This is why the novel ends with Oedipa waiting, with the "true" nature of the Trystero never established: a manifestation of the sacred can only be believed in; it can never be proved beyond doubt. (208–9)

This is a fairly exact description of the dialectical imagination's relation with ultimacy. For this imagination, the Ultimate is not manifested, analogically, in the always-already here and now; it is only proclaimed, dialectically, as that which is not-yet. The Tristero, the creative chaos envisioned by Nefastis, the drunken sailor, and other images do point toward that aspect of experience which Tracy defines as ultimate or "religious": "a dimension whose first key is its reality as limit-to our other everyday, moral, scientific, cultural, and political activities; a dimension which, in my own brief and hazy glimpses, discloses a reality, however named and in whatever manner experienced, which functions as a final, now gracious, now frightening, now trustworthy, now absurd, always uncontrollable limit-of the very meaning of existence itself" (*Rage* 108). But Thomas Pynchon has used what David Lodge calls the "endemic uncertainty" of the postmodern form to undo his images of this ultimate reality, and hence to suggest a deeply dialectical relation between the human world and the Ultimate or the whole.

An Analogical Imagination in a Postmodern Narrative

D. M. Thomas's *The White Hotel* is a textbook example of postmodernism. I have found that this novel, a best-seller when first published in 1981, is a good introduction to postmodernism for undergraduate students; after puzzling, infuriating, and in some cases offending readers, its unfolding layers seduce them into accepting that a story can be told and a character presented in a very disconnected way with radically disparate perspectives.

Comparing the novel to a Chinese box, Benzi Zhang asserts that its incompatible perspectives, its "re-re-visionism" (55), accomplish the postmodernist goal of revealing the "ineluctable fictivity of all versions/visions" (54). Zhang carefully distinguishes Thomas's postmodernist multiplied perspectives from the kind of modernist perspectivism of a Henry James: "[I]n Thomas's multi-vision novel, we discover that our eyes can deceive us, and that things do look different to different people. Through the rendering of numerous contradictory perspectives, the traditional Jamesian 'point of view,' as a facet of a text, becomes only an inescapable avoidance in Thomas's novel. . . . It becomes, in short, a view with no point" (57). It is not that Thomas just spins around an emptiness, writing about writing about writing; in Pynchon's terms, he does make "a thrust at truth." But for all its thrusts at reality—even the stark historical reality of the Holocaust—the novel, Zhang says, retains a postmodern decenteredness: "[O]utside all the vantage points of all the individual visions, there may be a constantly and asymptotically approachable framework of reality; but we cannot always see it directly—perhaps never" (57). In other words, the novel's uncertainties are, in David Lodge's words, "endemic."

The book's thrust at truth does lead some critics to assert that *The White Hotel* is not postmodern at all but is quite traditional. Richard Cross, in a fine analysis of Thomas's serious consideration of spiritual issues and even of life after death, argues that the novel is at core traditionally mimetic—that its shifting viewpoints are "not at all at odds with the representation of life" (22). Cross's analysis is quite

canny; nonetheless, the fact that Thomas is interested in real issues, including religious ones, does not in itself mean that he has not created a postmodernist text.
The fragmented design does not preclude a consideration of some external "reality." The book's design merely emphasizes that any experience of such reality—
historical, psychological, ultimate—is embedded in a context. The book's "construction," Mary Robertson says, "foregrounds the forms themselves and emphasizes the gaps, as if to say that there are many ways of 'writing' the reality of
a person, none more or less authentic, and that the reality of a person is always
'written,' that is, mediated by an arbitrary discourse" (461). Postmodernist form,
whether radically skeptical or open to some kind of faith, keeps in the foreground
the insight that for humans knowledge is always mediated: the in-itself, the center,
is always deferred, experienced and expressed not directly but through language
and symbol and metaphor. In this sense *The White Hotel*, for all its thrusts at
rounded psychological portraiture, at historical analysis of the Holocaust, and at
metaphysical speculation, is decidedly postmodern. By resisting any single discourse's attempt to totalize, the novel participates in postmodernism's celebration
of the plural rather than the univocal. This is precisely what Cross refers to when
he speaks of the "campaign" Thomas is waging "against the excesses of rationalism in our own day," and although Cross links this campaign with "the Ro-
mantics" and "the High Modernists" (such as Joyce), Thomas's decentered style
links him just as firmly with the postmodernists.

Such systematic resistance to totalization and excessive rationalism sounds a
bit like the resistance to a too-easy "contentment with the ordinary discourse on
rationality and the self" that, for David Tracy, links postmodernism with the great
religions (*Plurality and Ambiguity* 84). But it sounds even more like Paul Tillich's
"Protestant Principle," "the divine and human protest against any absolute claim
made for a relative reality" (*Protestant Era* 163). This principle, however, is
linked with the dialectical, not analogical, imagination. It may seem that D. M.
Thomas, whatever serious and sincere religious vision he may be conveying in
The White Hotel, imagines ultimate reality in a *dialectical* way: as that which
cannot be mediated through human symbol and metaphor, as that which is radically different from the fallen human world. Certainly in his graphic picture of
Nazi atrocities in the fifth section of his novel, Thomas portrays the *limit to* any
notion of human achievement and goodness. Considering this grim negativity and
the postmodern perspectival skepticism of the novel's structure, it may seem impossible to argue that Thomas presents a vision congruent with Andrew Greeley's
thumbnail description of the analogical imagination, which Greeley claims is
founded on an intuition that "[t]he world and all its events, objects, and people
tend to be somewhat like God" (*Catholic Myth* 45).

But this is exactly what I intend to argue. Yes, *The White Hotel*, with its perspectival skepticism and its vision of human depravity, contains a strong

dialectical kernel; this kernel, though, is part of (to pursue an awkward and perhaps silly metaphor) an ultimately analogical nut. David Tracy says that the
analogical imagination, if it is not to become fluffy and naive, needs to maintain
such a dialectical edge—the kind of edge that, as we saw, Joyce, Dubus, and Tyler
also maintain. As we have seen, Tracy asserts that without "that sense for the
negative, that dialectical sense within analogy itself," the analogical imagination
produces "the theological equivalent of 'cheap grace'" (*Analogical Imagination*
413). In the midst of the multiple perspectives, however, and in the face of a profound experience of the limit-to, an encounter with outright evil, *The White Hotel*
conveys a sense of David Tracy's gracious limit-of, a nurturing *being* that is
always already sacramentally present rather than just prophetically announced as
the not-yet. This analogically manifested graciousness is most obviously conveyed in the novel's final section, "The Camp," in which Thomas paints a playful
yet serious portrait of an afterlife and hence (within his postmodern design) suggests that this reality or possibility is as legitimately a part of the web of human
perspectives as any other.

But more important, Thomas's play of postmodernist perspectives is itself opti-
mistically analogical, for all its inherent skepticism. Thomas's dismantling of
mechanical chronological causality, represented in the novel's depiction of Freud
and Freudian theory, indicates that the possibility of future *wholeness*—as well,
granted, as the fact that physical existence has a beginning and an end—is always
already sacramentally present and active in the here and now. Indeed, the novel's
key image is of such a sacramental realization: at a crucial moment in the novel,
and again at the very end, protagonist Lisa Erdman realizes that a kind of analogy
of being flows through her life and gives it continuity. Although she has felt herself
to be fractured and even crushed (as we have found her, too, due to the book's
fragmented form and devastating content), an underlying being gives her life in-
tegrity. And this revelation is mediated, analogically and sacramentally, by the
very mundane sensory experience of a pine tree:

> [S]uddenly, as she stood close against a pine tree and breathed in its sharp, bitter
> scent, a clear space opened to her childhood, as though a wind had sprung up from
> the sea, clearing a mist. It was not a memory from the past but the past itself, as alive,
> as real; and she knew that she and the child of forty years ago were the same person.
>   That knowledge flooded her with happiness. But immediately came another in-
> sight, bringing almost unbearable joy. For as she looked back through the clear space
> to her childhood, there was no blank wall, only an endless extent, like an avenue, in
> which she was still herself, Lisa. She was still there, even at the beginning of all
> things. And when she looked in the opposite direction, towards the unknown future,
> death, the endless extent beyond death, she was still there. It all came from the scent
> of a pine tree. (252)

The novel's centerless leaps of perspective resist being pinned down to any one
propositional framework of causality or explanation, and Thomas uses this post-

modernist technique not to defer a glimpse of ultimate reality but rather to defer reductive explanations of proximate reality so that the Ultimate can be manifest. As Ellen Siegelman puts it, "Thomas is averring that we are more than what psychologists tell us we are, that any discipline or point of view that attempts to define the psyche is bound to be reductionistic. . . . 'Both/and' appears to be the motto rather than 'either/or'" (76). Hence, in *The White Hotel* D. M. Thomas uses postmodernist strategies to convey a vision of the world that is *both* mundane *and* holy—in which analogical, sacramental glimpses of the unnameable Ultimate gleam through the ordinary.

The book's prologue and first three sections, roughly half the novel, are written in forms of discourse that are very dissimilar to each other: a series of letters from, to, and about Sigmund Freud, with some reference to Carl Jung as well ("Prologue"); a surreal and perhaps obscene poem (section 1, "Don Giovanni"); a surreal and perhaps obscene narrative (section 2, "The Gastein Journal"); and a fictional case study, supposedly written by Freud himself (section 3, "Frau Anna G."). These texts seem to exist independently from each other; it is not until late in the third section that we realize that sections 1 and 2 have supposedly been composed by the mentally ill woman—with the pseudonym "Anna G."—whose case Freud is presenting. And yet, for all the disruption, there does seem to be an underlying structure: the structure of repetition itself. The multiple discourses are linked in that they convey the same images and narrative motifs over and over again: a train, a white lakeside hotel that eventually goes up in flames, an emerald lake, snow-capped mountains, drowning people, falling stars, breasts gushing milk, severed breasts and removed uteruses, a black cat, a pine tree, an avalanche that buries people alive, music, a proliferation of sexual detail that combines intense pain and pleasure ("The plum who marries / an ox," reads a haiku poem repeated in various forms throughout the book, "can anticipate / great sorrow, great joy" [86]).

In his book *Fiction and Repetition*, J. Hillis Miller—borrowing from Gilles Deleuze—describes two forms of repetition, one straightforward and mimetic and the other postmodern. Miller describes the mimetic form of repetition in this way:

> What Deleuze calls "Platonic" repetition is grounded in a solid archetypal model which is untouched by the effects of repetition. All the other examples are copies of this model. The assumption of such a world gives rise to the notion of a metaphoric expression based on a genuine participative similarity or even on identity. . . . This is, so it seems, the reigning presupposition of realistic fiction and of its critics in nineteenth- and even in twentieth-century England. (6)

On the other hand, the kind of repetition that I am calling "postmodern" is, Miller says, a Nietzschean mode in which resemblance to one fixed prototype is replaced by a play of difference without any absolute, authoritative center:

> The other, Nietzschean mode of repetition posits a world based on difference. Each thing, this other theory would assume, is unique, intrinsically different from every

other thing. Similarity arises against the background of this "disparité du fond." . . .
It seems that X repeats Y, but in fact it does not, or at least not in the firmly anchored
way of the first sort of repetition. (6)

Although for Miller the "Platonic" mode of repetition is the more clearly Christian mode, while the "Nietzschean" mode is radically skeptical, I would suggest that in *The White Hotel* Thomas uses a Nietzschean mode of repetition to upend not Christianity but rather Freudian reductionism, in order precisely to mediate a sense (albeit hypothetical, experienced but not dogmatized) of religious presence.

The book's third section, Freud's case study ("Frau Anna G."), is Freud's attempt to articulate the center, the clear and authoritative source, of the repeated images that swirl around his patient. The woman whom he calls Anna G. has come into his office with intense pain in her left breast and ovary and a tendency to hallucinate while engaging in sexual intercourse. As she brings to Freud the experiences and feelings of her past—memories imbued with the motifs that are scattered repetitiously through her fantasies—it is up to Freud to cure Anna by definitively naming the source, in Miller's terms the Platonic archetype, of the motifs dominating Anna's fantasies.

Freud accomplishes this in two ways—personally and generally. At the individual, personal level, Freud authoritatively diagnoses Anna's illness: she is homosexual, in love with her teacher and mentor (whom Freud calls "Madame R") and unable fully to repress this fact. The repressed truth keeps reemerging, repeating, in a variety of fantasy images and most painfully in the hysterical illness itself, which, says Freud, symbolizes "her unconscious hatred of her distorted femininity; . . . total self-hatred, a wish to vanish from the earth" (164). In other words, Freud asserts that all the repetitions point back to the unbearable truth of Anna's homosexuality. But then Freud introduces a more general theory about the mechanism of repetition itself, which is quite literally reductive; he claims that psychological repetition reflects a person's drive to be reduced back to an inanimate state: "Was there not a 'demon' of repetition in our lives, and must it not stem from our human instincts being profoundly conservative? Might it not therefore be that all living things are in mourning for the inorganic state, the original condition from which they have by accident emerged?" (150).

Already, however, there is some contradiction between Freud's two explanations; there is a difference or gap. The first explanation, that Anna is masking her own homosexuality, is very particular and personal; the second, that humans repeat because they crave the inorganic state, is downright metaphysical. And the novel as a whole poses a third possibility: that the woman has been experiencing these repetitions, including repetitious psychosomatic pains, not because of past personal events or because of a universal longing for pre-womb oblivion but because she has an uncanny ability to foresee the future. She is going to be murdered by the Nazis in a brutal way that includes being kicked by a jackboot in the left breast, raped with a bayonet, and then buried alive (293–94). If this final event in the woman's life is what her pains all along have prefigured, the novel is suggesting an alternative to *both* of Freud's interpretations and thus exposing the inadequacy of such definitive proclamations. In place of Freudian theory the book implicitly offers another system of discourse, which is not directly used in the novel (although it is hinted at in the letters of the prologue): Carl Jung's religious and metaphysical revision of Freudian psychoanalysis.

This is essentially Rowland Wymer's thesis about the novel. Wymer states: "The radical interpretive reorientation which takes place in *The White Hotel*, whereby the significance of symptoms points forward into the future as well as backward into the past, strongly favors a Jungian rather than a Freudian perspective" (62). For one thing, Jung (unlike Freud) would have seriously entertained the possibility that this woman has been foreseeing the future; as Wymer points out, Jung describes similar premonitions in his autobiography, *Memories, Dreams, Reflections:*

> [Jung] himself had visions of destruction in late 1913 and early 1914 which he at first interpreted as manifestations of a personal psychic disturbance but later saw as premonitions of the coming world war. Jung also accepted the validity of more precisely precognitive experiences, such as the pains in Lisa's left breast and ovary, and gives several examples of his own in which he foresaw the deaths of friends. (62)

But the issue goes beyond precognition itself; the woman's foreknowledge acts as a kind of trope for an orientation toward the future rather than toward the past, which the woman—whom we finally know to be named Lisa Erdman, a moderately successful opera singer—describes to Freud: "*Frankly I didn't always wish to talk about the past; I was more interested in what was happening to me then, and what might happen in the future*" (226). It is this, really, that is the Jungian revision of Freud that the novel suggests. As Wymer puts it, "In a Freudian analysis the past *is* the problem and hence the chief topic of investigation. In a Jungian analysis it is the present maladjustment of the patient and the prospects for a better adaptation which are more strongly emphasized" (62).

This is not to say that Thomas disposes of Freud once and for all, simply replacing him with Jung; such a strategy would itself constitute proposing an authoritative "Platonic" center to the repetitions, and my contention is that the book's postmodernist balancing act allows no such absolute solution to its ambiguities. Rather, the book offers a both/and, an affirmation of both Freud and Jung.[6] Freud

---

6 In his autobiography, similarly, Thomas imagines such a complementary, playful relationship between Freud (whom he considers "the greater poet," presumably because of the narrative brilliance of his case studies) and Jung, a both/and rather than an either/or: "Jung and especially Freud mingled with Pushkin in my imagination. . . . Jung could make cupboards bang and knives break; but Freud was the greater poet, it seemed to me. Avoiding an expected rendezvous, they passed one another in

is "right," in that by guiding Lisa through her own past he does relieve her pain and help her cope with her troubled life. But Jung is "right" as well, in that all along Lisa has been pointing toward the future, even a future existence beyond death—which Jung, very much unlike Freud, considered a serious possibility. What we have here, in other words, is a combination of postmodernist ambiguity and analogical imagining: endemic uncertainty eliminates all univocal reductions, allowing present mundaneness possibly to be a mirror of the multiplicitous mysteries of ultimate reality. The postmodern multiplicity ends up, in David Cowart's words, reproducing "at once the world of phenomenal appearances and the complex realities they veil: realities of history, realities of consciousness, and realities of spirit" (226). This both/and—or, rather, and/and/and—is an assertion that these various levels of reality, though irreducibly mysterious, are proportionate (*analogos*) to each other. The postmodern technique has, after all, retrieved—albeit in a playful and uncertain way—something like the medieval analogy of being that links the symbolic layers of Dante's *Divine Comedy*.

In the fourth section of the novel ("The Health Resort"), immediately after the fictionalized Freud's case study, we finally encounter the protagonist more or less directly, through straightforward third-person prose. It is only here that we learn the woman's actual name: "In the spring of 1929, Frau Elisabeth Erdman was travelling by train between Vienna and Milan" (171). This more formally realistic discourse, however, does not have absolute authority; it exists in playful postmodernist tension with the other discourses of the novel, both those that precede and those that follow.

One of the effects of the more straightforward narrative section is to qualify the certainty of the Freud case study. Indeed, this fourth section of the novel contains a letter that Lisa writes to Freud in which Lisa specifically lists the lies and half-truths she told Freud during her psychoanalysis with him. She lied about when she wrote the erotic verses on which Freud based some of his conclusions; she suppressed the fact of having observed her mother, aunt, and uncle having three-way sex, including anal sex, and she falsely ascribed the anal sex to a lover she had as a very young woman; and she failed to tell Freud that her first husband—with whom sex was painful and traumatic—was a rabid anti-Semite. Lisa's father was Jewish, and Lisa now confesses that she failed, throughout her psychoanalysis, to admit how painful her Jewishness has been to her; she was viciously molested by a group of sailors for being "*a dirty Jewess*" (221), and she blamed her father for making her a Jew. Lisa's correction of these lies, or bits of misinformation,

---

non-existent trains" (*Memories and Hallucinations* 23). Then Thomas quotes from a poem he wrote about Freud, Jung, and "a young woman . . . who would become Frau Anna": "Freud dined sombrely with the faithful Binswanger, / And pleaded a headache; Jung worked late. Owls hooted. / In their uneasy sleep the two exchanged their dreams" (*Memories and Hallucinations* 23).

strongly undermines Freud's analysis of her problems and prepares us for the book's shift from sexual to political themes. And Lisa's corrective letter stands as a reminder that everything in this book is a lie, a fiction; each section of the novel reshuffles the repeating motifs in a different, but never definitive, way. This is the dialectical aspect of Thomas's book: a postmodernist representation of the inadequacy of all linguistic statements. The book is a palimpsest of fictions; certainly Lisa's wild and erotic poem and "journal" are fictive, but so is the Freudian case study, with its falsification of Lisa's identity (in the case study she is not Lisa Erdman the opera singer but Anna G. the cellist), its faulty information (the "lies" she confesses to in her letter), and its wrongheadedly dogmatic theories about the causes of Lisa's illness. Even Lisa's own correspondence in this fourth section is based on fictions. When she writes to Freud, she foolishly imagines a reburgeoning relationship, which can never occur. Furthermore, she writes her key letter—to Victor Berenstein, accepting his proposal of marriage—in the form of a poem, an operatic aria, rather than in any kind of straightforward, factual way.

But if everything through the first four sections of the novel is relativized, exposed as fiction, the fifth section ("The Sleeping Carriage") is a harsh presentation of what Tracy would call a limit-dimension that slams us into the limits of fictiveness itself. This is the chapter in which we learn what Lisa has been painfully foreseeing all along—that she will die after being brutally raped and buried alive by Nazis at Babi Yar in Ukraine. Finally, it seems, in the face of all the play of lying, the novel presents reality itself, violent and terrible. Mary Robertson claims that the depiction of the massacre of Jews at Babi Yar definitively drives out the psychoanalytic theory of the previous sections of the novel: "The rhetorical force of that chapter," she says, "is greater than that of the rest of the novel put together" (460), and "the book seems to swerve into an argument for the weightiness of the documentary discourse" (462). The chapter is fierce and jarring, and its depiction of the death of Lisa and her stepson Kolya at the Babi Yar massacre, narrated in flat and straightforward prose, has the horrific impact of a documentary film on the Holocaust. This section of the novel does for a while seem to supersede all that came before it.

It would, however, be as reductive to say that the book settles, absolutely, on this as a final viewpoint as it would be reductive to endorse without qualification Freud's discourse. If Robertson is right and this chilling depiction of Nazi horror is the book's only real reality, then "reality" must be only stark objectivism— photographs of mutilated bodies rather than stories of individual people with their own quirky, subjective viewpoints and experiences. This is, in fact, what Robertson seems to believe about reality; Robertson duly notes that Thomas adds yet another chapter to his novel, a chapter depicting a hypothetical resurrection in an afterlife, but she thinks that this final turn cheapens the book and that Thomas has perhaps "resorted to the tired idealism of the modernists in the face of history"

(463). For Robertson, the documentary objectivism is the book's only authentic resting place; she asserts that the subsequent section's "religious transcendence is at least theoretically a palliative, but it will not be very credible in the twentieth century" (471).

But Thomas does not rest with such documentary realism (whether his alternative is a bland and incredible "palliative" is, I suppose, a matter of opinion). Thomas acknowledges the radical evil of the Holocaust, which surely stands as a *limit to* naive analogical images of immanent and universal goodness, but he goes an extra postmodernist step and suggests that even this is not the final "truth"; even this is relativized, part of a larger narrative web. Yes, the Holocaust forms a limit to the importance we can grant to Lisa's life as an opera singer, to Freud's analysis of her neuroses, and to her fantasies about a libido-driven White Hotel. But the fantasies and stories—the analogies that mediate Lisa the person rather than Lisa the Holocaust statistic—qualify the Holocaust discourse as much as that discourse qualifies the fantasies and stories. The novel asserts that such fantasies were part of the psyche of each person killed at Babi Yar and suggests that this reality undermines the documentary objectivism of this section of the novel as much as it undermines the certainty of Freudian theory:

> The soul of man is a far country, which cannot be approached or explored. Most of the dead were poor and illiterate. But every single one of them had dreamed dreams, seen visions and had had amazing experiences, even the babes in arms (perhaps especially the babes in arms). Though most of them had never lived outside the Podol slum, their lives and histories were as rich and complex as Lisa Erdman-Berenstein's. If a Sigmund Freud had been listening and taking notes from the time of Adam, he would still not fully have explored even a single group, even a single person. (294–95)

The narrator concludes his narration of the Babi Yar atrocity with chilling objectivity. He says the Babi Yar ravine was eventually filled in with concrete, and "above it were built a main road, a television centre, and a high-rise block of flats" (298). Then, however, as a transition to the novel's sixth and final section, he adds that the human soul supplements and overflows such reductiveness: "[A]ll this had nothing to do with the guest, the soul, the lovesick bride, the daughter of Jerusalem" (298).

To call anything "playful" after the grim presentation of Nazi atrocity may seem sacrilegious, but I think that in the book's final section Thomas is tentatively, even playfully, imagining a reality that could qualify even the radically objectifying reductiveness of the Holocaust. This concluding section, "The Camp," places all the novel's elements in a religious framework, a relation to the whole of reality, that goes beyond the dialectical limit even of the Holocaust to a graciousness that is *not* not-yet but that has always already been analogically present.

What is perhaps most striking about "The Camp" is that this leap to transcendence (this section of the book depicts the realm of life after death, or at least plays with that possibility) is not much of a leap at all. The book does not shift dialectically from the profane to the sacred, but rather it gathers together and repeats all the mundane images and motifs that have appeared again and again before. The afterlife, if this is what we are seeing, is merely a refugee camp, and people's lives continue in an ordinary but hopeful way. Lisa's conversation with her mother is altogether mundane; the serial killer Peter Kürten, who had once led Lisa to reflect on what a horrific curse human selfhood can be (it would be "unimaginably horrible," she had thought, to "have to spend every moment of your life, the only life you were given, as Kürten" [209]), is indeed still himself, but he is trying to undergo rehabilitation; and Lisa's conversation with her father is amusingly strained: "Well, let me know if you need anything," her father tells her. "Take care of yourself" (320). The motifs that appeared in Lisa's original erotic fantasies, and that were ostensibly explained during her Freudian analysis, are back: Lisa has traveled to the camp by train, she meets a young man, the camp looks "more like a hotel" (304), Lisa bleeds vaginally, she drinks milk gushing from her mother's breasts, and there is even a black cat. And these new forms of the motifs, although in many cases transfigured in a positive way, are not a "Platonic" repetition in Miller's sense of the term; the final version of the motifs is not really any more definitive than earlier versions. But there is a sense of connection through all the repetitions, a gracious trust that Lisa's fantasy of the burning White Hotel pointed forward to her final, Dantesque image of a glorious transcendent rose as much as it pointed backward to the fire in which her adulterous mother died. As Lisa and her mother walk together in this seeming New Jerusalem, the narrator says: "White was the wind that came off the hills. The sun set on the desert, and its light through a distant dust storm streaked into circles and formed the likeness of a rose" (319).

Indeed, by the end of the novel it seems that even the sex itself has earned this mundane/transcendent multivalence, and that what seemed lurid in the novel's first sections now retrospectively has a mystical cast. This may be Thomas's most stunning assertion of the analogical both/and. The book rejects the dialectical distinction between *agape* and *eros* and moves toward the kind of sacramental synthesis of the two that, as we saw, David Tracy endorses: "As grounded in that gift of trust, *eros* will be transformed but not negated by divine *agape*. That transformation is *caritas*" (*Analogical Imagination* 432).[7] The web of connections linking the wild sensual eroticism of Lisa's poem and journal with the mythic transcendence of "The Camp" suggests that each analogically contains the other. Indeed, in his autobiographical work *Memories and Hallucinations*, Thomas ex-

---

7 As we saw earlier, the dialectical theologian Anders Nygren condemns this "classical Catholic idea of love, the Caritas-synthesis" (722), saying that it "displays an *egocentric perversion*" (683).

plicitly embraces such a synthesis of *eros* with transcendence. In a discussion of sex, he says: "I prefer the word erotic. It's where we are most vulnerable and sensitive, most open to wonder and to the sacred. Where the microcosm opens itself to the cosmic" (161).

I do not mean to suggest that Thomas has tacked on an easy, unalloyed redemption of the sadness and pain that have preceded; as I have indicated, the world of "The Camp" is quite imperfect. The final section of the novel is still *inside* the story of Lisa's troubles, not a supernatural escape from them. But this fact, too, reflects the book's analogical imagination, its refusal to dialectically divorce the "beyond" from the here and now. Thomas depicts a sacred realm that is not radically distant from the secular. And yet, within this imperfect secularity and painfulness, there is a hopeful sacramental fact: Lisa's experience of another pine tree. Earlier, as we saw, the scent of a pine tree opened for Lisa "a clear space . . . to her childhood, as though a wind had sprung up from the sea, clearing a mist." This was a sacramental experience, truly making *present* both the no-longer and the not-yet: "It was not a memory from the past but the past itself, as alive, as real. . . . And when she looked in the opposite direction, towards the unknown future, death, the endless extent beyond death, she was still there. It all came from the scent of a pine tree" (252). Fittingly, the book ends with Lisa, in her mysterious life beyond death, again smelling the scent of a pine tree. The final words of the text suggest a healing analogical linkage of the past, present, and future, and, perhaps more important, of the earthly world and the transcendent: "She smelt the scent of a pine tree. She couldn't place it. . . . It troubled her in some mysterious way, yet also made her happy" (322).

The pine tree is not a center that undoes the novel's overall postmodern centerlessness; it is an analogical image, not an absolute proposition. And even the seeming "meaning" of the image, that Lisa is always there, is hypothetical rather than certain. Thomas's portrayal of an afterlife seems to owe much to the chapter "On Life After Death" in Jung's *Memories, Dreams, Reflections*, in which Jung argues that concepts of existence after death are based not on dogmatic assurance but only on an imaginative exploration of the myths, dreams, and images that percolate in the psyche. Jung listens openly to images and myths of the afterlife, but he allows them (in J. Hillis Miller's terms) Nietzschean play rather than dogmatically asserting that they refer to some external prototype that can be definitively and rationally described:

> I can't say whether these thoughts [of life after death] are true or false, but I do know they are there, and can be given utterance, if I do not repress them out of some prejudice. . . . Rationalism and doctrinairism are the disease of our time; they pretend to have all the answers. But a great deal will yet be discovered which our present limited view would have ruled out as impossible. Our concepts of space and time have only approximate validity, and there is therefore a wide field for minor and major de-

viations. In view of all this, I lend an attentive ear to the strange myths of the psyche, and take a careful look at the varied events that come my way, regardless of whether or not they fit in with my theoretical postulates. (299–300)

Thomas's portrayal of the afterlife in general, and in particular his suggestion of Lisa's immortality through the repeated image of a pine tree, is a way of truly but playfully—without "doctrinairism" or "theoretical postulates"—giving "utterance" to thoughts of life after death. And within the uncertainty and playfulness, *The White Hotel* expresses a genuine hopefulness, a sense that beyond the stern limit-to is a gracious limit-of. The final image of the pine tree suggests that pushing away reductive meanings need not leave nothing, nor need it leave us merely waiting for the crying of Lot 49. Rather, resistance to reductionism can open up the mundane to become sacrament, an analogical manifestation of an ultimate reality that postmodernism—in good apophatic fashion—cannot definitely name, but neither will it, in positivistic fashion, dismiss.

Conclusion

I avoid the temptation of suggesting that the analogical imagination thus subsumes and contains the dialectical. At the risk of remaining too dialectical myself, I wish to end as I began, with a claim that whatever the overlap there are significant differences between these modes of imagining ultimacy; my friend's initial insight that *Twin Peaks* and *Columbo* essentially differ remains valid and wise. Not to maintain this difference would, I think, be a denial of the power and insight—as well as the risks and limitations—of each mode of religious imagination. David Tracy himself specifically warns against attempts to subsume differences: "Because an analogical, not univocal, imagination is the need of our radically pluralistic moment, the dissimilarities are as important as the similarities-in-difference, the ordered relationships will emerge from distinct, sometimes mutually exclusive, focal responses of the different traditions and the focal questions in the situation" (*Analogical Imagination* 447). Tracy claims that when true conversation thrives (as I hope I have allowed conversation between the analogical and dialectical imaginations, and between theology and literature, to thrive in these pages), "the autonomy of each will be respected because each will be expected to continue, indeed to intensify, a journey into her/his own particularity" (*Analogical Imagination* 449).

But since Tracy believes in real conversation, he does not consider differences to be so unbridgeable as to halt dialogue; antinomies are real, but so are analogies. Hence, to overstate the differences between the analogical and the dialectical imaginations—as overly facile contrasts of Catholicism and Protestantism might—would deny the nuanced, playful, uncanny connections between them, the fact that each is the other's supplement in that marvelously paradoxical postmodern way. A supplement, as we saw, is part of and hence connected to that which it supplements, linked by the analogy of being, and yet it is also something quite new, not yet present in the supplemented: "a supplement adds itself as a surplus, appearing to work for completeness," and yet "[t]hat which requires supplementation already has within it a trace of what the supplement brings" (Hart 197). This, I think, is the relation of the dialectical and the analogical imaginations to each other. Each contains analogical traces of the other, and yet each adds itself to the other as a dialectically *other* surplus. Considering that these are modes of imagining nothing less than the Ground of Being and its relation to us dialectically fractionalized and yet analogically related beings, it is not surprising that the imaginations—and the literary works embodying them—would vary in rich, irreducible, and mysterious ways.

Works Cited

Altizer, Thomas J. J. *Mircea Eliade and the Dialectic of the Sacred.* Philadelphia: Westminster Press, 1963.

Bandera, Cesáreo. *The Sacred Game: The Role of the Sacred in the Genesis of Modern Fiction.* University Park, Pa.: Pennsylvania State University Press, 1994.

Barth, Karl. *The Epistle to the Romans.* Trans. Edwyn C. Hoskins. London: Oxford University Press, 1933.

Batchelor, John. *The Life of Joseph Conrad: A Critical Biography.* Oxford: Blackwell Publishers, 1994.

Billy, Ted, ed. *Critical Essays on Joseph Conrad.* Boston: G. K. Hall, 1987.

Bowen, Zack. *"Ulysses" as a Comic Novel.* Syracuse: Syracuse University Press, 1989.

Burgess, Anthony. *Re Joyce.* New York: W. W. Norton, 1965.

Calvin, John. *Institutes of the Christian Religion.* Vol. 1. Trans. Ford Lewis Battles. Philadelphia: Westminster Press, 1960.

Conrad, Joseph. *"Heart of Darkness" and Other Tales.* Oxford: Oxford University Press, 1990.

———. *Lord Jim.* Oxford: Oxford University Press, 1983.

Cowart, David. "Being and Seeming: *The White Hotel.*" *Novel: A Forum on Fiction* 19, no. 3 (Spring 1986): 216–31.

Cross, Richard K. "The Soul Is a Far Country: D. M. Thomas and *The White Hotel.*" *Journal of Modern Literature* 18, no. 1 (Winter 1992): 19–47.

Detweiler, Robert. *Breaking the Fall: Religious Readings of Contemporary Fiction.* San Francisco: Harper and Row, 1989.

Dubus, Andre. *Broken Vessels.* Boston: Godine, 1991.

———. *Voices from the Moon.* In *Selected Stories.* New York: Vintage, 1989.

Eliade, Mircea. *The Sacred and the Profane: The Nature of Religion.* Trans. Willard R. Trask. New York: Harcourt, Brace, 1959.

Gadamer, Hans-Georg. *Truth and Method.* New York: Continuum, 1975.

Gamache, Lawrence. "Defining Modernism: A Religious and Literary Correlation." *Studies in the Literary Imagination* 25, no. 2 (Fall 1992): 63–81.

Gifford, Don. *Notes for Joyce: "Dubliners" and "A Portrait of the Artist as a Young Man."* New York: Dutton, 1967.

Gifford, Don, and Robert Seidman. *Notes for Joyce: An Annotation of James Joyce's "Ulysses."* New York: Dutton, 1967.

Goldberg, S. L. *The Classical Temper: A Study of James Joyce's "Ulysses."* London: Catto and Windus, 1961.

Greeley, Andrew M. *The Catholic Myth: The Behavior and Beliefs of American Catholics.* New York: Macmillan, 1990.

———. "The Catholic Imagination and the Catholic University." *America,* 16 March 1991: 285–88.

Green, Martin. *"The Crying of Lot 49*: Pynchon's *Heart of Darkness." Pynchon Notes* 8 (February 1982): 30–38.

Guerard, Albert. *Conrad the Novelist.* Cambridge: Harvard University Press, 1965.

Gregory of Nyssa. *The Life of Moses.* Trans. Abraham J. Malherbe and Everett Ferguson. New York: Paulist Press, 1978.

Happel, Stephen, and David Tracy. *A Catholic Vision.* Philadelphia: Fortress Press, 1984.

Hart, Kevin. *The Trespass of the Sign: Deconstruction, Theology, and Philosophy.* Cambridge: Cambridge University Press, 1989.

Hayles, N. Katherine. "'A Metaphor of God Knew How Many Parts': The Engine that Drives *The Crying of Lot 49.*" In *New Essays on "The Crying of Lot 49,"* edited by Patrick O'Donnell, 97–125. Cambridge: Cambridge University Press, 1991.

Johnson, Elizabeth. *She Who Is: The Mystery of God in Feminist Theological Discourse.* New York: Crossroad, 1992.

Joyce, James. *A Portrait of the Artist as a Young Man.* Ed. Hans Walter Gabler with Walter Hettche. New York: Vintage, 1993.

———. *Stephen Hero.* New York: New Directions, 1963.

———. *Ulysses.* Ed. Jeri Johnson. Oxford: Oxford University Press, 1993.

Jung, C. G. *Memories, Dreams, Reflections.* Trans. Richard and Clara Winston. 1961; New York: Vintage, 1989.

Karl, Frederick R. *Joseph Conrad: The Three Lives.* New York: Farrar, Straus, and Giroux, 1979.

Kenner, Hugh. *Dublin's Joyce.* London: Chatto and Windus, 1955.

Kierkegaard, Søren. *Concluding Unscientific Postscript.* Trans. David F. Swenson and Walter Lowrie. Princeton: Princeton University Press, 1968.

Kuschel, Karl-Josef. *Laughter: A Theological Reflection.* Trans. John Bowden. New York: Continuum, 1994.

Lakeland, Paul. *Postmodernity: Christian Identity in a Fragmented Age.* Minneapolis: Augsburg Fortress, 1997.

Lawrence, Karen. *The Odyssey of Style in Ulysses.* Princeton: Princeton University Press, 1981.

Levenson, Michael H. *A Genealogy of Modernism: A Study of English Literary Doctrine, 1908–1922.* Cambridge: Cambridge University Press, 1984.

Litz, A. Walton. "Ithaca." In *James Joyce's "Ulysses": Critical Essays,* edited by Clive Hart and David Hayman, 385–405. Berkeley: University of California Press, 1974.

Lodge, David. *The Art of Fiction.* New York: Penguin, 1992.

———. *The Modes of Modern Writing: Metaphor, Metonymy, and the Typology of Modern Literature.* Ithaca: Cornell University Press, 1977.

Lonergan, Bernard. *Method in Theology.* New York: Herder and Herder, 1972.

Luther, Martin. "Heidelberg Disputation." Trans. Harold J. Grimm. In *Career of the Reformer,* vol. 1, edited by Harold J. Grimm, 39–70. Philadelphia: Huhlenberg Press, 1957.

Lynch, William F., S.J. *Christ and Apollo: The Dimensions of the Literary Imagination.* 1960; Notre Dame: University of Notre Dame Press, 1975.

———. *Christ and Prometheus: A New Image of the Secular.* Notre Dame: University of Notre Dame Press, 1970.

———. *Images of Faith: An Exploration of the Ironic Imagination.* Notre Dame: University of Notre Dame Press, 1973.

———. *Images of Hope: Imagination as Healer of the Hopeless*. 1965; Notre Dame: University of Notre Dame Press, 1974.

———. *The Integrating Mind: An Exploration into Western Thought*. New York: Sheed and Ward, 1962.

———. "The Life of Faith and Imagination: Theological Reflection in Art and Literature." *Thought: A Review of Culture and Idea* 57, no. 224 (March 1982): 7–16.

McFague, Sallie. *Metaphorical Theology: Models of God in Religious Language*. Philadelphia: Fortress Press, 1982.

———. *Models of God: Theology for an Ecological, Nuclear Age*. Philadelphia: Fortress Press, 1987.

McMichael, James. *"Ulysses" and Justice*. Princeton: Princeton University Press, 1991.

Mendelsohn, Jane. "The Devil in Miss Spark: Muriel's Wicked, Wicked Ways." *Village Voice Literary Supplement*, December 1990, 25–26.

Mendelson, Edward. "The Sacred, the Profane, and *The Crying of Lot 49*." In *Individual and Community: Variations on a Theme in American Fiction,* edited by Kenneth H. Baldwin and David K. Kirby, 182–222. Durham: Duke University Press, 1975.

Miller, J. Hillis. *Fiction and Repetition: Seven English Novels*. Cambridge: Harvard University Press, 1982.

———. "*Heart of Darkness* Revisited." In *Joseph Conrad: "Heart of Darkness," A Case Study in Contemporary Criticism,* edited by Ross C. Murfin, 209–224. New York: St. Martin's Press, 1989.

———. "Presidential Address 1986: The Triumph of Theory, the Resistance to Reading, and the Question of the Material Base." *PMLA* 102 (1987): 281–91.

Morse, J. Mitchell. "Proteus." In *James Joyce's "Ulysses": Critical Essays,* edited by Clive Hart and David Hayman, 29–49. Berkeley: University of California Press, 1974.

Noon, William T., S.J. *Joyce and Aquinas*. New Haven: Yale University Press, 1957.

Nygren, Anders. *Agape and Eros*. Trans. Philip S. Watson. Philadelphia: Westminster, 1953.

Olsen, Lance. "Pynchon's New Nature: The Uncertainty Principle and Indeterminacy in *The Crying of Lot 49*." *Canadian Review of American Studies* 14, no. 2 (Summer 1983): 153–63.

Polkinghorne, John. *The Faith of a Physicist: Reflections of a Bottom-Up Thinker*. 1994; Minneapolis: Fortress, 1996.

Pynchon, Thomas. *The Crying of Lot 49*. 1966; New York: Harper and Row, 1990.

Rahner, Karl. *Foundations of Christian Faith: An Introduction to the Idea of Christianity*. Trans. William V. Dych. New York: Seabury, 1978.

Raschke, Carl A. "The Deconstruction of God." In *Deconstruction and Theology*. Thomas J. J. Altizer, Max A. Myers, Carl A. Raschke, Robert P. Scharleman, Mark C. Taylor, and Charles E. Winquist, 1–33. New York: Crossroad, 1983.

Robertson, Mary F. "Hystery, Herstory, History: 'Imagining the Real' in Thomas's *The White Hotel*." *Contemporary Literature* 25, no. 4 (Winter 1984): 452–77.

Rorty, Richard. *Contingency, Irony, and Solidarity*. Cambridge: Cambridge University Press, 1989.

Schlossman, Beryl. *Joyce's Catholic Comedy of Manners*. Madison: University of Wisconsin Press, 1985.

Schwarz, Daniel. *Reading Joyce's "Ulysses."* New York: St. Martin's Press, 1987.

Scott, Nathan A., Jr. *The Broken Center: Studies in the Theological Horizon of Modern Literature*. New Haven: Yale University Press, 1966.

———. *Negative Capability: Studies in the New Literature and the Religious Situation*. New Haven: Yale University Press, 1969.

———. *The Poetics of Belief: Studies in Coleridge, Arnold, Pater, Santayana, Stevens, and Heidegger*. Chapel Hill: University of North Carolina Press, 1985.

———. "Theology, Poetics, Psychotherapy: The Field of the Imagination. Some Reflections on the Legacy of William F. Lynch, S.J." *Logos: A Journal of Catholic Thought and Culture* 1, no. 1 (1997): 60–77.

———. *Visions of Presence in Modern American Poetry*. Baltimore: Johns Hopkins University Press, 1993.

———. *The Wild Prayer of Longing: Poetry and the Sacred*. New Haven: Yale University Press, 1971.

Sherry, Norman. *Conrad*. New York: Thames and Hudson, 1988.

Siegel, Jules. "Who Is Thomas Pynchon . . . And Why Is He Taking Off with My Wife?" In *Lineland: Mortality and Mercy on the Internet's Pynchon-L@Waste.Org Discussion List*. Jules Siegel and Christine Wexler, 83–96. Philadelphia: Intangible Assets Manufacturing, 1997.

Siegelman, Ellen Y. "*The White Hotel*: Visions and Revisions of the Psyche." *Literature and Psychology* 33, no. 1 (1987): 69–76.

Spark, Muriel. *Curriculum Vitae*. New York: Houghton Mifflin, 1992.

———. "The Desegregation of Art." In *Critical Essays on Muriel Spark,* edited by Joseph Hynes, 33–37. New York: G. K. Hall, 1992.

———. "My Conversion." In *Critical Essays on Muriel Spark,* edited by Joseph Hynes, 24–28. New York: G. K. Hall, 1992.

———. *The Prime of Miss Jean Brodie*. 1961; New York: Plume, 1984.

———. *Symposium*. 1990; London: Penguin, 1991.

Steiner, George. *Real Presences: Is There Anything in What We Say?* London: Faber and Faber, 1989.

Sultan, Stanley. *The Argument of Ulysses*. Columbus: Ohio State University Press, 1964.

Thomas, D. M. *Memories and Hallucinations: A Memoir.* New York: Viking, 1988.

———. *The White Hotel*. 1981; New York: Pocket Books, 1982.

Tillich, Paul. *The Protestant Era* (abridged ed.). Trans. James Luther Adams. Chicago: University of Chicago Press, 1957.

———. *Systematic Theology*. Vol. 1. Chicago: University of Chicago Press, 1951.

Tompkins, Jane. "Masterpiece Theater: The Politics of Hawthorne's Literary Reputation." In *Falling Into Theory: Conflicting Views on Reading Literature,* edited by David H. Richter, 119–28. Boston: St. Martin's, 1994.

Tracy, David. *The Analogical Imagination: Christian Theology and the Culture of Pluralism*. New York: Crossroad, 1981.

———. *Blessed Rage for Order: The New Pluralism in Theology*. New York: Seabury Press, 1975.

———. *Plurality and Ambiguity: Hermeneutics, Religion, Hope*. San Francisco: Harper and Row, 1987.

Tyler, Anne. *Saint Maybe*. 1991; New York: Ballantine, 1992.

Updike, John. "A Disconcerting Thing." *America,* 4 October 1997: 8–9.

———. *Roger's Version*. 1986; New York: Fawcett Crest, 1987.

————. "Ungreat Lives." *New Yorker,* 4 February 1985, 94–101.

Voelker, Joseph C. *Art and the Accidental in Anne Tyler.* Columbia: University of Missouri Press, 1989.

von Hügel, Baron Friedrich. *Essays and Addresses on the Philosophy of Religion.* 1921; Westport, Conn.: Greenwood Press, 1974.

Watt, Ian P. "The Ending of *Lord Jim.*" In *Critical Essays on Joseph Conrad,* edited by Ted Billy, 85–102. Boston: G. K. Hall, 1987.

Woolf, Virginia. *The Common Reader.* New York: Harcourt, Brace, 1925.

Wymer, Rowland. "Freud, Jung, and the 'Myth' of Psychoanalysis in *The White Hotel.*" *Mosaic: A Journal for the Comparative Study of Literature* 22, no. 1 (Winter 1989): 55–69.

Zhang, Benzi. "The Chinese Box in D. M. Thomas's *The White Hotel.*" *International Fiction* 20, no. 1 (1993): 54–57.